GALEN
On the Properties of Foodstuffs

This book presents a translation of and detailed commentary on Galen's *De alimentorum facultatibus*, his major work on the dynamics and kinetics of various foods. It is thus primarily a physiological treatise rather than a *materia medica* or a work on pathology. Galen commences with a short section on the epistemology of medicine, with a discussion on the attainment, through *apodeixis*, or demonstration, of scientific truth – a discussion which reveals the Aristotelian roots of his thinking. The text then covers a wide range of foods, both common and exotic. Some, such as cereals, legumes, dairy products and the grape, receive an emphasis that reflects their importance at the time; others are treated more cursorily. Dr Powell, a retired physician, discusses Galen's terminology and the background to his views on physiology and pathology in his introduction, while John Wilkins's foreword concentrates on the structural and cultural aspects of the work.

OWEN POWELL is an Honorary Research Fellow in the Department of Classics and Ancient History at the University of Queensland. He is a retired physician who worked as Medical Superintendent for sixteen years at the Princess Alexandra Hospital in Brisbane and subsequently as Director of Research and Planning at the Queensland Department of Health. He is a Fellow of the Royal College of Physicians of Edinburgh and the Royal Australasian College of Physicians.

JOHN WILKINS is Reader in Greek Literature at the University of Exeter. He has published *The Boastful Chef: the Discourse of Food in Ancient Greek Comedy* (2000) and, with Shaun Hill, produced a translation and commentary on the surviving work of Archestratus in *The Life of Luxury: Europe's Oldest Cookery Book* (1994). He has also co-edited, with David Harvey and Mike D~~~~ ~~~~~~ ~~~~~~~~~ (1995). He is currently producing a new text c~ *facultatibus* for the Budé classical texts series.

GALEN
On the Properties of Foodstuffs
(De alimentorum facultatibus)

INTRODUCTION, TRANSLATION AND COMMENTARY BY

OWEN POWELL

Department of Classics and Ancient History,
The University of Queensland

WITH A FOREWORD BY

JOHN WILKINS

University of Exeter

CAMBRIDGE
UNIVERSITY PRESS

CAMBRIDGE UNIVERSITY PRESS
Cambridge, New York, Melbourne, Madrid, Cape Town, Singapore, São Paulo

Cambridge University Press
The Edinburgh Building, Cambridge CB2 8RU, UK

Published in the United States of America by Cambridge University Press, New York

www.cambridge.org
Information on this title: www.cambridge.org/9780521812429

First published 2003
This digitally printed version 2007

A catalogue record for this publication is available from the British Library

ISBN 978-0-521-81242-9 hardback
ISBN 978-0-521-03620-7 paperback

To the memory of my parents
Herman Powell (1889–1964)
and
Mary Powell née Eaton (1891–1974)

ὀφείλοντα γὰρ ἀποδοτέον, οὐθὲν δὲ ποιήσας ἄξιον τῶν ὑπηργμένων δέδρακεν, ὥστ᾽ ἀεὶ ὀφείλει. *Arist. EN 1163b20–1*

Contents

Foreword

John Wilkins

Owen Powell is the latest in a long line of scholarly doctors who have interpreted the works of Galen for later practitioners and readers. Orib-asius in the fourth century and Kühn in the nineteenth are two of the most famous, but behind these two lie many others who commented upon, translated or commissioned treatises or excerpts that still, in some cases, survive as manuscripts and printed books. All these doctors continue the work that Galen himself set in place as he tried to make the texts of the Hippocratic and Hellenistic doctors work for his own time. Powell in his introduction and commentary describes clearly the phys-iology of Galen's digestive system, and how that system compares with human digestion as now understood by medical science. Galen does not explain his system in full in this treatise, but refers to it in the introductory chapter and at various later points. It is a feature of the work to define its terms of reference and direct the reader elsewhere if an item falls outside those guidelines. I return below to navigational aids provided by Galen in his text. The purpose of this foreword is to complement Powell's in-troduction by exploring some points that he makes only in passing. The two major areas I aim to address concern the social and cultural world in which Galen was writing and the methods he used in attempting to collect and classify foods in the treatise.

The work is divided into three books: the first contains cereals and pulses, the second other plants and the third animals and fish. The largest number of items is to be found in the plant book. How did Galen decide on his order and what to include and what to leave out? 'Value' (something *chrêsimos*, literally 'useful', is the term Galen uses) appears to be the main criterion. Dietetics as a whole is declared the most valuable form of medicine (K. 453), and wheat the most valuable (that is, widely used) food (K. 480). At the beginning of the second book (K. 555), Galen explains that some authors move on from cereals and pulses to consider meat from animals, birds and fish, placing other plants last, since they are the least valuable nutritionally. One of those authors was the Hippocratic author of *Regimen II*, on which more below. Galen elects to differ, and has plants follow the seeded plants of cereals and legumes.

It is not always clear what belongs where. There is a revealing chapter near the beginning of book III (K. 669–70):

> **On the snail**. It is quite clear that we should count this animal among neither the winged nor the aquatic creatures. But if we do not include it among terrestrial animals either, we shall be saying absolutely nothing about the food from it. Nor again is it sensible to ignore it as we ignore woodworms, vipers and other reptiles that they eat in Egypt and some other countries. For none of those people will read this, and we ourselves would never eat any of what to them are foods. But all Greeks eat snails on a daily basis…

The comment on snail consumption is only part of the interesting content of this passage. In trying to find a place for the anomalous snail, Galen reviews other creatures which do not come into consideration at all, namely woodworms and reptiles. This treatise is no more a work of zoology than of botany, so Galen does not explore the classification of the snail any further. He might have cited a zoological source, just as he resorts to a botanical source, Theophrastus, for problematic plants in K. 516 and elsewhere. For Galen, though, in this treatise, the key question is not biological but cultural, in two senses: do we eat this? Who are 'we', the community of writer and readers? Woodworms and vipers are beyond the pale, since they belong to another culture, namely Egypt, whose people, apparently, will not be reading Galen's book. There is no sharing of cultural practice, whether of food or of text, with these Egyptians. Galen has other problematic cases for the received diet in the world of the eastern Roman Empire in the second century AD. Again, these help to shape his terms of reference. At K. 615 we read:

> **On carobs**. Carobs [*keratia*], which have the third syllable spoken and written with the letter *tau*, are nothing like cherries [*kerasia*], with the letter *sigma*. They are a food that is unwholesome and woody, and necessarily difficult to concoct for nothing woody is easy. But the fact that they also are not excreted quickly is a considerable defect with them. So that it would be better for us not even to import them from the eastern regions where they are produced.

Carobs are a bad food, not to be recommended by the doctor; but, because people do eat them, they are included. The comment on the spelling of the term I address below. A third example will complete the picture (K. 664):

However, some people also eat the flesh of very old donkeys, which is most unwholesome, very difficult to concoct, bad for the stomach, and, still more, is distasteful as food, like horse and camel meat; which latter meats men who are asinine and camel-like in body and soul also eat!

Some people even eat bear meat, and that of lions and leopards, which is worse still, boiling it either once only, or twice. I have said earlier what twice-boiled is like.

As to dogs, what must I also say? That in some parts very many people eat young plump dogs...

These extraordinary foods, the carob, donkeys, camels, bears and dogs, define the limits of the civilized diet as far as Galen is concerned. These foods are eaten, but are all open to question. To eat old donkeys and camels betrays less than full human faculties. Bears, lions and leopards are so much wild animals that they need to pass through the civilizing process of cooking twice before they are suitable for human consumption. It is not quite clear who the dog-eaters are. Galen refers to certain *ethnê*, but where these tribes or peoples live and whether they are Greek-speaking is not made clear. The dog-eating peoples may be outside the Greek world altogether, like those Egyptians who eat woodworms. Galen is attempting to set boundaries, even though they cannot be clearly defined, since the Roman Empire included so many peoples and languages. Alexandria was largely civilized in its diet (K. 486, donkey- and camel-eating; K. 539, a young man on an uncooked vegetarian diet; K. 540, consumption of *lathyroi* (grass peas); K. 612, pistachios; K. 616, sycamore fruit; K. 617, *persea*-fruit), some other parts of Egypt apparently were not. Galen is not much interested in what might be termed excessively civilized, that is, luxurious foods, that had concerned Plato when he was discussing food and medicine (*Gorgias* 517a7–518c1). There is the odd puzzled comment, as on the livers of red mullets (K. 716), but there appears to be no objection to doctors and chefs pursuing similar interests (K. 638). Galen quotes twice from a *Symposium*, a medical work by his predecessor Herakleides of Tarentum, the important Empiricist, which also ranged more widely than a strict medical brief might suggest.

Galen's interests, surprisingly, turn out to focus on the reverse of the luxurious diet, namely the food of half-starved peasants. At K. 685–6, on milk, he turns his attention to wet nurses:

For unwholesome milk is so far from producing healthy humour that even when people with healthy humour use it, it makes them full of unhealthy humour. Indeed, in an infant, when the first nurse had died, and another who was full of unhealthy humour was providing the milk for him, his whole body was obviously infected with numerous ulcers. When famine had taken hold in the spring, the second nurse had lived on wild herbs in the field. So she and some others in the same country who had lived in the same way were filled with such ulcers. We observed this in many other women who were nursing children at that time.

Galen rarely addresses gender-specific dietary questions in this treatise. When it comes to working people, however, he has much to say. These wet nurses, like many of the poor in Mediterranean countries, often faced food shortages in the spring. (Galen comments on the phenomenon also at the beginning of his treatise *On Good and Bad Humour*.) In this season, the economically vulnerable also ate tare and vetch, which the farmers normally stored as cattle food (K. 551). The same went for oats (K. 523) which 'is food for draught animals, not for men, unless perhaps at some time when, being at the extreme of hunger, they are forced to make bread from this grain'. These are not foods that are *chrêsimoi*, 'valuable' or 'useful', at least for nutrition. They may, however, have other uses, as Galen observes of another bad seed (K. 546)

On bitter vetch. With ourselves and many other countries [*ethnê*], cattle eat bitter vetch which has first been sweetened with water, but people absolutely avoid this seed; for it is distasteful and produces unhealthy humour. But some-times in a severe famine, as Hippocrates wrote, from force of necessity they come to it. We ourselves use bitter vetch with honey as a drug...

It can cut through thick humours, and so can have a pharmacological benefit, as can also the nutritionally poor caper (K. 615). One reason, then, for the inclusion of these plants is that the treatise shares an interest in the pharmacological powers of plants with Galen's extensive treatise *On the Mixtures and Powers of Simple Drugs*. A comparison between the two is instructive. Another reason for including these unpleasant seeds normally used for cattle food is that they help to define a further boundary for the human diet in the Graeco-Roman world. Like the dog and the bear, these foods are not normally eaten; in this case, only under dire duress. This idea is supported by Galen's term for the seeded plants, the plants of Demeter. These are the plants of life, supplied by the great corn goddess who oversees Greek culture and agriculture. Demeter presides over the cereals of cultivation. Galen is happy to include wild plants in his list in book 11, but some of these are harmful, as the wet-nurses revealed; others turn out to be marginal, for example the extremely astringent nightshade (K. 635) and curled dock (K. 635), which no one would eat except pregnant women and curious children in country areas. Here,

Galen's approach is inclusive of all classes of citizen and the full range of the diet (compare the assessment of Garnsey (1999) 36–41). Only, in a secondary sense, he is using these peasants as a kind of guinea pig for the elite to discover what the human frame can stand, as my colleague David Braund once suggested to me.

Broad cultural concerns bring us to the second point. In discussing a further unpleasant plant, *arakoi*, or wild chickling, Galen observes (K. 541),

> We find that the final syllable of the name of *arakos* is written with a *kappa* in *The Merchant Ships* of Aristophanes, where he speaks of 'wild chickling, wheats, ptisane, emmer, darnel and *semidalis*'. The seed is very like the seed of the grasspea, and indeed some think they are of the same family. In fact its every use and property are close to those of grasspea, except to the extent that it is harder and more difficult to cook; and consequently it is more difficult to concoct than grasspea is. People in our region call the wild one that is spherical, hard, smaller than bitter vetch, and found among cereals, *arachos*, pronouncing the final syllable with a *chi* and not a *kappa*; and they pick it out and throw it away as they do axeweed.

Many of Galen's forays among the country people who lived around Pergamum were undertaken for the purpose of autopsy, that is, personal observation and verification. He went to inspect the plants with his own eyes, for a double purpose: to see how the plants were eaten by country people and how they named and commented upon them. Dioscorides in the preface of his *De materia medica* had emphasized the importance of looking with your own eyes at the way plants and other drugs changed according to season, location and other factors. For Galen, such autopsy complemented his own research. He could observe medical phenomena, such as the effects of a vegetarian diet (K. 539) or vomit after eating certain mushrooms (K. 656); but much research came from reading. The importance of books and his own library is made clear in, among other places, his treatise *My Own Books*. The present entry on *arakoi* is remarkably scholarly. Galen begins with the spelling of the last syllable and justifies his spelling with a quotation from a lost play of Aristophanes. What has such a sentence to do with medicine? The problem concerns correct identification of the plant, which in different forms is spelt in different ways. Correct identification *is* a medical matter, for error may lead to a plant with the wrong powers being administered to the patient. Compare the entry on carobs above, where the confusion rests clearly in the sound of the word, not in botany. The plant is similar to the grasspea (*lathyroi*), we are told, while some claim it is a variant or at least of a related

species (*genos*). In practice it is like the grasspea but worse, particularly
for the digestion. There is thus some difficulty with identification, which
may lead to error. There is also a wild variety, but this is spelt differently
and is apparently discarded, 'like axeweed'. This wild variety grows 'in
our region'. As often, Galen uses the testimony of Pergamum and its
hinterland, which was part of Mysia.

A number of things need to be said about Galen exercising his autopsy principally in Asia Minor rather than in Greece or Italy. There
is some autopsy from Italy, particularly on the variation in pollution of
the Tiber and its tributaries (K. 722), but Asia Minor and the East are
much more important. The country people in his area provide the evidence for, among other things, wheat and milk mixtures (K. 495), what
wheat porridge does to the stomach (K. 499), and the effects of chickpeas
(K. 533) and grasspeas (K. 540). Evidence comes too from Alexandria
(see above), Syria, Bithynia and Thrace. And the evidence, we should
note, is not only physical and physiological. Galen notes the different
spelling of *arachos* in his area. When he goes to Thrace to try to identify
wheats, he learns of a cereal called *briza* (K. 514), and describes it and
spells the local name. Terminology is as much a concern as botanical
categories: the right name must be applied to the right plant.

Sometimes his research extends over many centuries of Greek thought.
The names for *arakos* (K. 541) and for *zeia* (K. 522) are partly confirmed
by Aristophanes and Homer respectively. In other words, in the search
for the true term, a literary author can make a contribution as well as a
technical author in a relevant field, such as Theophrastus or Dioscorides.
Aristophanes is an interesting choice since his testimony is to the term
in use in the Attic dialect in the fifth century BC. We know from Galen's
list in *My Own Books* that Galen had studied comedy. He had also written
essays on political terms in Eupolis, Aristophanes and Cratinus as well as
Examples of words specific to the writers of comedy and *Whether the texts of ancient
comedy are a worthwhile part of the educational curriculum.* Comedy, then, for
Galen was an educational cornerstone something like Homer. Nevertheless, Aristophanic usage brings him into the realm of the Atticists who
insisted on pure Attic even in the second century AD, and against whom,
as Powell notes, Galen regularly fulminates. Examination of the places
where the Atticists are referred to makes it clear that Galen's concern
was a matter of clarity rather than of principle. They are often contrasted
with medical needs or the more useful names used 'by us' in Pergamum
and Mysia, by 'all Greeks' or by peasants: see K. 490, K. 585, K. 605,
K. 606, K. 612 and K. 633. There are more neutral references at 1.12

and 2.41. The Atticists, according to Galen, simply got in the way of accurate identification and good medicine through the obfuscating effect
of archaizing terminology.

It remains the case, however, that for Galen in this treatise, the
Athenians are people with a dialect and not people with a diet that
he wishes to examine. The treatise is not addressed to a great Roman
patron, as are many of Galen's treatises. It draws little on Rome, but at the
same time talks in broad and general terms. It is addressed to Greeks
and what is current in Greek; this does not seem to be at the expense of a
Roman audience. It seems that the great court doctor can address a problem as easily from his homeland in the Greek East as from metropolitan
Rome. Nutton's comments (1991) on the contrast between the first part
of *On the Therapeutic Method* (composed in Rome) and the second part
(composed in Pergamum) are revealing in this respect.

When discussing *arakoi*, Galen noted that they were similar to grasspeas
(*lathyroi*) (K. 541), the previous item in the treatise, which in turn are said
to be similar to cowpeas and birds' peas (*phasêloi, ochroi*, K. 540). Galen
orders his items by botanical relationship, placing similar with similar.
This was the system of order in Dioscorides, as that author sets out in his
preface. But this was not the only order that Galen had at his disposal.
He could have followed an alphabetical order, as he does in the related
treatise *On the Mixtures and Powers of Simple Drugs* (see Barnes (1997) 10–11).
That he did not may suggest a more skilful clientele, who could find their
way round the text and did not need the ready terms of reference afforded
by alphabetical order. There are aids to navigating the text. First, there
are references forward and back to tie in a point with something relevant
said elsewhere. Then there are references to other works by Galen, in
particular to the closely related *On the Mixtures and Powers of Simple Drugs*,
On Mixtures and *On Hygiene*. The first two in particular set out some
of the physiological background to which the reader may need to be
referred. Then there is reference to predecessors. Galen's treatment of
them is most interesting. Galen covers a number of these topics in an
important passage in K. 457. He refers his reader to *Mixtures* for what
they need to know about the 'mixtures' [*kraseis*] of humours in human
beings and their foods and to *On the Mixtures and Powers of Simple Drugs* for
various properties of foods. He then comes to the Hippocratic *Regimen II*,
which was written, according to Joly, the Budé and *CMG* editor, in about
400 BC. Galen reviews the difficulties of this text. The authorship is
disputed; the text of the beginning of the treatise is disputed; the texts with
which it is bundled up are of varied quality. Galen gives the opinion that

Regimen II is worthy of Hippocrates (whether he wrote it or not); the whole discussion is a scholarly review of sources. Galen saw, as we can, that, whatever its authorship, this was a perfectly serviceable treatise which said broadly what he wanted to say in a very brief compass. What it says in nineteen Budé pages of Greek text Galen says in two hundred *CMG* pages. What was the need for this massive inflation? There are many things that Galen wishes to take into account. He does not contradict the Hippocratic text but often amplifies properties of foods to cover a wider range of needs, or to provide colour from his own observation. Foxes provide an example of the latter. *Regimen II* declares that 'foxes have a moister flesh than hares and are diuretic' (46.4). Galen writes, 'amongst ourselves, hunters often eat the meat of foxes in the autumn, for they are being fattened by grapes' (K. 665). Personal observation is not used here to contradict, but confirms and gives a location, the now familiar one of Pergamum and Mysia, 'amongst ourselves'. Galen refers to the Hippocratic author elsewhere. It is notable, though, that later medical authorities are criticized for confusions and omissions in a way that the Hippocratic author is not. If the Hippocratic author omits an item, the fact is passed over less harshly (K. 511). *Regimen II*, however, is not the only Hippocratic text used. Galen refers in K. 743 to his commentary on *Regimen in Acute Diseases*, and, as we saw on bitter vetch (K. 546), he also refers to a passage in the *Epidemics*, one of the Hippocratic texts for which Galen produced a written commentary.

Diocles of Carystus and Mnesitheus of Athens are sometimes criticized for confusions and omissions but elsewhere they are referred to respectfully. Less so are Phylotimos and his teacher Praxagoras of Cos who are frequently censured. This links with the other main concern, difficulties of identification. Two cases in which this is evident concern the classification of fish and the identification of the beans known as *dolichoi*.

Galen has this to say on Phylotimos on fish with soft flesh (one of the categories of fish used by Aristotle and Diocles, among others, K. 720):

In the third book of *On Foodstuffs* Phylotimos wrote as follows about soft-fleshed fish, in these very words: 'Gobies, wrasse, rainbow wrasse, perch, Murry eels, *kichlai, kottyphoi*, horse-mackerel and again, hake; and, as well as these, bonito, sole, *hepatoi, kitharoi*, maigre and the whole family of tender-fleshed fish are dealt with better in the stomach than all others.' So it is worth wondering how he neglected the parrot wrasse, although they hold first place in the rock-fish family, all of which have flesh that is very soft and most friable when compared with other fish.

Clearly this is a problem of classification. Galen has various views on the strictness or otherwise that is required. He sometimes says that he is not concerned with detail but with the general principle, or it does not matter which term is used provided everyone understands it. A particular example occurs in K. 464:

It will make no difference whether we refer to things eaten as 'eatables' or as 'nutriments'. In fact, so too do people call them 'foodstuffs' or 'comestibles' just as often as the former names, in the way that Hippocrates also wrote in the *Epidemics*: 'Comestibles and drinks need trial as to whether they persist for the same time...' And again elsewhere: '...labours, foods, drinks, sleep and sexual activity – all in moderation'. Now, as I always say, we should not concern ourselves with names [*onomata*], nor worry about which to use, since they are familiar to every Greek, but it is proper to strive to understand the matter.

At other times, he censures an Atticist or a wrong attribution, or a wrong *onoma*, as here. Jonathan Barnes (1997) has commented on this kind of inconsistency. We have to accept that Galen is looking for clarity, but at times gives a little leeway. Such licence is rarely accorded the unfortunate Phylotimos, who is censured again later in K. 720, 724 and in K. 727, 728, where he has failed to take account of the Roman *galaxias*, to which I return below. In K. 732, he and Praxagoras are found to be in error over physical processes rather than classification. Galen's verdict on Phylotimos is damning, but not completely so.

Clarity is patently what is lacking in the case of *dolichoi* (K. 542). Here there is a confusion of both terminology and plant that is difficult to resolve. The terminology is particularly problematic:

The name *dolichos* was included in the writings of Diocles, together with the names of other seeds that nourish us, and also in the *On Regimen* of Hippocrates, which work I have already discussed. I think that they were speaking in this way about the seed of a cultivated plant which nowadays is referred to by most people in the plural, in two ways. For some call them *loboi* [pods] but others *phasêoloi*, producing a word with four syllables and in this way making a name different from *phasêlos*, with its three. Some say that *phasêlos* [cowpea] is the same as *lathyros* [grasspea], but others say that it is a species of it.

Galen quotes Theophrastus in an attempt to identify the plant, and then refers again to the Hippocratic author and Diocles to establish where in the natural and medical order they place *dolichos/dolichoi*. Phylotimos and Praxagoras do not mention the plant at all. Galen presents the evidence and implicitly concurs with his quoted predecessors by placing *dolichoi* next after the members of the cowpea and grasspea families. He also adds further material of his own, on storage, using as evidence the practice of his own father, and, characteristically, on a local variation: 'One of my friends who lives in Rome used to say that in Caria, in his own city which is called Ceramos, *dolichoi* are planted in cultivated land like the rest of the legumes, and have a more elongated shape than grasspeas.' In his attempt to be as clear as possible, Galen draws on the standard combination of the books in the library, both medical and botanical, and on the testimony of 'most people' and a report from his friend, who, like him, was a man of Asia Minor who spent some time in Rome. There is also the report of his father's storage policy. He has again extended a passing reference in the Hippocratic text into a major item. He makes it his own with his autopsy and observation of local practice, as in the case of *briza* (K. 514). He extends over classes to a greater extent than we can detect elsewhere, and reports peasant names as readily as any other class's terms.

Confusion over names continues with the telling case of *seris*, which Powell translates as 'chicory'. Galen's entry on these plants is quite brief. He says (K. 628): 'I cannot say precisely whether the earlier Athenians gave the name chicory to what among the Romans are called endive, or to some other wild vegetable plants. Chicory has a property very much like lettuce, while being inferior to them in flavour and the other features previously mentioned concerning lettuce.' Once again, Galen includes a wild plant of no apparent status, and the slight difficulty of identification between the old Attic name and the current term in Latin. He had in fact said more on *sereis* in his earlier treatise *On the Thinning Diet*, and appears not to wish to repeat that material, though we might at least have expected a cross-reference at this point. The version in *On the Thinning Diet* runs as follows:

There is another kind of 'wild herb' which is less cutting than those mentioned; this kind appears to belong between the two, having neither a definitely cutting nor a thickening effect. The general name for these is *seris*; but the individual species are given different names by rustics, such as lettuce, chicory, the Syrian *gingidia*, and the countless similar ones in every region. The Athenians use the term *seris* indiscriminately for all of them; for the ancients did not allot any names to the individual species. (trans. Singer)

In addition to noting a similar approach to problems of terminology in *On the Thinning Diet* to those we have seen in the present treatise, we might note, also, that once again rustics' names for plants need to be taken into account. Terminology is not the sole preserve of scientists and

taxonomists, as far as Galen is concerned. The Roman perspective brings
new complications, and, apparently, new refinements in taxonomy, presumably either because the plants were more widely used or because
more varieties had been brought on since the fifth century BC. Why did
Galen not draw on Roman authors to assist with some of these problems? Pliny might have been of assistance on the identification of both
seris and the problematic *zeia* of K. 511 (Pliny, *Natural History* XVIII.19).
Certainly, he, Celsus and Columella faced the difficulty of identifying
Greek plants in Latin, for which see, for example, Celsus 11.18, 19, 33,
Columella VIII.14.2, André (1985) and Langslow (2000: 76–139). We
might explain the absence of Latin authors in our treatise by supposing
either that Galen believed that technical medical language should remain a Greek preserve or that he rejected these authors as insufficiently
incisive technically, when compared with authors he does use, such as,
for example, Theophrastus or Dioscorides. The latter is, however, only
quoted once. It is certainly the case that Galen is more interested in Rome
than in Athens or mainland Greece since he reviews food consumed at
Rome (K. 507, K. 603, K. 637, K. 697, K. 727) and not merely Roman
terms (K. 484, K. 628, K. 638). Other references to Rome are to Galen's
Carian friend who resided there (K. 546), and to the polluted Tiber
(K. 722). It is notable that, as the great metropolis, Rome is considered
in these passages in terms of its language, environment, army and mar-
kets, and as a place to stay for a time; but for country life and reference
to the practices and terminology of peasant farmers Galen draws exclusively on Mysia. He has no interest in Latin or the Roman idealization of
the Italian countryside, so prevalent in Latin literature. That said, Italy is
referred to (K. 524, K. 620, K. 650, K. 666), whereas mainland Greece
is not, with the exception of a reference to the consumption of acorns
in Arcadia when all the other Greeks were eating the grains of Demeter
(K. 621).

Galen's relationship with the countryside may explain why he lists
more plants as separate items with headings in book 11 than fish in
book 111. Many of the plants in the first two books are unpleasant to
eat, as I remarked above. Galen seems to have included them not so
much in order to achieve a full coverage of every plant imaginable but
rather to link them with the related pharmacological work *On the Mixtures
and Powers of Simple Drugs*, to which I referred. A plant may be 'useful'
even if it tastes nasty and has negligible nutritional value. The plants
may also have been more likely to be consumed by most people than
the myriad varieties of fish. It may also be the case that Pergamum, like

Rome, traditionally identified itself with its surrounding farmland and did not see itself as a major centre for the consumption of fish. It was, after all, some 24 km from the sea. If Galen had wished to present the greatest list of foods that anyone had ever seen, then fish would have been a prominent element of that list, because of the many species and names of Mediterranean fish. But that is closer to the project of Galen's near-contemporary Athenaeus of Naucratis (*Deipnosophistae*, book VII) than to Galen's in this treatise. Pergamum is not mentioned in Athenaeus' list of fish and cities where fish were eaten. Unlike Athenaeus, however, Galen has no interest in cheap, small fish. For him, fish tend to be large and at the luxury end of the market, such as the *galaxias*, which he claims was so beloved of Roman gourmets. Galen claims to list the fish that 'men regularly eat' (K. 708). It is his usual claim about utility. But, in contrast with his treatment of cereals and other plants, this time 'men' appears not to include all classes.

What is Galen trying to do in this treatise? It seems, in the first instance, that he is writing a practical guide that includes all the foods that a physician is likely to come across in his patients or an interested amateur in his own diet. A patient is more likely to eat lettuce than a rare form of crayfish. We have seen from the example of the snail that Galen is interested in a coherent classification; but we have also seen that he does not try to include absolutely everything. The work is partly practical, identifying as clearly as possible a terminology and classification for the modern imperial world. Mnesitheus and Diocles were no longer sufficient. In addition they may have had a narrow geographical range, as does the author of *Regimen II*. Hippocratic authors have a large interest in geographical matters, as can be seen in *Airs, Waters and Places* and *Epidemics*, but this is less evident in *Regimen II*, in which place names give way to general geographical considerations. Galen covers the whole empire, as we have seen, from a Mediterranean perspective. He has almost no interest in mainland Greece and the islands; rather more in Rome and Italy; his terms of reference extend to Spain and Syria, Thrace and Alexandria, with the main evidential base set in Asia Minor, in Bithynia and the part of Mysia closest to Pergamum. He also covers the normal diet, with the limits of civilization being set. Lions and donkeys are preferably not eaten, nor are certain pulses except in times of famine. Extremes of poverty and foreignness thus define the foods of 'civilized' diet, which human beings can expect to eat without ill effect if they are in good health. The point of the travelling identified in Nutton (1995) and of the anecdotes that do not involve travelling is that Galen is bringing to bear what van der Eijk (1997) has identified as 'qualified experience'. He has seen the effect of wheat porridge on his own bowels; he has seen the student who ate no meat for four years; he is well aware that capers are not nourishing but are beneficial in other respects, whether as medicine or food. His theoretical approach enables him to judge correctly one piece of evidence against another, as in the case of the rock fish mentioned above. Foods are complicated and challenge neat classification. Above all, the human body depends on its humours and the ways in which they assimilate the juices of plants and animals. This is perhaps best seen in the case of the wet nurses. So a correct understanding of the complicated picture presented by observation is Galen's key aim. Fieldwork complements research. With this method, Galen is also claiming authority and status. When placed beside his predecessors, he has gone to places they had not included, and he has spoken to classes of person not normally considered, such as the ditchers and harvesters of Mysia (K. 498). In addition, he has the command of Greek literature and thought from Homer, through Aristophanes to the Hellenistic period, that enables him to out-gun any critic who comes his way.

Powell notes some interest in the treatise in specific conditions that derive from bad or inappropriate diet. Sometimes this relates to morbidity among the poorer classes, but normally the concern is fairly specific: the focus is on thick and sticky foods, which damage the channels of the liver and kidneys. I note this since the area of concern is the same as that treated in his earlier treatise *On the Thinning Diet*. The item on milk in book III (K. 687) is a good example. It is not clear to me whether the dangers of thickening the humours far exceed those of thinning them (this would explain why Galen emphasizes what he has already treated in detail) or whether there is some other reason for not giving space to the dangers of excessive thinning of the humours, and the conditions that arise from that. Conditions derived from excessive thickening include arthritis, liver and kidney conditions, headaches and epilepsy. But now I trespass on the territory of Dr Powell.

Preface

Owen Powell

The text of *On the Properties of Foodstuffs* upon which this translation is based is that edited by Georg Helmreich in 1923 for the *Corpus Medicorum Graecorum* series. As has now become conventional, the pagination of the much older edition of Karl (sometimes Carl) Gottlob Kühn is given in the margin. This has advantages both for greater precision in internal cross-referencing where this is needed, and for tying the commentary to the text. Items that receive mention in the commentary are identified by asterisks in the text.

The titles of all ancient sources are given in English. These, with the more traditional Latin titles, appear in a separate list of ancient sources. Throughout the translation and commentary, all Greek words and phrases are given in conventional transliteration. I have kept transliteration of terminology to a minimum but, given Galen's frequent discussion of alternative spellings (or names), some transliteration is necessary to make sense of his statements, as it is for the very few terms that resist satisfactory translation. In a few footnotes the Greek font is used where this seems likely to be helpful. All translated quotations from ancient sources are attributed to their translators, and where there is no such attribution the translation is my own.

Throughout the translation I have made use of both round and square brackets. The former enclose what I take to be in the nature of parenthetical remarks by Galen. The latter are used where Galen's statements need the actual Greek in order to be understood. These are generally matters to do with peculiarities of spelling, or with the etymological questions that were one of his particular interests.

Throughout the book several abbreviations recur:

CMG   *Corpus Medicorum Graecorum* (Lepzig and Berlin, 1908–)

K.   Kühn, C. G., *Claudii Galeni opera omnia* (Leipzig, 1821–33; repr. Hildesheim, 1965)

LSJ   Liddell, H. G., Scott, R. and Jones, H. S., *A Greek–English Lexicon* (9th edn, Oxford, 1968)

OCD[3]   Hornblower, S. and Spawforth, A. (eds.), *Oxford Classical Dictionary* (3rd edn, 1996)

SM   Marquardt, J., Müller, I. and Helmreich, G. (eds.), *Claudii Galeni Pergameni scripta minora* (Leipzig, 1884–93; repr. Amsterdam, 1967)

SOED   *Shorter Oxford English Dictionary* (3rd edn, revised 1969).

I am, of course, indebted to a number of people. Quite early in the exercise Dr John Vallance looked at a draft of the translation and the commentary on book 1. His comments re-directed me to a more thoughtful and rigorous approach. It was not to be as simple as I had thought. I am most grateful to him.

In dealing with a work of such diversity no one person can hope to be expert across the board. I am therefore grateful to Emeritus Professor Trevor Clifford for advice on botanical taxonomy and for pointing me to a modern definitive work on that subject; to my daughter Dr Judith Powell for the same attention to fish; and especially to Dr Hilton Deeth, Director of the Food Science and Technology Unit of the University of Queensland, for giving up time to discuss all manner of things to do with dairy products. It would also be remiss of me not to mention the help I received from the suggestions of the two anonymous readers of the Press. Without the careful attention of the copy-editor, Jan Chapman, whatever value this book has would have been greatly diminished. Jackie Warren, too, has handled its production (to say nothing of myself) with efficiency, patience and good humour. I thank them both.

In particular, I must thank Dr John Wilkins, of the University of Exeter, for agreeing to contribute a foreword that stands against a background of scholarship quite different from my own, but which greatly enhances whatever value this book has. Dr Michael Sharp of Cambridge University Press suggested this and for that, as well as other courtesies, I am most appreciative.

Above all I owe so much to my erstwhile supervisor and present friend, Michael Dyson of the Department of Classics and Ancient History at the University of Queensland. His influence throughout the translation may be hidden to others but I am very aware of it, and grateful for it, as I am also for his capacity for lateral thinking, which so often helped me to make sense of Galen's sometimes convoluted discussion.

Nevertheless, with all that help so generously given, the responsibility for errors of omission or commission, or of interpretation, remains with me.

Finally, it is no mere formality to thank my daughters for their continued enthusiasm for the project, and my wife Glenda, who has supported and encouraged me from the outset – not, it must be admitted, in the expectation of a deathless work of classical scholarship, but rather because, as a geriatrician of long experience, she is a committed member of the 'use it or lose it' school of preventive geriatrics!

Acknowledgements

Owen Powell

The quotation from the Menon Papyrus on p. 6 has been reproduced from W. H. S. Jones, *The Medical Writings of Anonymus Londinensis* (Amsterdam, 1968) by permission of Adolf M. Hakkert. The quotation from Galen's *On the Thinning Diet* on p. xviii has been reproduced from P. N. Singer, *Galen: Selected Works* (Oxford, 1997) by permission of Oxford University Press. The quotation from Aristotle's *Posterior Analytics* on p. 154 has been reproduced from Jonathan Barnes, *The Complete Works of Aristotle* (Princeton, 1984). © Princeton University Press. Reprinted by permission of Princeton University Press. The quotation from Galen's *Institutio Logica* on p. 156 has been reproduced from John Spangler Kieffer (ed.), *Galen's Institutio Logica* (Baltimore, 1964) by permission of Johns Hopkins University Press. The quotation from the Hippocratic Corpus on p. 6 has been reprinted by permission of the publishers and of the Trustees of the Loeb Classical Library from Hippocrates, volume IV, Loeb Classical Library L 150, translated by W. H. S. Jones, Cambridge, Mass.: Harvard University Press, 1931. The Loeb Classical Library ® is a registered trademark of the President and Fellows of Harvard College.

Introduction

For one and one half millennia Galen of Pergamum influenced the practice of medicine in the Western world, and for rather longer in some parts outside it. That in the hands of his successors this influence became stultifying and inhibitory of progress was no fault of his, although critics, from Paracelsus in the sixteenth century to others in the present day, have tried to diminish his importance.[1] Yet even fifty years ago, when antibiotic therapy was in its infancy and synthetic pharmaceuticals were far less common than now, any pharmacy in the Western world would have stocked a range of basic medicaments known as 'galenicals' – tinctures, syrups, extracts and the like – which were the building blocks for many of the prescribed medicines of the time. Nor was the term merely a memorial, for many of these galenicals stood in a direct line of succession from Galen's own medicaments. Indeed some were virtually identical, and used for much the same purposes that he had recommended. And to this day his views on foods from vegetable sources are referred to with obvious sincerity in some modern herbals.[2]

I commence this introduction by discussing the man and his work in general terms. After this I deal with several matters that arise so frequently throughout the book that it seems better to discuss them now than to make repeated comment as the work proceeds.

GENERAL

I shall not attempt to provide a more comprehensive biography of Galen than to say that he lived from AD 129 until perhaps 210; that he had an excellent, and doubtless expensive, education in medicine and philosophy in several of the great centres of the Eastern Mediterranean; that he

---

[1] For Paracelsus see Pagel (1964) 315; for modern critics see, for example, Baum (1989) 607, although the criticism of Galen here is more for his alleged subservience to Aristotle.
[2] E.g. McIntyre (1988) 21.

I

spent the greater part of his mature professional life in Rome and was
for a time the personal physician of the Emperor Marcus Aurelius; that
he was prickly, combative and self-opinionated; and that he read widely
and wrote voluminously.[3]

This present work, probably written late in his career, is of value for
a number of reasons, and John Wilkins has given a valuable account of
some in his foreword. There is no doubt that it holds much for a social
historian of the times, such as the evidence it provides, and which has
been used, for example by de Ste Croix, of the exploitation of the rural
poor by the urban well-to-do[4] or, as a bizarre sidelight (at III.1; K. 663),
on the rascally practices of certain innkeepers. As well, and importantly,
it reveals some of Galen's views on the nature of medical knowledge and
how that knowledge was logically to be validated. As Frede[5] has pointed
out, Galen had a sufficiently confirmed place in the general philosophical
tradition for professional philosophers to take note of, if only to disagree
with, his views, and Barnes[6] accords him 'an honourable place in the
history of logical science'. Finally, in this as well as in his other books
Galen is often our only surviving source, frequently in direct if fragmentary quotation, for the words of other medical writers of antiquity whose
works have been lost. Naturally enough, he was frequently selective in
his references, which were usually made, approvingly or otherwise, to
argue for his own theories. Selective or not, without them we would be
a great deal more ignorant of ancient medicine than we are.

But all these benefits are secondary to what Galen himself must have
regarded as the main purpose of the book, which was to describe the effect
of particular foods or classes of foods upon the body, and the reciprocal
effect of the body upon the foods. Aside from the obvious fact that depri-
vation of food leads to death, there were two reasons for this approach:
first, because in antiquity there was a clear connection between food and
pharmacology; and second, because of the perceived importance of regimen, of which diet was an important component, in the maintenance
of health and the management of illness.

THE PLACE OF FOOD IN THE MEDICINE OF ANTIQUITY

As the ancients saw it, foodstuffs (or many of them) had a dual role – on the
one hand as nutriment necessary for life and to provide the wherewithal

---

[3] For his early life see Nutton (1973).   [4] De Ste Croix (1981) 13–14; 219.
[5] Frede (1981) 66.   [6] Barnes (1991) 56.

for growth and reproduction; on the other as a drug (*pharmakon*), or better, pharmacological agent, with an effect, good or bad, upon the physiological processes of the body. To understand nutrition meant to understand what the body did to the food (as nutriment) in order to assimilate it into its tissues. To understand pharmacology meant to understand what the food (as drug) did to the body, and Galen makes a clear and logical distinction between the two activities, which were essentially those that modern pharmacology refers to as the phenomena of pharmacokinetics and pharmacodynamics. In fact he went a good deal further than this. He identified as 'foods' those items that the body assimilated into its own tissues. The rest were 'drugs' (*pharmaka*), and these were of four types. The first remain unaltered, but change and overcome the body, in the way that the body does foods; these drugs are 'absolutely deleterious and destructive of the animal's nature . . .'; that is, they are poisons. Also poisons are those of the second group, which 'take the cause of change from the body itself, then are putrefied and corrupted and in consequence then at the same time putrefy and corrupt the body . . .' The third and fourth groups are non-poisonous. The third warms the body but does it no harm, and the fourth, after acting upon the body, is eventually assimilated, and is both drug and food. In practice, poisons aside, there were items that invariably acted as drugs, and others that were invariably nutriments, but most lay somewhere along a line between those extremes, their role at any one time depending upon the circumstances at that time.[7] Within this last group he makes a further distinction between foods that were also 'cold' drugs and those that were also 'hot' drugs, the latter acting pharmacologically during the time that they were undergoing concoction in the veins and becoming foods when concoction had been completed.[8]

It should be said at this point that Galen's definition of 'food' was broad, embracing substances that we certainly should not now regard as such (for example, Indian hemp or marihuana) as well as others that were merely embellishments to food such as, then as now, poppy seed. But a great variety of foods was thought to have a therapeutic role. Some were believed to have a specific pharmacological action like promoting the flow of bile or thinning viscid mucous secretions, while others were thought to have a more general effect. To anticipate later discussion, all foods were considered to exhibit varying degrees of warmth and cold,

---

[7] *On Mixtures* K. 1.656 = Helmreich 92; see also Harig (1974) 90–1; Singer (1997) 271.
[8] *On Mixtures* K. 1.681 = Helmreich 107 = Singer (1997) 283.

moistness and dryness, and since many disease states were, it was believed, due to or at any rate manifested by aberrant mixtures of these
qualities, on the principle of treatment with opposites foods were a valuable adjunct to other therapy, or even the only therapy available. This
principle of treatment by opposites antedated Galen, at least as long
before him as *Nature of Man*,[9] which was one of the Hippocratic works
on which he wrote a commentary. In this present work, however, Galen
deals only briefly with therapy, and for a more systematic treatment one
should turn to his *On the Mixtures and Properties of Simple Drugs* or, as he did
himself, to the *On the Materials of Medicine* of Dioscorides, written in the
previous century.

REGIMEN

Rather than therapeutics, the bulk of this book has to do with such matters as the nomenclature of plants used for food, the nutritional value
of their products and also of many non-vegetable foods, and the physiological and pathological effects arising from their use. Such an approach
found its rationale in the kind of medicine that Galen implicitly advo-
cates. This was as much concerned with the prevention of illness and the
maintenance of good health as it was with the treatment of established
disease. Its aim was to ensure that the individual was kept in the best possible physical condition, with an important qualification that the degree
of training necessary for the extreme fitness of the athlete was not normal
and was indeed potentially dysfunctional. This qualification had been
made even in Hippocratic times, and was repeated by Galen in several
of his works.[10] It has been revived in our own time with the recognition
of the fact that over-training may have such unintended consequences
as disturbed endocrine function (such as amenorrhoea in young women
athletes), the early onset of osteoporosis and even sometimes a degree of
immunological deficiency.

   The way to this state of excellence, many believed, was through *diaita*,
which we usually translate as regimen, and which meant much more
than the word diet that is derived from it, embracing as it did virtually
everything to do with the lifestyle of the individual. According to Celsus
it was one of three forms of therapy available to the physician (although
therapy was only a part of its purpose) – the others being surgery and

[9] Hippocrates, *On the Nature of Man* 9 = Loeb *Hippocrates* IV, 24–5.
[10] Hippocrates, *Aphorisms* 3 = Loeb *Hippocrates* IV, 98–9; Galen, *Thrasybulus* K. V.820 = *SM* III.43
and *Exhortation to Study the Arts* K. I.30 = *SM* I.123.

pharmacology.[11] The concerns of regimen were with the whole of an individual's activities, covering such things as how often and when one should bathe; the nature of one's work and leisure; sexual activity; and, of course, the food one ate and its preparation. This was a holistic approach to personal health two millennia before the word was coined and the concept popularized in the twentieth century. In Plato's *Charmides* it was said to be the attitude of the Thracian physicians, for whom treatment of the eyes involved treatment of the head, but treatment of the head without treatment of the body was folly, and so 'they apply their régime to the whole body and try to treat and heal the whole and the part together'.[12] This is much like the aphorism of the great Canadian physician Sir William Osler, to the effect that it was more important to know what sort of patient has a disease than what sort of disease a patient has.[13]

The idea of regimen in Greek medicine, it was said, originated with a certain Herodicus of Selymbria (a Megarian colony on the shores of the Propontus, now the Sea of Marmara), an athletic trainer whom Plato mentions several times, although not always with respect, as when, in the *Republic*, he has Socrates relate that Herodicus, out of concern for his own health, 'mixed physical culture with medicine and wore out first himself and then many others'.[14] Nor was the author of the Hippocratic *Epidemics VI* any more impressed: 'Herodicus killed fever patients with running, much wrestling, hot baths. A bad procedure.'[15]

But whatever such critics thought of it, regimen came to mean what Plato's Thracians had demonstrated, namely, that the patient was to be looked at as a totality, an entity in his or her own right, and not as a stereotype of some particular disease, and this attitude was just as applicable to the healthy person. We cannot tell now how deeply this view penetrated Greek medical practice. Greek doctors having, no doubt, the human failings of their modern successors, one can guess that it was ignored by some, given lip service by others, and observed with varying degrees of conviction by most. On the face of it, Galen seems to have recognized its value without abandoning other more active measures such as blood-letting and, of course, the time-honoured treatment by opposites.

Herodicus' theory is explained in the so-called *Anonymus Londinensis*, thought to be derived from a pupil of Aristotle and sometimes called the '*Menon Papyrus*':

---

[11] *On Medicine* proem 9 = Loeb *De medicina* 1, 6–7.   [12] *Charmides* 157a-b (Jowett's translation).
[13] Cushing (1940) 489.   [14] *Republic* 406b (Grube's translation).
[15] Hippocrates, *Epidemics* VI.3.18 = Loeb *Hippocrates* VII, 243 (Smith's translation).

But Herodicus of Selymbria thinks that diseases come from regimen. Regimen, he says, is according to nature when it includes exercise, and the proper amount of discomfort too, so that the nourishment is digested, and the body continually receives its increase as the nourishment is absorbed according to nature. For he thinks that health results when the body enjoys a natural regimen, and disease when the regimen is unnatural...It is said too that this writer called the art of medicine 'scientific guidance to the natural condition'.[16]

The author of the Hippocratic *Regimen I* also held closely to this theory, and the following extract could almost be taken as the *raison d'être* for this present work of Galen's:

I maintain that he who aspires to treat correctly of human regimen must first acquire knowledge and discernment of the nature of man in general...and further the power possessed severally by all the foods and drinks of our regimen, both the power each of them possessed by nature and the power given them by the constraint of human art...[but]...eating alone will not keep a man well; he must also take exercise. For food and exercise, while possessing opposite qualities, yet work together to produce health. For it is the nature of exercise to use up material, but of food and drink to make good deficiencies.[17]

GALEN AS RESEARCHER

Although regimen in the general management of illness as well as in the maintenance of health was clearly prominent in Galen's mind through-out this book, it is not a textbook of therapeutics in the sense of dealing in any systematic way with specific diseases. Nor is it a research-based work like his treatise on functional anatomy, *On the Use of the Parts*. His research in the present work lay in his (apparently exhaustive) trawling of the earlier literature – sometimes with attribution but more often, probably, without.

However, there are strong indications from time to time of his interest in epidemiological research, using that term in its broad modern sense to cover more than merely the investigation of disease transmission. There is good evidence, for example, that Galen had an instinctive grasp of one of the canons of modern statistical epidemiology. This is that, in order to identify the effect of an independent upon a dependent variable, all extraneous variables must be as far as practicable eliminated, or at least 'controlled' or if possible held constant. Indeed, Galen had already put this quite clearly in his treatise *On Mixtures*, in which, investigating the

---

[16] *Anonymus Londinensis* 49 (Jones's translation).
[17] *Regimen* 1.2 = Loeb *Hippocrates* IV, 226–7 (Jones's translation).

influence of age upon the natural warmth of a child, he insists upon the need to ensure that the children under examination should be identical in all things except those two variables, for example, they should be of the same degree of plumpness. From what he writes in the present work one can guess that such views on statistical inference had been stimulated by the agricultural experimentation of his greatly respected father, which he describes in 1.37 (K. 552).

He was also an experimental physiologist. Thus, keeping our attention on the alimentary tract, in *Natural Faculties* he describes how, using a vivisected pig, he investigated the factors involved in the retention of ingested food in the stomach. He decided that it had less to do with the extent of liquefaction of the contents than with their degree of concoction, and that it was a matter of the food being changed into something proper to the animal that was being nourished.[18]

It is therefore not idle to speculate upon the factors (apart from the inevitable one of age) that might have inhibited Galen from making further progress in such investigations.

There are two obvious culprits. The first relates to what was in effect a cultural taboo on human anatomizing. As is well known, Galen's dependence on primate surrogates such as the ape, and non-primate mammalian subjects such as the pig, led him into errors in describing human anatomy. Most were of no great practical significance in the context of the times. Of much greater importance was the fact that the taboo removed all possibility of developing the study of human morbid, or pathological, anatomy. The purpose of this discipline, which was consequently unavailable to Galen, is to relate the perceived signs and symptoms of illness to anatomical changes in organs not normally accessible to observation but obtainable by post-mortem examination. Inability to do this inevitably leads to incorrect and sometimes fantastic hypotheses, although it must be said that Galen at times comes uncannily close to reality when one might have thought that fantasy would have been the next step. A good example in the present work is his association of splenic with hepatic pathology.

The second culprit was the almost complete absence of technological assistance and, most notably, of technology related to measurement. In the instance cited earlier, of the age/heat relationships of children, Galen had no means of objective measurement of body temperature. Had this been available to him, he must have realized at once the falsity of his

---

[18] *On the Natural Faculties* K. 11.155 = Loeb *Galen on the Natural Faculties*, 240.

theory; indeed, most probably the 'theory' itself would have been still-born. The purpose of measurement in medicine is essentially one of comparison, whether it be comparison of repeated measurements of the same variable in the one individual to detect change over time, or the comparison in an individual of the measurement of a particular variable with its so-called 'normal range', in other words as measured in a population of 'normal' individuals. It is certainly true, as Harig has pointed out,[19] that Galen was concerned to measure the intensity of effect of qualities, and that he used a terminology of gradation to do so. But this of its nature was a completely subjective exercise, quite unsuited to the purposes just mentioned. Physiological variables are continuous in their nature, but for comparative purposes must be expressed digitally. In practice there would have been almost nothing of the sort available to Galen, except for some physical measurements – height, span and so on, and there is no evidence that he used them – and a crude measure of the pulse rate.

The absence of technology had another effect, for technological and theoretical innovation interact reciprocally, each driving the other. One has only to consider the relationship between technological advances in gastroenterological endoscopy and advances in our knowledge of gastro-oesophageal pathology.

Medicine has always progressed in two ways. The first is through the accretion of knowledge resulting from painstaking research. The second is by conceptual leaps of such nature that they occur but rarely, perhaps centuries apart – in antiquity, the Hippocratic *On the Sacred Disease*, which took medicine out of the temple and eventually differentiated the physician from the priest; in the seventeenth century Harvey's *Circulation of the Blood*; Mendelian genetics and Pasteur's germ theory of infection in the nineteenth; perhaps the human genome in the twenty-first. Galen made no conceptual leaps. The advances he initiated were of the first category. But his research hardly explains the long and influential life of his work. Something about it, clearly, must have so satisfied his students and his students' students that his writings were reproduced (and translated) in the numbers necessary to survive the ravages of rats, floods, fire and neglect, while the work of other eminent physicians disappeared or survived only as fragments.

That something, I suggest, was a combination of his wide-ranging repertoire, his meticulous and detailed observation especially in his

[19] Harig (1974) 117.

anatomical work and, above all, the self-conscious aura of omniscience which pervades his work and to which, then just as now I suspect, the medical student always responds.

At this point it may be helpful to discuss several matters that recur throughout the text and which would otherwise demand repeated reference to the commentary.

PROPERTIES

This is an awkward word in English. We may speak of the property (or attribute) of something in terms of its physical characteristics, for example, that iron is hard and has a certain specific gravity. We can also speak of the property of a thing in terms of its chemical characteristics, for example, that under certain conditions iron can combine with sulphur to form iron sulphide. Beyond this chemical property, with certain substances, is their physiological property, for example, that in a certain chemical combination iron forms haemoglobin, which has the property of carrying oxygen in the blood to the tissues. And, of course, the substance may need to be described in terms of a pathological property, for example, that in certain states excess iron in the body can result in the condition known as haemochromatosis, with damage to the liver and other organs.

The last three examples are close to the meaning that Galen gives to the Greek word *dynamis*, which I have translated as 'property', and which is traditionally called 'faculty'. This word, which at times means power, might or force, also has the sense of capacity, ability or potentiality, as might be expected from its cognate verb which means, amongst other things, have the ability to. As so often, Galen is following Aristotle, who used the word as part of his technical vocabulary. As Aristotle explains,[20] the word has a twofold meaning. On the one hand it indicates a potentiality to produce change in something (an unexceptional Greek meaning); on the other, it indicates the potentiality in a thing to undergo change or, as Ross[21] puts it, 'of passing from one state to another'. It will be recognized that this precisely describes the twin activities of pharmacodynamics and pharmacokinetics, which were mentioned above. Not surprisingly, the existence of a particular property (*dynamis*) is assumed, and the property identified by its effect or activity (*energeia*). So aloes, which is able to increase the *tonos* (tension; tone) of the oesophagus has a *tonikos* (tonic) property.

[20] Aristotle, *Metaphysics* IX, 1046a5.   [21] Ross (1995) 182.

There is little fundamental difference between Galen's views on chemical, physiological and pathological properties and our own. However, there is a great difference in respect of his attitude to physical appearances (these were not, strictly, *dynameis*). Unlike ourselves, Galen held that physical characteristics (say, colour) were reflected in physiological properties. So that in III.39 (K. 744) of the present work we learn that good red wine produces good red blood. It was, after all, a reasonable belief for the times.

HUMOURS AND QUALITIES

Throughout this work there are many references to humours – that they are healthy or unhealthy; thick or thin; easily produced from some foods and poorly from others. Sometimes such statements are general in their application while at others times they refer to particular humours.[22] Similarly, much is made of *kraseis* (mixtures, blends) of qualities – in foodstuffs, in the body as a whole, in individual parts of the body or in body fluids – referring to the different proportions of two pairs of contrarieties, moist and dry, warm and cold, which were dominant in the foods, body parts and body fluids (or humours); just as they were in the natural world of climates and seasons.[23] These two related concepts, of qualities and humours, went back a very long time. To trace their origin and subsequent development in any detail in the present context would be a tedious and unhelpful exercise. But the relevance of the fully developed concepts to Galen's view of medicine is undeniable. Moreover it was the authority of Galen that ensured their long life as a coherent, if ultimately untenable, theory.

Of course Galen was heavily in debt to a long line of predecessors – medical and non-medical – for his views. The notion of health as the product of a dynamic equilibrium between opposing influences goes back at least to Alcmaeon in the sixth century BC, and had been widely held by the Hippocratic writers. Plato took it and extended the notion beyond medicine to the cosmos. Aristotle developed and refined the concept of a *mesotês*, a middle state, in which the individual organ functioned well or otherwise according to whether or not the elements of which it was composed (earth, air, fire and water) were properly proportioned

---

[22] There are useful discussions of humours by Vallance in *OCD*[3] and by Nutton in Bynum and Porter (1993) chap. 3, 14.

[23] The fourfold pattern of humours, qualities and seasons is discussed at length in Schöner (1964).

and blended; and since these elements were characterized by different qualities, this concept was extended to include the balance of hot and cold, or of moist and dry. Tracy has written the definitive work dealing with this subject and his concluding chapter is a succinct summation of the arguments.[24]

The notion of humours (or body fluids) and the idea that disease was related to some imbalance of them was only one of many theories in antiquity, some of which completely ignored them. For Galen the definitive theory was that articulated in the Hippocratic *Nature of Man*. We know this to be the case since he wrote a detailed, line-by-line, commentary on the work.[25] Galen believed that it was a genuinely Hippocratic work, or at the least the product of Hippocrates' pupil (some say his son-in-law) Polybus. It commences with arguments, which Galen characteristically converts to vigorous polemic, against those who had taken a monistic approach to the physiology of the body. The monists had asserted that man was composed of a single substance – for the philosophers, one of the elements (air, fire, water or earth); for the physicians, one of the humours. If this were true, so the Hippocratic argument went, it would mean that it would be impossible for such a one to feel pain (which Galen elsewhere defines as anything contrary to nature), nor could generation take place, since generation required two components. The truth, it was concluded, was that the nature of man was made up of blood, phlegm (i.e., mucus), yellow bile and black bile, and it was through these that he felt pain and maintained health. If their balance was disturbed, the body experienced disease.

While *Nature of Man* makes frequent mention of the four standard qualities – hot and cold, moist and dry – it was the balance of the humours that took prominence in that work. However, Galen's *Commentary* paid at least as much attention to the qualities as it did to the humours. Galen, who revered the name of Hippocrates, was not beyond reading more into the Master's words than the Master may have intended, and was inclined to call upon Hippocrates to bear witness to the soundness of his own views or to demonstrate that he was following in the right tradition. At any rate, both here and elsewhere, as Nutton has pointed out,[26] while Galen accepted the humours as underlying his physiology, so far as diagnosis and therapy were concerned he emphasized the qualitative changes in

[24] Tracy (1969) 334–43.
[25] Hippocrates, *On the Nature of Man* IV.2–51 = Loeb *Hippocrates* IV, 2–41. Galen, *On Hippocrates' 'On the Nature of Man'* K. XV.1–173 = *CMG* V.9.1.
[26] Nutton (1991) 15, n. 21.

the body. Given that each humour was characterized by a specific mix
of qualities, perhaps the difference was really only one of emphasis.

By his own reckoning Galen was both physician and philosopher, but
as a practising physician he saw little profit in discussing the more fundamental elements. Fire, air, water and earth were necessary for producing
the first links of the food chain, namely plants, and by passing along the
chain they eventually become part of the human organism. This seems
to have been almost the limit of his interest, although there are occasional hints to the contrary when he speaks of 'earthiness' of substance,
as in 1.29 (K. 547) of the present work regarding bitter vetch. But the
really important matters to Galen were the qualities, associated with the
elements, that inhered in food and became manifest in the body when
concoction of the food in the veins and liver produced, in actuality, the
humours that until then had existed only potentially. Still less did he
regard Plato's ideas in the *Timaeus* about the geometrical representation
of the elements as being of practical consequence. This, he thought, was
a matter for theoretical philosophy and not for medicine.[27]

As for the humours themselves, these were blood, phlegm, yellow bile
and black bile, and some need further comment. The humour blood,
Galen points out in *On Hippocrates' 'On the Nature of Man'*, was not the
blood usually seen in blood-letting or trauma, for that contained both
biles and phlegm, as well as blood in the strict sense, which seems to have
been conceptualized as a theoretical fluid without separate existence.[28]
Phlegm covered what we now would call mucus. Yellow bile seems to
have varied considerably in colour, from quite pale to the colour of egg
yolk or greenish, and sometimes the term seems to be covering a range of
similar fluids. But there was no doubt of its separate existence, nor of the
fact that it was collected in the gall bladder and passed via the cystic and
common bile ducts into the small bowel. Black bile has always been a
problem for translators. At times one has the sense that it existed only to
make up four items, the number that figured so largely in Greek scientific
thought, be it to do with elements, qualities or seasons. At other times

---

[27] Plato, *Timaeus* 53c–56d. Galen, *On the Doctrines of Hippocrates and Plato* K. v.668 = *CMG*
v.4.1.2,496.

[28] *On Hippocrates' 'On the Nature of Man'* K. xv.60–1 = *CMG* v.9.1,33. The reference is to the role
of menstrual blood in generation. Later, at K. xv.73–4 = *CMG* v.9.1,39, he says that blood is
of two types – one containing mucus and the biles, as it appears in blood-letting, the other pure
and completely unmixed with any other humours. Actual blood, he tells us in *On the Doctrines of
Hippocrates and Plato* K. v.674 = *CMG* v.4.1.2,498, takes the name of the predominant humour
contained in it. Nutton, in Bynum and Porter (1993) 287, uses the term 'elemental humour',
which effectively expresses the sense.

it seems that it indicated one or all of the various black or dark fluids that must have been as common then as now – the black, tarry stool of an intestinal bleed, the dark urine of haematuria or, in a land where malaria must have been common, of blackwater fever. Nor is the difficulty made easier by the existence of what Galen refers to as *ta melana* – black things – which sound like what nineteenth-century physicians, who were addicted to culinary similes, called 'coffee grounds', that are found in the vomitus in a variety of conditions in which denatured blood has collected in the stomach.

The four humours, most emphatically, were not present in the foods themselves, except potentially, as Galen makes clear in *Natural Faculties*.[29] Honey, he points out for example, produces yellow bile because it undergoes a change that enables it to be converted to bile, not because the bile is contained within it. He goes on to say that when nutriment is changed in the veins by the innate heat of the body, blood is produced when the innate heat is in moderation, otherwise either yellow bile or phlegm is produced, the final result depending, respectively, upon whether warmth or cold predominated in the particular food. Seasonal factors also played a part, for different humours tended to predominate in different seasons. As for black bile, in a treatise devoted to that humour Galen tells us that it results from overheating of yellow bile. But it must be said that much that Galen says about black bile is as puzzling as one might expect when he is dealing with such a mysterious fluid. For example, he appears to agree with what is apparently an ancient distinction between a black bile that is corrosive and a normal black humour. What does seems clear, as Nutton points out, is that the existence of black bile as an 'elemental' humour explained its invisiblity in the body.[30]

GALEN'S THEORIES ON DIGESTION AND NUTRITION

Galen pointed out in his *Natural Faculties* that nutrition is 'the assimilation of that which nourishes to that which is being nourished'.[31] It is curious, in a work dealing with the properties of foods, including their potential to become 'that which nourishes', that there is so little information about the actual physiology of nutrition in *Properties of Foodstuffs*. To find out how

---

[29] *On the Natural Faculties* K. 11.115–18 = Loeb *Galen on the Natural Faculties*, 178–82.

[30] *On Black Bile* K. v.112 = *CMG* v.4.1.1,75. On its invisibility, see Nutton in Bynum and Porter (1993) 287. On the distinction from black humour, *On the Natural Faculties* K. 11.136 = Loeb *Galen on the Natural Faculties*, 210. On seasonal factors see Schöner (1964).

[31] *On the Natural Faculties* K. 11.24 = Loeb *Galen on the Natural Faculties*, 38 (Brock's translation).

Galen saw the processes by which substance in the external environment became part of and identical to substance in the animal body we must look elsewhere in his writings. For this *On the Natural Faculties*, *On the Use of the Parts* and to a lesser extent *On the Opinions of Hippocrates and Plato* are invaluable. Making use of these sources we can most economically examine Galen's theories of digestion and nutrition by following the progress of food from the external environment to its eventual assimilation in the tissues of 'that which is being nourished'.

Before doing so we might note two things that were fundamental in his theory. The first was the teleological approach exemplified by Aristotle's belief in a Nature 'which makes nothing in vain',[32] to which Galen wholeheartedly subscribed. The second was his extension of Aristotle's concept, as expounded in his *On the Soul*, of faculties (*dynameis* – properties; attributes) of the soul (*psychê* – as we might say, 'life force'). The most primitive of these, present in every form of life, was the nutritive faculty or property. To serve this, Galen provided second-order *dynameis* of a general nature – attractive, retentive, alterative and expulsive – which applied to the body as a whole as well as to its constituent parts. Beyond these again were more specific attributes such as the haematopoietic or blood-forming property. Galen was quite agnostic so far as the *psychê* was concerned, and was disarmingly frank about his *dynameis*: 'so long as we are ignorant of the true essence of the cause which is operating (*tên ousian tês energousês aitias*) we call it a faculty'.[33] In other words, if an activity X produces an effect Y, let us say an active change in something, there must exist in that something a potential Y^a for this change to take place. In Aristotelian terms X is the efficient cause (*aitia*) of Y, but Y is the final cause (*to hou heneka* – the for the sake of which) of Y^a. And the *dynamis* takes its name from that.

In the light of Galen's coolly dispassionate remark about *dynameis* that has just been quoted, one may question the depth of his commitment to Aristotle's concept. Indeed what Galen was describing, and for all we know this may well have been his aim, was an analytical model that permitted the conceptual isolation of otherwise inseparable components of a complex activity. At one place in *Natural Faculties*,[34] he may be doing just that when we find him identifying two (admittedly hypothetical) sorts of attraction – *horror vacui* (where something moves to fill emptiness), and

[32] *Parts of Animals* 658a9 (Ogle's translation in Barnes (1984)).
[33] *On the Natural Faculties* K. 11.9 = Loeb *Galen on the Natural Faculties*, 16 (Brock's translation).
[34] *On the Natural Faculties* K. 11.206–7 = Loeb *Galen on the Natural Faculties*, 318–19.

the mutual attraction of things that are of 'appropriate' quality.[35] But such theorizing need not concern us here.

In the ordinary course of events an animal extracts food from its external environment in response to the stimulus of appetite. Galen believed that the stomach, and especially the cardio-oesophageal area, was the one site for the symptomatic expression of the need for food. However, the stomach, which has no power of perception, must be informed of this need by messages from the sensorium (*apo tês aisthêtikês archês* – from the source of sensation[36]). These messages are conducted through the two vagus nerves that end in plexuses around the stomach. In this way the animal becomes aware of appetite. But appetite cannot be indiscriminate. For each species there is food that is proper to it, and food that is not. Man does not normally eat grass, nor a donkey flesh. So Nature has arranged it that grass is distasteful to a man, and flesh to a donkey.[37]

When the proper food has been taken by the individual, a sequence of changes commences under the influence of the alterative faculty. Of course, where necessary, the first change would have been the preparation of the food before eating. Passing over that, the alteration that takes place in the mouth is essentially a physical change, brought about by the action of chewing and the presence of saliva (referred to as phlegm). This change prepares the food for its onward passage to the stomach. Galen regarded the passage of food down the oesophagus on swallowing as a function of the attractive property of the stomach. He berates the long-dead Erasistratus for denying this and insisting upon the importance of oesophageal peristalsis. In a splendid piece of imagery he envisages the stomach extending its upper portion like a hand to clutch the food and draw it back into itself.

Once the food is in that organ, as well as whatever liquid has been taken with it, the retentive property of the stomach ensures that it stays there while the alterative property, acting through the process of *pepsis*, converts it into a fluid (*chymos*) or chyme of a quality appropriate to that individual. *Pepsis* was thought of in much the same light as cooking, and resulted from the action of the body's innate heat. For this reason it is translated here as concoction, rather than the digestion of some translators, as I discuss later. The stomach, Galen says, is the particular instrument (*organon*) of concoction.[38]

---

[35] *On the Natural Faculties* K. 11.206–7 = Loeb *Galen on the Natural Faculties*, 318–20.
[36] *On the Use of the Parts* K. 111.277 = Helmreich 1.203 (May's translation).
[37] As Galen points out at 1.6 (K. 567).
[38] *On the Use of the Parts* K. 111.284 = Helmreich 1.208.

We may note at this point one instance in which *The Properties of Food-stuffs* contributes to our understanding of Galen's physiology. Frequently throughout this work he refers to a food being subject to 'corruption' in the stomach and relates this to the ease or otherwise of its concoction. The words he uses to describe this are derivatives of *diaphtheirein*, which variously means to destroy, corrupt, spoil or ruin and also, in the passive, to be decomposed. Unfortunately he gives too little information about the actual process to permit an unequivocal translation. For better or worse I have chosen to use 'corrupt' but 'spoil' would be as acceptable. We are told that it takes place more readily under certain conditions such as the presence in the stomach of bile, and with certain foods such as the colocynth. But what actually happens is left unstated because, no doubt, it would have been obvious to his contemporaries even if it is obscure to us. The important feature is that, apart from certain anomalous situations, such as the pankration fighters of K. 487, corruption and concoction seem to have been, so to speak, in competition. Concoction was a time-related process and the less susceptible a food was to corruption the more time was available, he must have thought, for complete concoction and vice versa.

The stomach eventually exercised its expulsive property, in two directions. In a small way, the squeezing action of the stomach initiated a process of *anadosis* or distribution that saw a proportion of the chyme entering the portal venous system leading to the liver. However, the greater part of the chyme was expelled through the pylorus into the duodenum and so on to the jejunum which, Galen also tells us, was the particular instrument (*organon*) of distribution (*anadosis*) which took place by way of the superior mesenteric vein to the portal vein and so to the liver. As stated earlier, Galen believed that he had shown experimentally that the factor determining the emptying of the stomach was the completeness of concoction rather than the degree of fluidity of the chyme. That is to say, it had a chemical rather than a physical basis.

One curious point emerges at this stage. Before the stomach gets rid of its contents it was thought to have extracted from them what was necessary for its own nutrition by contracting around the food, from which it drew 'the fluid proper to itself'. Which raises the question, if nutriment for the remainder of the body needed further processing in the liver (as will be seen shortly), why was this unnecessary for the nutrition of the stomach? Especially since, in starvation, the liver sends (presumably processed) nutriment to the stomach by retrograde flow in the portal vein. Galen does not explain and indeed may not have recognized any anomaly.

As just stated, the jejunum was the particular instrument of *anadosis*, the place from which distribution begins, as the nutrient fluid is extruded from the gut into the superior mesenteric vein and so into the portal venous system leading to the liver. What was not so extruded, the residues or waste products (*perisômata*), was expelled as excrement. The veins were thought to terminate in the gut wall in invisible openings, and in this present work (at 1.12; K. 508) it is implied that nutriment could be hindered in its distribution due to a lack of match between the invisible holes and the solid particles. However, the fluid passed through them under the combined influence of the expulsive property of the gut (expressed through its peristalsis) and the attractive property of the liver. The veins themselves were also thought to have a propulsive property of their own.

From this point the metabolic pathway becomes somewhat obscure. It seems that a preliminary working up of the chyme took place in the portal vein, but that the major change occurred in the liver. The liver was important for two reasons. First, it was thought to be the origin of the veins that extended throughout the body and so carried nutrient material to all parts. Second, it was the site of the major alteration of the nutriment from the gut, when this was converted to blood under the influence of the liver's haematopoietic property. It was obvious that blood from the portal system must find its way through the liver into the hepatic veins leading from the liver into the vena caval systems (the superior vena cava to the upper body, the inferior to the lower). How this was accomplished, of course, could only be guessed at. Galen's guess involved a hypothetical network of channels within the liver, so fine as to be invisible, connecting the portal and the caval systems' veins. This network had the further advantage of slowing the flow and so enabling more thorough concoction. Taking a cue from the Hippocratic *On Nutriment*, he believed that passage through this network was facilitated by the existence in blood of a thin clear fluid which was the transporting agent or *ochêma*.[39] The clear serum that is extruded from clotting blood may have been the origin of this notion. This acted by dilution in much the same way that ingested drink had diluted, and so made more fluid, the chyme that concoction produced in the stomach. Excess of this clear fluid was eventually got rid of as urine.

Following its final processing in the liver, the nutrient blood, as the chyme had now become, was directed into the vena caval system which drains the body and so passed in retrograde fashion (as we now know) to

[39] *On Nutriment* 55 = Loeb *Hippocrates* 1, 360.

the periphery. Galen then postulated a final three-stage process that was a tribute to both his logic and his imagination. Somehow the nutrient blood had to become tissue such as bone, flesh and tendon. To reach this outcome Galen envisaged the nutrient material undergoing, at the tissue level, first, a stage of application (*prosthesis*); next, one of attachment (*prosphysis*); and lastly, one of assimilation (*homoiôsis*),[40] when it finally became part of, and indistinguishable from, the tissue it was nourishing or for which it was providing the substance of growth. When growth was occurring, this assimilation took place with a corresponding expansion in bulk; but when nutrition alone was concerned, in the absence of growth, we must assume that Galen had in mind, correctly, that the assimilated tissue was replacing tissue that had been lost in the wear and tear of life.

ATTICIZERS

This subject has nothing to do with either medicine or nutrition, but on no fewer than five occasions in this work 'Atticizers' are the explicit objects for Galen's jeers, and on several other occasions the implied ones. In this he was a participant, intentionally or not, in a debate upon the issue of what Swain refers to as 'the language consciousness of the Greek elite in the second sophistic period' – an issue which in some ways anticipated the *katharevousa* (or puristic) versus demotic struggle of later Greek linguistic history. In what follows I am heavily in debt to Swain's lucid account.[41]

At the time of the Athenian hegemony of the Greek world in the fifth and fourth centuries BC there was a linguistic exchange between the Attic and Ionic dialects, which resulted in Attic being regarded as the literary language, while Ionic was the prestige language of philosophy and science (including the Hippocratic *corpus*). But Ionic influence was powerful outside science, and by the time of Alexander's conquest of Persia it was the Ionic/Attic blend which was becoming the language of the new Greek civilization of the Near East, and this common (*koinê*) tongue progressively diverged from a dying, pure Attic.

However, during the period of the so-called second sophistic movement there arose a tendency among the intellectual elite to re-emphasize the supposed virtues of the ancient literary Attic dialect. Swain makes the point that the effect of this, by design or otherwise, was the same

---

[40] *On the Natural Faculties* K. 11.24–5 = Loeb *Galen on the Natural Faculties*, 38–40.
[41] Swain (1996) chaps. 1 and 2.

as the effect of the puristic–demotic split of more recent times, namely, to put political and economic power in the hands of an elite; and to withhold it from the rest. It is surely no coincidence that Galen at 11.11 (K. 584) makes a similar point about those who prefer money to knowledge.

In no sense was the *koinê* a separate language. In fact it covered a wide spectrum from the educated to the uneducated and doubtless beyond that, to the spoken tongue. Thus Galen's (educated) *koinê* is not that of the Gospel of St Luke. Indeed, Galen's *koinê*, and educated *koinê* generally, was closer to 'pure' Attic than it was to less educated *koinê*. But, as is implicit in all his comments, where even educated *koinê* parted company with Attic was in its vocabulary. Given that Galen wrote to be read by his contemporaries, his overriding desire for clarity demanded the use of contemporary rather than obsolete terms, as John Wilkins has pointed out in his foreword. It was this matter of terminological divergence which most got under his skin and produced his most vigorous vituperation.

Galen's medical and scientific terminology

Translation of ancient Greek 'scientific' texts presents a number of problems and reliance upon the standard dictionaries is risky. These depend upon the accuracy of sources of information that may have been dubious to start with or, more likely, may have been superseded by advances in knowledge or changes in terminology or taxonomy.

In *On the Properties of Foodstuffs* the problems relate both to the medical and to the non-medical content. For my part, however, the medical content has been the more difficult to interpret, and this despite my professional life having been spent in medicine. Or perhaps because of it!

Questions of interpretation aside, there is the prior problem of translating terminology, and here there are some difficulties that apply specifically to the translation of ancient medical texts. A good deal has been written on this subject by philologists such as Chantraine as well as by a number of other classicists, of whom Lloyd has made the most valuable contribution in English, dealing especially with anatomy. The translator of Galen's *On the Use of the Parts* has also given an account of the problems she faced.[1] Among the identified causes perhaps the most important is the Greek lack of an agreed, consistent, stable and unambiguous *scientific* language. In our own time we have been able to use Greek or Latin (sometimes Arabic) to provide names, or elements for word-building, but the Greeks had nothing (or did not think of using anything) of the sort. As a result they employed their ordinary language for extraordinary purposes, or as metaphor.[2] This lack of a scientific language had major consequences, resulting in inconsistency between authors and even within the same author's writings; and leading to instability of terminology over time.

At the modern end of the translation equation other problems arise. Concepts and nomenclature have been retained in the lexicon when they

---

[1] Lloyd (1983) 149–67; May (1970).   [2] Skoda (1988).

are long obsolete, and a name which once held a general meaning in Greek, and perhaps at first held much the same meaning in English, over time has no longer retained it in the modern tongue. For example, to the Greeks *cholera* was a non-specific term for a type of diarrhoea; to us cholera is a specific infectious disease. This narrowing of focus over time is not rare.

As regards the scientific, but non-medical, elements in the present text the position is a little different, although it varies with the discipline. Broadly speaking, there is no great problem with the nomenclature of terrestrial animals, of which in any case the ancient name has often carried into modern Greek. There is little problem with birds, rather more with fish, and very much more with plants. Much identification hinges upon collateral evidence from other ancient authors, and sometimes considerable gaps remain. With the birds and fishes, one cannot but be grateful to that great polymath D'Arcy Wentworth Thompson.[3] Although his taxonomical details may now be dated, his identifications generally remain secure. However, in the case of plants some identifications inevitably remain in the 'most likely' category.

Concentrating therefore on medical terminology, I shall examine several Greek terms that occur frequently throughout this work, particularly those of gastroenterological or nutritional reference.

anadosis – ἀνάδοσις. This is derived from the verb *anadidōmi* and both words occur frequently in *On the Properties of Foodstuffs*. The verb has a range of possible meanings in English – 'deliver up', 'give up', 'send up' and, in the context of food, 'distribute'. In the same way the noun can mean 'distribution'. The question is whether it has another technical meaning that is different from any of those given above. Vallance referred to 'the absorption of nutriment into the veins, ἀνάδοσις...',[4] and there is some support in Galen for this approach. It has been noted in the introduction that in his *On the Use of the Parts* Galen states that the small bowel (*enteron*) is the *organon* of *anadosis*. Now *organon* carries a sense of instrumentality and is, indeed, most properly translated as 'instrument'. There is clearly a case for 'absorption' here.

But the question remains whether this was the exclusive meaning, and there is clear evidence in *On the Properties of Foodstuffs* that this was not so. For example, the verb is used to describe *chymos* passing up to the liver (11.9; K. 574) or to 'the liver and the body as a whole' (11.61; K. 650), and this goes well past absorption. Distribution is clearly implied.

---

[3] Thompson (1936; 1946).   [4] Vallance (1990) 66.

Further, as with *pepsis* and digestion (to be discussed shortly), the range of activity implied by the term is too complex to be encompassed by a single modern *technical* term. In its modern gastroenterological context absorption is such a term: it refers to a specific physico-chemical process by which nutrient material is carried across the mucosal lining of the small bowel. Even at this initial intestinal level Galen's *anadosis* described a process that was completely different from what we know as absorption. To translate *anadosis* as absorption is to indicate something that does not exist.

Since there is no comprehensive English technical term to describe the process Galen envisages, I have of necessity done what Galen himself did of necessity, and have used the usual 'distribute' or 'distribution' throughout. I have some support from the fact that the first published English translator of Galen, A. J. Brock, had come to much the same conclusion, commenting that the process of *anadosis* involved two stages: '(1) transmission of food from alimentary canal to liver (rather more than our "absorption"); (2) further transmission from liver to tissues...'[5]

koilia / gastêr – κοιλία/γαστήρ. There is no problem with the fact that both of these words could be used, virtually interchangeably, to indicate the anatomical stomach, although *koilia* tended to be restricted to situations in which the container aspect of the stomach was at least implied. Nor need there be concern with Galen's occasional use of one or the other word in its more ancient sense of belly or abdomen.

The problem arises from Galen's information in his introductory chapter (1.1 at K. 467) that the meaning of either word can be extended to include the intestines (*ta entera*), which he supports by introducing two, possibly slang, words – *progastôr* and *megalokoilos*. Two difficulties arise from this.

The first is that while in English the word stomach can certainly apply to the belly in general, it does not carry the additional meaning implied by *entera*. *Entera*, and therefore *gastêr* or *koilia* when used in such a context, must be translated as intestine(s), bowel(s) or, less elegantly but common in medical jargon and rooted in embryological terminology, gut. But, unlike the Greek, there is no single word in English that covers the anatomical stomach together with the small and large intestine.

The second difficulty arises from the first, for it is remarkable how seldom one can be certain whether, in any particular instance, Galen is referring to the anatomical stomach, the belly or the bowel. When we

---

[5] Brock (1916), Introduction to *On the Natural Faculties*, Loeb *Galen on the Natural Faculties*, 13, n. 5.

read, as we often do, of the mouth of the *gastêr/koilia*, we can be certain that he refers to the anatomical stomach. Again, when, in the same chapter at K. 467, the effect of scammony juice is to purge (*hypagein*) *tên gastera*, the likelihood is great, but one cannot be certain that it is the bowel that is affected since scammony is a recognized purgative (as we understand the term). But in many other places it would be unwise to adopt too dogmatic a view about this and similar phrases. A modern physician may well be doubtful whether the rate of gastric emptying can be assessed by a patient's history or on physical examination, but this does not mean that Galen had the same view. His system of physiology, after all, contains many such assumptions about invisible events. That said, however, in a context of *hypagein* (or similar) a meaning of bowel is probably more common.

There are three possible ways to handle this uncertainty – either consistently to translate *koilia* and *gastêr* as 'stomach'; or as 'intestine' (or similar); or to make judgements based upon context. Consequently I have commonly used phrases such as 'move the bowels' or 'act as a purgative' unless the context suggests the stomach, when 'increase gastric emptying' has often seemed appropriate. Such translations are necessarily subjective and may not be universally acceptable. But this is the approach that I have adopted.

pepsis – πέψις. This is very commonly translated as 'digestion', and it may seem pedantic to cavil at this. After all, the *SOED* definition of digestion is 'The process whereby the nutritive part of the food is, in the stomach and intestines, rendered fit to be assimilated by the system.' However, the process that Galen describes under the name *pepsis* takes place not only in the stomach but continues in the portal vein and especially in the liver. As with *anadosis*, there is also a difficulty because 'digestion', as nowadays understood, is a process that results in the chemical breakdown of food into simpler, absorbable, components, and this was certainly not what Galen would have understood by *pepsis*. In a non-medical context the word means 'ripening', 'changing (by heat)' and 'cooking', and this is very much the sense in which Galen uses it. He envisaged the food, under the influence of the innate heat of the stomach, undergoing a process much like cooking, and hence the translation as 'concoction'.

stomachos – στόμαχος. In his *On the Use of the Parts* Galen tells us that this word can refer to any narrow passage leading to a cavity, but that in the alimentary tract it was 'the common name' (*to koinon onoma*) for 'the thoroughfare' that passed from mouth to stomach, which was called, more specifically, the *oisophagos*.[6] Chantraine thought that in Homeric times *stomachos* meant throat, but that in the Hippocratic *Sacred Disease* it had come to mean the entrance of the stomach, the phrase in question being *tou stomachou tês gastros*.[7] Fortunately Praxagoras, a near contemporary of Hippocrates, gives the precise anatomical relationships, describing the trachea lying in front of it before it passes to the lungs; with the *stomachos* behind, attached to the vertebrae in the neck and 'implanted' into the stomach.[8] Anatomical relationships are the only certain way to identify a structure, and there can be no doubt at all that for Praxagoras the word indicated the oesophagus in its full length. Aristotle, in his two major biological works – *Parts of Animals* and *History of Animals* – uses both *oisophagos* and *stomachos*, with some preference for the former.

Closer in time to Galen, Rufus of Ephesus quite explicitly refers to the *stomachos* as the means by which food and drink pass to the stomach; and in another passage he suggests that the term includes the upper portion, at least, of the stomach, that is, our gastric cardia.[9] Which brings us to Galen.

We have seen that Galen regarded *stomachos* as the common term for *oisophagos*, but in *On the Use of the Parts* he much more frequently uses the latter term. However, in *On the Properties of Foodstuffs* he never once uses it. The word he employed to describe the use of the term *stomachos* was *koinon*, meaning shared, common, everyday. It was used in *hê koinê glôssa* to describe the everyday language of his day (see the remarks on Atticizers in the introduction). This may suggest that the more 'scientific' *oisophagos* was used for the restricted audience of an extremely technical work on functional anatomy, whereas the present work, on the face of it for a wider and not necessarily professional audience, received the *koinê*.

Nevertheless throughout this translation on a number of occasions I have left the word *stomachos* untranslated and transliterated, for reasons that are given in the following section.

to stoma tês koilias/gastros – τὸ στόμα τῆς κοιλίας/γαστρός. 'The mouth of the stomach' is a phrase that occurs with great frequency throughout the present work. It bears an interesting relationship to the *stomachos*. In one place (11.22 at K. 600) Galen speaks of the stomach emptying itself (or being emptied) when astringent food is eaten in the

[6] *On the Use of the Parts* K. 111.267 = Helmreich 1.195 – ὄνομα δὲ . . . τὸ μὲν ἴδιον οἰσοφάγος, τὸ δὲ κοινὸν στόμαχος . . .
[7] Chantraine (1975) 40; *Sacred Disease* 10 = Loeb *Hippocrates* 11, 160.
[8] Steckerl (1958), fr. 10.
[9] *On the Nomenclature of the Human Body* 155, 7–8; *On the Parts of the Human Body* 178, 6–11.

presence of a relaxed *stomachos*. In another (11.64 at K. 652), a particular
food is said to stimulate appetite in a relaxed *stomachos*. In a third place
(11.26 at K. 607) we can go further, for Galen remarks, à propos of
gnawing sensations at the 'mouth of the stomach', that he has often said
that physicians frequently call the mouth of the stomach *stomachos*, and
he repeats this elsewhere (K. 600, 608). Then, in his *On the Pulses for
Beginners* he refers to such usage as *dia tên tôn pollôn synêtheian* – 'by general
custom'.[10] But he also says in *On the Use of the Parts*, in May's translation,
that 'the Creator did not connect the cavity of the stomach directly to
the oesophagus [*stomachos*], but made the so-called mouth of the stomach
a receiving channel...'[11] But further, in K. 604 of the present work he
remarks that the area around the mouth of the stomach is also called the
kardia (as indeed it is to this day). As De Lacy points out in a note to his
translation of *On the Doctrines of Hippocrates and Plato*,[12] the same usage is
to be found in a work by Nicander of Colophon, of the second century
BC.

It seems therefore that to some physicians, including Galen himself
on occasions, the meaning of the word *stomachos* had been or was being
extended to indicate what is now called the gastro- or cardio-oesophageal
junction. Moreover, on the above evidence Galen was not completely
consistent in his nomenclature, for he appears to vary his use of the
phrase between the cardia and the actual gastro-oesophageal junction.
In other words, on some occasions at least, Galen used the word to
include oesophagus, gastro-oesophageal segment and the upper part (or
cardia) of the stomach itself. So rather than commit to something like
cardio-oesophageal region, I have thought it better in such a situation
to transliterate *stomachos* rather than translate it, leaving translation as
oesophagus (and once as gullet) where the context is less equivocal. As
with *koilia/gastêr* this too involves subjective judgement. Which raises the
question of:

eu- and **kako-stomachos** – εὐ- and κακο-στόμαχος – two words
which recur throughout this work. In an alimentary context the dictionary gives the meaning of these words as 'good' or 'bad for the stomach';
and throughout the present translation I have obediently, if reluctantly,
conformed to this. But if *stomachos* did not at the time mean the total
anatomical stomach (and it seems unlikely that it did) how can a simple prefix have made it so? There is perhaps a clue in LSJ, where the

[10] *On the Pulses for Beginners* K. VIII.489.   [11] *On the Use of the Parts* K. III.315 = Helmreich 1.231.
[12] De Lacy (1984), note in *On the Doctrines of Hippocrates and Plato*, 182, 23.

verb *eustomacheô* has a single reference to the first-century B C philosopher
Philodemus, in which the word is said to have meant 'have a good appetite'. Then, we are told by Galen that the stomach is the sole source
of appetite, 'and particularly the parts at its mouth', and in a splendid
piece of imagery he describes the stomach drawing down food to itself
by means of its *stomachos* 'as if by a hand'.[13] So that it seems very possible
that the true meanings of *eu*- and *kako-stomachos* may well have been 'good
for' and 'bad for the appetite'.

Which may make one wonder, was St Paul (if it was he) recommending
to Timothy that he 'take a little wine for your stomach's sake (*dia ton
stomachon sou*)',[14] or as an aperitif?

chymos; **chylos** – χυμός; χυλός. The problem with these words is
due to the vagaries of transliteration over the years and, in the case of
chymos especially, to the fact that it covers a variety of meanings in English
which in the Greek are only implied in the context. For *chymos* can mean
flavour and does so on a few occasions in this work (as does *chylos*, in a
quotation from Diocles at 1.1; K. 455). But its other meaning is a fluid and
it is here that the difficulty lies. For the word was originally transliterated
into English from its Latin equivalent, *umor*, to give humour, but it is
wrong to translate it invariably in this way. Indeed, *chymos* occurs in
several distinct medical contexts (as well as in its general meaning of a
fluid), that is, as *chymos* to indicate the contents of the stomach, or as one
or other of the various *chymoi* or natural body fluids that traditionally have
been called humours. Sometimes the two contexts have been allowed to
merge, so that as well as the four *chymoi* or humours which are the basis
of Galen's humoral theory, there has been a tendency for some to give
the same name humour to the *chymos* within the gut. But in his *Natural
Faculties* Galen quite explicitly denies the existence of humour (as we
use this admittedly anachronistic term) before it has been formed in the
portal venous system. In fact a transliteration of the Greek – *chyme* –
gives the precise term used today for the fluid contents of the stomach.
Curiously, this quite accurate translation of *chymos* in that context seems
never to have taken hold. Indeed I am unsure whether it has ever been
used! As to humour, there is no single word in Greek that means, *and
that only means*, what we now call humour. Either the actual humour such
as blood or bile is explicitly stated, or the word *chymos* is qualified in
such a way as to indicate which humour is intended. In fact, 'humour'

---

[13] *On the Use of the Parts* K. 111.275 = Helmreich 1.201 (May's translation); *On the Natural Faculties*
    K. 11.174 = Loeb *Galen on the Natural Faculties*, 270 (Brock's translation).
[14] 1 Timothy 5.23.

might better be replaced by 'body fluid', as Temkin has done in English, or as Harig, for example, has done in German with *Körpersaft*.[15] De Lacy also, not invariably but from time to time, imitates Galen and simply uses 'fluid'.[16] But there is a heavy weight of tradition on the side of humour, and since it cannot be confused with anything else (the remaining vestigial uses relate to the eye and, decreasingly, to 'humoral' in contrast to 'cellular' antibody) perhaps it may be left in peace. I have also applied the same reasoning to one of the humours – phlegm – a traditional term transliterated from *phlegma*. This really means mucus or at least mucoid material, which occurs in a variety of sites. But phlegm as we now understand the term is a mucoid material restricted to the respiratory tract. Nevertheless in the present translation I have yielded to tradition. As a related question we should note several derivatives of *chymos*: *eu-* and *kako-chymia*, which indicate a good (healthy) and bad (unhealthy) humoral state, the sense that I use here; and *eu-* and *kako-chymos* for which LSJ has 'productive of healthy [and unhealthy] humour', but also 'wholesome' and 'unwholesome', which latter I most often use.

Chylos is a different matter. It also means a fluid or juice, or the sap of a plant, and is so used in this work. A related noun, *chylôsis*, can be translated as liquefaction. Unfortunately, this has been interpreted by some to mean that while *chylôsis* of food within the alimentary tract results in fluid, when this fluid passes via the portal vein to the liver it can be referred to as chyle.[17] Unfortunately, in today's physiology chyle is quite a different thing, being the fatty fluid that is absorbed from the small bowel into a receptacle called the *cisterna chyli* in the abdomen, from which it passes up the thoracic duct to enter the bloodstream at the root of the neck. To speak of chyle in any other sense is wrong. On the few occasions in the present work when faced with *chylos*, I use fluid or juice or sometimes, in a botanical context, sap. An exception is the occasion mentioned earlier when it means flavour.

leptomerês – λεπτομερής (lit., finely particulate). An ordinary word that, when used in a technical sense, did not necessarily mean the same thing to everybody. Vallance has examined the, perhaps idiosyncratic, use of *leptomerês* by Asclepiades of Bithynia some two hundred years before Galen.[18] Its use by Galen was explored by Debru in a paper based especially on his *On the Mixtures and Properties of Simple Drugs*,[19] and her

---

[15] Temkin (1973) 17; Harig (1974) 35. [16] De Lacy (1984), e.g. at 529, 3.
[17] E.g. *On the Use of the Parts* K. 111.270 = Helmreich 1.205 (May's translation); De Lacy (1984) *On the Doctrines of Hippocrates and Plato* 411, 20.
[18] Vallance (1990) 59. [19] Debru (1997a) 85–102.

conclusions can be summarized as follows. *Leptomerês*, and its less common opposite *pachymerês*, found their greatest application in Galen's pharmacology, especially the pharmacology of externally applied medicaments. He thought that it was important to understand the consequences of a liquid substance being thin or thick, or of a solid substance being light (or rare, or fine) or dense. In a liquid, *leptomerês* implied fluidity and a capacity to form solutions; in a solid, lightness and a capacity for reduction to fine powder. Clearly he is referring to qualities of the substance additional to the canonical warm, cold, moist and dry.

The pharmacological importance of *leptomereia* is that a *leptomerês* substance is thereby enabled to penetrate to the depths of the body. Conversely, a *leptomerês* waste-product is more easily excreted, the finest material in the insensible perspiration, coarser material in sweat, or the urine, or the faeces. Inability to excrete waste material because it is at the *pachymereia* end of the scale is pathological.

Although Galen's (and Debru's) emphasis is pharmacological, the matter of *leptomerês* also bears upon nutrition, and we shall find later (at 11.34; K. 615) what, on the face of it, appears to be a curious anomaly, namely, Galen's opinion that *leptomereia* hinders concoction. The conclusion seems to be that this must be the consequence of more rapid elimination.

Throughout this translation I have usually followed P. N. Singer's 'fine in its substance', or something similar.[20]

krâsis – κρᾶσις. There is no problem with this word, as such. In the present context it simply means a mixing or blending of the four qualities. I include it because it may be asked, if we continue to use the traditional 'phlegm', albeit with some reservations, why can there be any objection to using the traditional 'temperament', a word whose Latin root implied a balanced mix or blend? Unlike phlegm, however, which at least is one variety of mucus, temperament these days has had stripped from it so much of its Galenic meaning that all that remains is a description of personality. To use it in this way is of course a distortion of Galen's intent, and a confusing trap for the newcomer. In his recent translation of Galen's *Peri kraseôn* (traditionally *De temperamentis*) Singer has rightly used the modern *On Mixtures*, and I have followed him, occasionally using 'blend' or 'blending' for variety.

---

[20] Singer (1997).

Translation

BOOK I

1 Many of the finest physicians have written about the properties of K. VI foods, taking the subject very seriously since it is about the most valuable 453 of any in medicine. For while we do not invariably make use of other resources, life without food is impossible, be we well or ill. So it is understandable that most of the best physicians have been concerned to 454 examine its properties in some detail, some alleging that they had come to know them from experience alone, others wanting to employ theoretical argument* as well, while still others considered this latter to be the most important.

Now, if in their writings about food they were in agreement about everything (as is the case with people who write about geometry and arithmetic), there would now be no need for me to take the trouble to write again about the same things in addition to so many such men. But since by holding differing views they have raised suspicions about one another (for they cannot all be speaking the truth!) we must become impartial judges and put what they have said to the test. For without demonstration* it is wrong to put one's confidence in one more than the others.

Since the starting points for demonstrations are twofold in type (for every demonstration and confident position has its origin either in perception or in a clear mental concept) it is necessary for us also to use one or the other, or both, of these for the elucidation of the problem in question. But since judgements using reason are not equally easy for everyone, for one must be both naturally intelligent and trained 455 from childhood in subjects which sharpen reasoning, it is better to start from experience, and especially because many physicians have declared that the properties of foodstuffs have been discovered by this means alone.

Now perhaps one might look down on the Empiricists, who have made it their task and pursuit to speak out vigorously against what has been discovered with the aid of reason. Nevertheless Diocles,* though he was a Dogmatist, wrote as follows in the first book of his *Hygiene for Pleistarchus*:

Those who suppose that things with the same flavours, smells, warmth, or anything else of the sort have the same properties are in error. For one can point to many dissimilar effects resulting from things that are similar in this way. Neither should one assume that every aperient or diuretic or whatever has any other property is as it is because it is warm or cold or salty; since not every sweet, bitter or salty thing, or anything else like this, has the same 456 properties. Instead, one should acknowledge that it is its nature as a whole that is the explanation of whatever usually results from each. For so might one least go wrong. Those who think that for each food they must give a cause why it is nutritious, laxative, diuretic or anything else like that seem to be unaware, first, that such information is not often necessary for their use; and second, that many things that exist in some way resemble in their nature certain principles, so that they do not admit of reasoning about cause. As well as this, people sometimes go wrong when, making assumptions about things that are unknown, disputed or untrustworthy, they believe that they are adequately stating the cause. One should therefore pay no heed to those who account for causes in this way, or to those who think it imperative to give an explanation for everything. One should rather believe what has been learnt from long experience and seek a cause of things that admit of one when, as a result of this, what is said will be better known or more credible.

This passage from Diocles is from one who believes that the properties of food are comprehended only from experience, and not from indication in 457 respect of either mixtures or humours. But he did not mention that there is also another type of indication* in respect of the parts of plants. I mean by 'indication in respect of the parts of plants' one by which, in addition to the others he employed, Mnesitheos* shows that some properties exist in the roots of plants, but different ones in the stems; just as there are others in the leaves, fruit and seeds. Now everyone, even if poorly endowed intellectually, is aware that just as experience teaches many other things, so too it teaches about foods that are digestible and indigestible, wholesome and unwholesome, and laxative and constipating. However, they fall into great error by using experience in these same matters in the absence of distinguishing criteria, as I showed in *On the Properties of Simple Drugs* and the third book of *On Mixtures*; and really the errors are much the same in each case. This is why I do not choose to describe in detail here, as I did in those works, the distinguishing criteria* by which, 458 if one takes note of them, he will more certainly discover the properties;

since it is my custom to write once and for all about each subject, and not retail the same things about the same subjects in multiple treatises. Nor shall I now neglect what has been my usual practice, which is to use the principal criteria only so far as it is possible to combine conciseness with clarity to the greatest extent. I shall start with what is generally agreed, and has been correctly reported by Erasistratus,* namely, that *melikrat** does not purge the stomach in every case nor do lentils check it; but that there are some people who, as well as experiencing neither effect, even encounter the opposite,* inasmuch as while the stomach is checked after *melikrat* it is emptied by lentils. Also, he says that one finds people who digest beef more easily than they do rock fish.

I myself always enquired of such people (for I shall start with the latter) what sort of symptom occurs which shows them that rock fish are indigestible. Is there any heaviness in the stomach that feels like lead, 459 stone or clay pressing down? For this is how some people describe the sensation in this type of indigestion. Or does a gnawing feeling manifest itself in it; or flatulence; or a sense of distressing belching? Some say that in their own case the belching is rather greasy; others, that there is a gnawing feeling; and some, that both occur.

On carefully considering the physical evidence in these people I found in the stomach a great accumulation of yellow bile, relating to some ill-mixture or to a constitutional peculiarity. I say 'constitutional peculiarity' because in some people the bile flowing into the intestine from the liver goes back up to the stomach; and I mean that the mixture is defective when their innate heat* is sharp, irritant or, as one might say, feverish. So it is likely that these people more easily concoct foods that are difficult to corrupt than they do those that are easily corrupted, since the foods that are easy to concoct are readily altered and corrupted whereas those that are difficult to concoct are altered with difficulty and are hard to corrupt. So these latter foods, whenever they are associated with great warmth, are concocted more than if they were to be in contact with a 460 stomach of moderate warmth. In terms of this argument, then, some people concoct beef more easily than they do rock fish.

In some people lentils disturb the stomach more than they restrain it, in accordance with the following theory. I have shown in my work *On the Properties of Simple Drugs* that just as among the medicaments we prepare some are compounded of opposing qualities and properties, in the same way not a few drugs that appear to be single are by nature compound. This sort of situation occurs with many foods. For not only lentils, but cabbage too, and of seafood almost all the so-called 'pottery-skinned' animals* have natures which are compounded from opposing properties. For the actual solid component of each is slow to pass and astringent to the stomach; but the liquid part promotes its emptying. Precise demonstration of this occurs as a result of boiling, when the water in which each has been boiled empties the stomach, but the actual solid parts check it. In this regard you will hear some people say   461 that if, before other foods, you eat cabbage that has not been boiled too much, transferring it all at once from the kettle into a vessel holding oil and fish sauce,* the stomach will be emptied. But some others prepare what is called 'twice-boiled' cabbage to check it.

The preparation of such cabbage is as follows: having first boiled it in water they remove all this water from the container, replacing it with more clean water in which they boil it a second time, so that if any liquid is left from the previous boiling it will all be got rid of. For with everything boiled in water it is the case that it partakes of the property of the water at the same time as it contributes its own property to the water. And since this is a regular occurrence with things that are boiled in broth, you can learn whether what is being boiled is a pulse, part of an animal or a vegetable. For what has been boiled shows by taste and smell the quality and property of the broth, and the broth shows the property of what has been boiled in it. You can test the truth of the whole proposition I am now presenting by boiling up lentils or cabbage or any of the marine animals I referred to, then seasoning the decoction with   462 oil, fish sauce and pepper, and giving it to anyone you like, to drink, just as with twice-boiled cabbage. For you will observe that the bowel moves after the drinkable portion, but is constipated after the solid part.

So it is no wonder that sometimes both colic and flatulence occur after foods of this sort when the solids are taken in their entirety, together with their own juices; for there is conflict between them, with the solid material restraining and retarding, but the fluid portion pressing for excretion. If the irritant is expelled, the symptom ceases. While it remains, the bowel inevitably experiences colic and flatulence, and eventually there is evacuation of these contending influences.

Again, since in some people their stomachs are ready for evacuation but in others they are dry and excrete with difficulty, each group has   463 symptoms following such foods according to its own particular nature, as if sometimes the stomach is reinforcing the property of the juice, and sometimes that of the solid material. For when there are two opposing influences, victory must go to one of the two and defeat to the other. This happens with certain conditions of the stomach which are not natural to it but have arisen at a particular time. Sometimes there is an accumulation in it of phlegm, and at other times of bile. Of the phlegm itself, some is acid, some sweet and some is without any perceptible quality; and some is watery, some thick, some viscid and some is readily dispersible. Of the bile, some is yellow and some is pale, both admitting of great variation in degree; leaving aside the other biles* that are manifested in already 464 diseased bodies. So with each of the humours mentioned being readily disposed either to the evacuation or restraint of the stomach, when the solid parts of the above foods arrive there, complete with their specific juices, they reinforce humours with the same property as themselves, but counteract those with the opposite property.

It has been remarked previously that there are two classes of explanation why, in the case of the same foods, the contents of the stomach appear to be handled differently.* And now, as well as the natural constitution and the fluid and solid parts of what is eaten, one has discovered a third. It will make no difference whether we refer to things eaten as 'eatables' or as 'nutriments'. In fact, so too do people call them 'foodstuffs' or 'comestibles' just as often as the former names, in the way that Hippocrates also wrote in the *Epidemics*:* 'Comestibles and drinks need trial as to whether they persist for the same time...' And again elsewhere: 'labours, foods, drinks, sleep, sexual activity – all in moderation'. Now, as I always say, we should not concern ourselves with names, nor worry about which to use, since they are familiar to every Greek, but it is proper to strive to understand the matter.

It seems that these foods have a speedy or a slow passage either because 465 of our fundamental nature, or because of the acquired disposition of the stomach, or because of the particular substance. I mean the particular substance of the things that are eaten and drunk, since some are liquid but some are dry, some are tenacious while others are easily broken up and dispersed, and some possess an intrinsic pungency but others acidity, bitterness, sweetness, saltiness, harshness or astringency; or some, aside from these, have pharmacological properties of the same group as the purgative drugs. For example, orach, blite, mallow and the round gourd, through being sticky and moist, pass more quickly than those that are not so, especially in people who walk about quietly after food, on moderately yielding ground. For food slips through more on being shaken up than if one is reclining motionless.

One could also put mulberries and sweet cherries in this class, as also the thick, sweet wines. Both melons and what are called apple-melons 466 are good for evacuation because of their moistness and slipperiness, and

have a moderate cleansing power, the melons more so than the apple-
melons, which you can confirm by rubbing a dirty part of the body; for
they cleanse it of its dirt immediately. These also, you should know, are
among the items that stimulate micturition.

Also amongst moist, watery substances are the so-called apricots,
peaches and, in general, things that appear to have no pronounced quality of taste or smell, which, if the stomach is fit for emptying, pass easily; if
not, they remain unconcocted* and give it no assistance with this. For this
sort of food material, being somehow midway between what restrains
and what stimulates the stomach, inclines a little in one or other direction
when it chances on a stomach that is either not very sluggish in emptying
or is very strong in distribution. Of course, sometimes these foods also
restrain it.

Melikrat also, in those individuals in whom it is first to be speedily distributed, not only does not impel the stomach [*gastêr*] towards emptying,
but even brings about the distribution of foods that are mixed with it.
But if it is not first speedily distributed, it provokes excretion like yellow   467
bile does, because it contains within itself something bitter and irritant.
So foods and drink of such sort, merely by being irritant, stimulate bowel
[*koilia*] evacuation.*

It is clear that the substance of the intestines [*entera*] is also included in
the statement. Certainly people use the terms 'pot-bellied' [*progastôr*] and
'large-gutted' [*megalokoilos*] in this way. Certain foods that are purgative
of the gut [*gastêr*] have pharmacological properties mixed within themselves, like that in scammony, gourds, hellebore and the like. The nature
of such things is a mix of food and drug, just as if you yourself were to
throw a small quantity of scammony juice into the liquid of a barley
water.* For while in this way it is not appreciated by the senses, it will not
escape notice as regards its activity, but will obviously be purgative. Some
think that this is what was stated by Hippocrates – 'purging in foods is
best...'* – but others thought one should not take it in this way alone;
rather, it seemed to them that the statement can also have been made
of those foods that have neither any nutritive nor any cleansing property
for the animal.

In fact they also say that these often act not only as foods but also   468
as drugs, clearly warming, cooling, drying and moistening us; so that
whenever one of them is not acting upon the human body but is only
nourishing it, under these circumstances it will not be defined as a drug.
Now foods like these are very few in number; but, whatever they may
be, they only have the precise definition of a food when there is no

qualitative alteration* of the body of the consumer. For what has been warmed, cooled, dried or moistened has been altered qualitatively; but what has taken from food a mass of substance like that which has been dispersed, has benefited from it as from food alone.

Accordingly, things that are average in mixture without any predominating quality are food only, and not drugs, neither moving the bowels 469 nor checking them; neither strengthening nor relaxing the *stomachos*; just as they are neither sudorific, nor diuretic, nor productive of any other bodily disposition as regards warmth, coldness, dryness and moistness. But in all respects they maintain the body of the animal being nourished just as it was when it received them. But here there is a certain very useful point of distinction, and this was not described by Diocles, just as neither was any of the others I have dealt with so far.

For if a human body were precisely average in mixture, it would be maintained in its existing condition by food that is average in mixture. But if it were either warmer or colder, or drier or moister, one would do harm by giving this body food and drink that is average in mixture. For every such body needs to be altered in the opposite direction to the same extent that it has departed from the precisely average condition; and this will occur with foods that are the opposite of the existing ill-mixture. In each opposing situation the opposites stand the same distance from the mean. As, for example, if the body departed by three measures from 470 the well-mixed and average condition to a warmer one, it would be necessary for the food also to shift by the same amount from the well-mixed condition to the colder state. And if the body moved to a moister state to the extent of four measures, the food should by the same degree be drier than what is well proportioned.

Again, in this regard, one can find many people making the most contradictory statements about the same foods. At any rate, recently a certain two persons were debating with one another, the one declaring that honey is healthy, the other that it caused illness. Each made his judgement according to how he himself was affected by it, not considering beyond this, that all men do not have a single mixture from the beginning or, if they did, that they do not keep it unchanged in old age; just as they do not do so during seasonal or geographical changes – for the moment ignoring the fact that by their customs and ways of life they also change the innate dispositions of their bodies. At any rate, to come straight to the point, one of those men who were at odds with each other about honey was older, more mucous by nature and lazy in his lifestyle and all other activities (not least in regard to exercise before bathing). Consequently

honey was of benefit to him. But the other was by nature bilious, thirty 471
years of age and endured many hardships in his daily activities. So it was
likely that in his case the honey had been quickly converted to bile and
so was more harmful.

I myself also knew someone who complained about the region at the
mouth of the stomach, when I calculated from what he said that phlegm
had accumulated in it.* I recommended that leeks and beets be taken
with mustard, and when they had cut the phlegm, the stomach emptied
better and he was relieved of all symptoms. On the other hand again,
when he once suffered from indigestion and gnawing abdominal pains
after bitter foods, not only was he not helped with the gnawing by taking
beet and mustard, he was actually made worse. And then, wondering
how he was so badly affected by what previously had given great benefit,
he approached me to learn the reason.

Now it is reasonable enough in medicine for laymen to be mistaken 472
about such matters. But one would not excuse physicians who have left
undefined many very useful propositions. For it is not proper simply to
say that rock fish are well-concocted by most people but that some are
found who concoct beef more easily. Rather, they should define each
group. Just as it is not proper to speak about honey in a general way,
but rather with the additional feature that it is beneficial or harmful in
certain age groups, natures, seasons, regions and lifestyles. For example,
that it is most adverse in those who are dry and warm, but very beneficial
in those who are moist and cool – whether they are like this in mixture
because of age, nature, region, season or lifestyle.

So that in relation to the present enquiry it seemed most necessary
to examine the mixtures both of men and of foodstuffs. How many of
these there are in men and how one should diagnose them has been told
in my treatise *On Mixtures*; just as with drugs, in that work* which deals 473
with their properties. But in the present study it might be timely to speak
of the mixtures of foods, as has been written in the book *On Regimen*,
the work of Hippocrates according to some, but according to others the
work of Philistion, Ariston, Euryphon or Philetas, all men of old.* In
some copies its beginning is as follows:

One must know the property of every food and drink, both natural and acquired
through art, thus . . .

but in others:

One must diagnose the situation and nature of each region thus . . .

Now when this book is taken on its own it is entitled *On Regimen*,* being the second part of a whole which is divided into three. But when what was put together from the three parts is found as an undivided entity, it is entitled *On the Nature of Man and Regimen*. Now one might perhaps consider the second book, in which there is discussion about food, worthy of Hippocrates; the first is very far from his thought. But this is by the way. Whichever of the men mentioned it belongs to, it appears to bring 474 regimen back into the general enquiry concerning foods.

For he who knows that barley is cold and moist by nature, and also understands how to recognize the mixtures of bodies, both those that are innate and those that occur in an acquired condition, will use barley for food appropriately; not only in the case of healthy bodies but also in those that are diseased; and whoever understands their mixture might also happily employ barley meal in poultices.

Not only should one recognize the most important and primary mixture of each foodstuff but also, as was explained in *On Drugs*, the mixtures which arise from the primary ones; not least of which are many (if not indeed all) of those related to flavours, and also some related to smells. For as a result of each having been mixed in some way from so much 475 warm, so much cold, and so much dry and moist, one of them seems sweet, another sharp, or salty, or sour, or harsh or bitter. 'Saline' means nothing other than 'salty', and the same characteristic is revealed by both words; and the common class of 'sour' and 'harsh' is called 'astringent'. I have spoken at very great length about all flavours in the fourth book of *On the Properties of Simple Drugs* and whoever intends to follow what is now being said must assuredly have read that work in advance, so that I am not forced to repeat in this one the same things about them.

As I stated a little earlier, while some foods exhibit no noteworthy quality of smell or taste (ones which are in fact the sort people refer to as insipid or watery), others have very obvious astringency, or innate sweetness, or bitterness; just as others also appear rather salty, and some partake of a distinct pungency. So it is clear that foods like these have the 476 same property as those drugs which they resemble in flavour. In *On Drugs* I have given an explanation why some astringent ones do not produce the same effects as others; for instance, bitter aloes, burnt copper, bluestone, flower of copper, copper scale and copper ore.* For in each case, as a result of some other things having been mixed with their astringent property and substance, they undergo change in their particular functions; just as if you yourself were to mix scammony with quince, as of course we sometimes do when we carve out the parts around the seed of the quince, fill the hollowed-out part with scammony, plaster it with dough and bake it, and then offer it as food. For what has been prepared in this way evacuates the bowel without disturbing the *stomachos* since the cathartic property in it that is derived from the scammony predominates, while the familiar property of the quince persists. For it would not otherwise seem both pleasant *and* astringent, and suitable for the *stomachos*.

So it is that some foods have some slight property mixed within them- 477 selves, whether purgative, or naturally having some other action. In their case one should not entertain doubts about the properties associated with their flavours on the grounds that the effects are not those they have naturally. For anything that has an astringent quality, to the extent that it exists on its own, contracts, constricts and cools the substances associated with it. But sometimes the same substance can have parts of itself that are warming and parts that are cooling, as I pointed out in *On the Properties of Simple Drugs*, since nature has mixed them in this way, just as sometimes some physicians mix pyrethrum or pepper with one of the cooling agents.

As I said, this has been gone through very fully in my work *On Drugs*, and is most valuable for what is being taught now. In fact the various methods of preparation of each foodstuff are discovered by those who have already understood these things. I myself sometimes administer a beet and lentil dish, and before me Herakleides of Tarentum* frequently gave it to many people, not only to those in excellent health but also to those with some complaint. First we put in plenty of beets, and next either a small amount of salt or sweet fish sauce,* for in this way it 478 is more aperient. If, however, when you have pounded the lentils and boiled them twice, pouring off the first water, you then mix in a little salt or fish sauce and add a small quantity of something costive (to the extent that it does not upset the taste), you will make a drug, and at the same time a food, that is most useful for many who are troubled by chronic diarrhoea. I said 'for many', being careful not to say 'for all', because here too there is need for distinguishing criteria by which the dispositions of those who suffer from chronic diarrhoea will be identified.

Generally speaking, one cannot properly test anything empirically without first accurately working out, by reasoning, the disposition to which he is applying what is being tested, be it food, drink or drug. For the knowledge of such dispositions* is the stuff of remedies, not the knowledge of the remedies themselves; but since, without knowing 479 precisely the properties of the materials we use, it is impossible to help those in need of them, it is necessary here to discuss the properties in foodstuffs, as it was elsewhere to discuss those in drugs. Knowledge of them is achieved with difficulty by a defining test over a long time, and from the nature of the odours and flavours which the foods being tested appear to have; and as well, from the consistency they have acquired in respect of viscidity, friability or loose texture; and solidity, lightness or heaviness. All these contribute to their elucidation so that if, on arrival in a foreign country, you were to see some food you have never seen before, you would have a significant starting point towards knowledge of its property. What Mnesitheos wrote about roots, stems, leaves, fruits and seeds does not admit of a very secure distinction if you are differentiating them by a defining test in a manner that will become clear from what follows. For I have determined to go through each of these foods separately, in detail, even if the discussion is going to take longer. At any rate, I shall be able to give later, in another shorter work, a synopsis that will be valuable for those who have learned the art. For only extensive practice and training bring craftsmen to perfection. This is why I think that the 480 majority are correct who say that the best instruction is through personal contact, and that it is impossible for anyone to become either a helmsman or an expert in any other craft from a book. These are reminders for those who have previously studied and understood, not complete instruction for the ignorant. Just the same, if any of the latter who lack instructors are willing to attend carefully to what has been written clearly and in detail as I am doing, they will profit greatly, especially if they do not hesitate to read it over and over again.

2 On the naked wheats*

Reasonably enough, most physicians seem to me to have commenced the instruction in question with the wheats, since this grain has very many uses both for Greeks and for most foreigners. The most nutritious 481 of them are the dense ones with their whole substance compacted, so that it is difficult to split them by biting. They give bodies the most nutriment from the smallest bulk, just as their opposites, which are easily broken up by biting and after biting appear loose-textured and porous, produce little nutriment from great bulk. If you care to weigh an equal bulk of each you will find the dense ones by far the heavier. They are also more yellow in colour than the loose-textured ones. But one should test their nature, not simply by examining the external appearance, but by dividing them and breaking them up as I said. For although many from the outside appear yellowish and compact, inside they are seen to be loose-textured, porous and white. These latter have the most bran and, when milled, if one sifts out the very fine meal and makes what are called bran loaves from the remainder, trial will show that while they are poorly nutritive they produce much residue in the stomach and consequently 482 it is passed easily. At the same time, because the bran has a cleansing property, elimination of the residues, as you would expect, takes place quickly since the bowel is stimulated to excretion.

The loaves that are the opposite of these are extremely pure, bringing the greatest weight to the smallest bulk, but of all the breads they pass through the most slowly. Indeed you will also observe that their dough is quite tenacious, since, when it is drawn out to the greatest extent, it is not torn apart, which is characteristic of a tenacious substance. And so these naturally need more leaven and require more thorough kneading, and should not be baked soon after leavening and kneading.* But with bran loaves a small amount of leaven, light kneading and a short interval are sufficient. So too, while the pure loaves need a longer period of actual baking, the bran loaves need a shorter one. Between the most pure and the least pure is a wide range where there is more or less purity, some called, and in truth being, pure, and others impure.   483

As well, there is a precisely halfway form of these loaves which goes by the name of wholemeal. The older physicians called them unbolted. Now it is clear that these are from meal in unsifted form, when the bran-like material has not been separated from the pure flour. That is why they called them wholemeal, since the whole wheat itself is made into loaves, and unbolted, because when they are being prepared the meal is brought together without being sifted. But even among these themselves which seem to have been set precisely at the mid-point of the range, between the breads derived from bran and those of extreme purity, there is marked variation according to the nature of the wheat. For breads from the compact, heavy wheats are better; those from the loose-grained and lighter wheats are poorer.

Among the Romans, as also among just about everybody else over whom they rule, the purest bread is called *silignis*, and the next is called 484 *semidalis*. While *semidalis* is an ancient Greek name, *silignis* is not Greek but I cannot give it any other name. Now *silignis* is the most nourishing of them; next is *semidalis*; and the one in the middle, wholemeal, is third. Fourth is the group from unwinnowed grain, of which the bran loaf is the worst. It is indeed the least nourishing, and of all the breads it moves the bowels most.

The best-concocted breads are those that have been most leavened and very well kneaded, and baked in an oven with moderate heat. Greater heat scorches at once when first applied, and produces a pottery-like appearance on the outside; and the loaf turns out to be of poor quality on two counts, with its inside raw and inadequately baked, and its crust overbaked, dry and like pottery. With heat that is less than moderate the bread is not well baked, but the whole loaf is left rather raw, the inside most of all. Those that are baked uniformly throughout in moderate heat for a longer time are also very well concocted in the stomach and 485 are most suited to the sequence of activities that occurs following concoction. Clearly, the worst breads are those to which none of the above applies.

Now that I have distinguished the extremes among them in both excellence and badness, it is no longer difficult for anyone on his own, without assistance from me, to grasp that some breads are close either to the best or to the worst extreme, that some are further away; and that others, as I said, are placed midway between both extremes. It is just as I was saying earlier about honey, namely that one should not say simply that it is good or bad for health, but rather that it is good for a phlegmatic nature, one that is moister or colder than a well-mixed nature, even if it is only colder without much moistness, or moister without much coldness; and that it is unsuited for warm mixtures, and even more so for warm, dry ones. So among breads too, while one that has not been very well baked nor has much leaven is suitable for an athlete, and one that has been very well baked in the oven and has much leaven 486 is suitable for an ordinary individual or an old person, one which is absolutely unleavened is not fit for anybody. But if one also adds cheese to the bread, as holiday-makers among our country folk usually prepare it (which they themselves call unleavened), there is certain harm for everybody, even if some of them are very strong in body constitution, such as those who are by nature the best reapers and ditch-diggers. For these people are observed to concoct unleavened breads better than the strongest athletes (as they also do beef and the meat of he-goats). What further need is there to mention sheep and female goats as well as these?

In Alexandria they eat donkey meat as well, and there are also some people who eat camel. For while custom contributes to their concoction, of no less importance is the small amount taken and the depletion of the body* as a whole that necessarily accompanies those who toil throughout the day at their proper activities. For the depleted flesh snatches up from the stomach not only half-concocted, but even, when they work after a meal, sometimes absolutely unconcocted chyme. This is why these people later suffer very troublesome illnesses and die before they reach old age. Ignorant of this, most people who see them eating and concocting what none of us can tackle and concoct congratulate them on their bodily strength. Also, since very deep sleep occurs in those who undertake much hard labour, and this helps them with concoction to a greater degree, they are consequently less injured by harmful foods. But if you were to force them to stay awake for more nights in succession they would immediately become ill. So these people have but this one advantage in the concoction of harmful foods. 487

Athletes take very wholesome foods, but the heavyweights among them, especially, take foods that are fatty and glutinous. People refer in this way especially to wrestlers, *pankration* fighters* and boxers. Since their whole preparation is with a view to contests in which sometimes they must wrestle, or fight in *pankration*, all day long, for this reason they also need food which is both difficult to corrupt and not easily dispersed. 488 The nutriment from thick, glutinous humours* is like this, especially the sort from pork and from breads prepared as I have described, which professional athletes consume exclusively. If the ordinary untrained individual keeps using food like this he will very quickly come down with a plethoric disorder; just as also, if a man in training were to subsist on vegetables and barley-water, he would very soon be in a sorry plight and wear out his whole body. The humour from breads like those which I said the athletes use, if one of us ordinary people eats them, is thick and cold like that which we usually refer to, specifically, as 'crude'. Now it is also the case that phlegm is crude and cold, but not thick since it contains a good deal of moisture as well as flatulence-producing wind. That specifically referred to as crude is like this, and appears like that which sometimes settles out in urine and resembles pus. But while pus is 489 foul-smelling and tenacious, the crude humour resembles it only in consistency and colour, being neither foul-smelling nor tenacious. Certainly it does not settle in the urine in febrile patients only, due to the quantity of the crude humours I spoke of, but also in healthy persons who are engaged in heavy work and who take foods that are hard and difficult to concoct.

There will be later discussion regarding other foods, but as to the breads,* since we set out to discuss them first, let us now also speak about these in addition to what has already been said. The best of them are the *kribanitai*, when baked (and previously prepared for baking) in the manner that I have described. Those baked in an *ipnos* are second to these, having had the same sort of preparation. But since they are not baked right through like those in the *kribanos*, they are inferior to them. The ones baked on the coals, whether on the hot ashes or by using the tiling of the hearth like a *kribanos*, are all unsatisfactory through being unevenly cooked; the crust is overdone but the inside is underdone. And from having been baked covered in ash, the latter adds something 490 unpleasant to the so-called 'ash-hidden' loaves. So that, of all the breads, these last are liable to be the worst from the point of view of style of baking, even if they use the same ingredients. For in every instance of the topic under consideration you should take note that what are being compared with one another have been altered in respect of those features only,* since if you were to compare things that differ in many ways they would have, taken together, everything that has been described in each of them severally.

Now everything to do with the differences between breads has been dealt with sufficiently.

3 On pastries

Now might be the time to speak of the other sweetmeats that they make from wheaten flour. What are called girdle-cakes [*tagênitai*] by the Athenians but griddle-cakes [*têganitai*] by us,* the Asiatic Greeks, are prepared with olive oil alone. The oil is placed in a frying pan that is put on a smokeless fire, and when it has become hot the wheaten flour, soaked in a large amount of water, is poured into it. When cooked in the oil, it rapidly sets and thickens, resembling soft cheese solidifying in wicker baskets. At this point those making it turn it to bring the upper surface 491 underneath, in contact with the pan, bringing what was previously underneath, which has been sufficiently cooked, to the top; when the under part is now set, they turn it again, perhaps two or three times, until it seems to them that the whole has been cooked evenly.

It is obvious that this has thick juice, restrains the stomach and gives rise to crude humours.* This is why some mix honey with it, and there are those who also mix in sea salt. This, then, would be a class (or species, or however you want to refer to it) of flat-cake, just as country folk and very poor town-dwellers make many other such flat-cakes from whatever is to hand. For that reason those unleavened sweetmeats which they bake 492 in a *kribanos* and immediately remove and put into warm honey, so that they are saturated with it, are also a type of flat-cake; and so too are all such items made with honey.

4 About cakes

There are two sorts of cake: the better sort that they call 'pour-cakes', and the inferior 'broad-cakes'. Everything made up of these and *semidalis* is slow to pass, produces a thick humour which is obstructive of the food passages in the liver, causes enlargement of the sickly spleen and produces kidney-stones; but if they are concocted and properly turned into blood, they are quite nutritious. Things prepared with honey are of mixed property, since the honey itself has fine juice that thins whatever it is associated with.

So it is understandable that those cakes that had received more honey in their preparation, and which had been baked for a longer time, are less slow to pass and give rise to a humour that is a mix of thick and thin, and in healthy people are better for liver, kidneys and spleen than those that have been prepared without honey. But in people with incipient obstructions, 493 whether due to inflammation or induration, they are just as harmful; sometimes, rather, they are even more harmful, most especially all those in which the flour is somewhat sticky. For the humour from them is not only held back and prevented from progressing due to its thickness, but also, being plastered inside the narrow extremities of the vessels, produces a stubborn blockage. The viscus damaged in this way produces in patients a certain heavy sensation, which requires the assistance of thinning foods and drink. This has been discussed elsewhere in my *On the Thinning Diet.**

Nothing prepared in this way harms the chest or lung. But later I shall discuss the foods that generate thick, sticky humour. The present account requires that you keep in mind the other things I have gone through up to this point, and especially everything to do with the property of breads, since we use them continually. And there is no harm in recalling, in summary, what has been said about them.   494

So then, the healthiest bread, in a man who is neither young nor in training, is that with the most leaven and the most salt, which has been kneaded by the baker to the greatest extent until it has been prepared for baking, and has been baked in a moderately hot pan in the way I spoke of previously. Let taste be your criterion of 'most' in regard to the leaven and salt; for in a stronger mixture of these the unpleasant taste indicates that it is unhealthy. So it is better to increase the amount of them to just short of when taste recognizes unpleasantness from the mixture.

5 On light bread*

Those who want to make light bread find that while the food is less nourishing it has, to the greatest possible extent, avoided harm due to obstruction. For this bread is the least thick and sticky, since it has become more airy rather than more earthy. Its lightness is revealed by its weight, and by the fact that it does not sink in water; rather, it floats like a cork.

You should know that many of our country people bake a mixture of wheaten flour and milk, and this food belongs to the adhesive group. 495 Even though all such foods are wholesome and nutritious, because of this they hurt those who use them continually, producing obstructions in the liver and generating kidney-stones. Since the crude humour is added to the glutinous component, whenever the kidney passages in some people are naturally very narrow, by delaying the very thick and very glutinous humour here, it is likely to produce stone, like that formed in the vessels in which we heat water and that which is coated around the stones in many natural hot springs. The mixture of the kidneys themselves also contributes particularly to this, when the warm in them is of the fiery, sharp sort. The stones that are developed in joint conditions are also of this type. For it is always the case that everything superfluous in the body runs to the weakest sites* and produces effects in them according to its own nature. I will return to this in the discussion on milk and all its uses, 496 as also about the thickening foods, since there are certain other foods with this type of property.

6 On groats

Groats belong to the wheat family.* They have juice that is quite nourishing and tenacious if, when they have been cooked in water alone, they are taken with honeyed wine,* or with sweet or even astringent wine (the critical time for use is specific for each), and if salt and oil have been stirred in. Sometimes, too, vinegar is added to it. Physicians say that groats prepared in this way are seasoning à la ptisane.* But some say that the patient is nourished by ptisane made from groats; and some of the old physicians, like Diocles and Phylotimos, call groats prepared in this way 'wheaten ptisane'. This is why the name is rarely used amongst the older physicians, as also that of spring wheat. They refer to them by the common name of 'wheat'. In Hippocrates' *Regimen* it was stated that breads made from groats, while very nutritious, are less aperient. It was also said that *semidalis* and boiled groats are strong and nutritious.*

So it is well to be wary about much use of them for those people in whom 497
the liver is easily obstructed or the kidneys prone to the development of
stones.

One should particularly pay attention to gruel made from what are
called 'washed' groats. For this is their liquor when they have been mixed
with water, but, although it needs lengthy boiling, it tricks those preparing
it into believing that it has been sufficiently cooked, and does considerable
harm to sick people, the very ones for whom they are preparing it. For
because it is viscid it quickly becomes firm and thickened. Accordingly
cooks, when they have mixed the groats with a good deal of water, should
boil them on the coals for a longer period, stirring in dill, until they are
nicely cooked, and at that time also put in salt. If you also have mixed in
olive oil right at the beginning, you will do no harm.

But take this as a side-issue with application to therapeutics and not
to our present concern. For healthy people, whenever they need gruel
because of severe irritation of the stomach, or the passage of much biliary
material, or anything of that sort, once you have boiled the groats to the
greatest extent so that they are softened, and have then stirred them so 498
that they come to resemble the strained liquor of ptisane, give it then as
a draught. The seasoning is the same as with washed groats.

7   On wheat boiled in water

If I had not once eaten wheat boiled in this way, I should not have
expected food from it to be of use to any one. Not even in famine would
anybody come to this sort of use, for if wheat is in good supply one can
make bread from it. At dinner people eat boiled and roasted chickpeas
and other seeds for want of so-called desserts, preparing them in the
same fashion, but nobody eats boiled wheat in this way. This is why I
should not have expected anyone to eat boiled wheat.

But once when walking in the country not far from the city, with two
lads of my own age, I myself actually came upon some rustics who had
had their meal and whose womenfolk were about to make bread (for
they were short of it). One of them put the wheat into the pot all at once 499
and boiled it. Then they seasoned it with a moderate amount of salt and
asked us to eat it. Reasonably enough, since we had been walking and
were famished, we set to with a will. We ate it with gusto, and felt a
heaviness in the stomach, as though clay seemed to be pressing upon it.
Throughout the next day we had no appetite because of indigestion, so
that we could eat nothing, were full of wind and suffered from headaches

and blurred vision. For there was not even any bowel action, which is the only remedy for indigestion. I therefore asked the rustics whether they themselves also ever ate boiled wheat, and how they were affected. They said that they had often eaten it under the same necessity that we had experienced, and that wheat prepared in this way was a heavy food, difficult to concoct. It was obvious that this could be worked out even by someone who had not tried it. For as I said earlier, where its flour, when eaten, is not easy to concoct unless it has been thoroughly worked up with salt and leaven, and mixing and kneading, and baking in an oven, how could one not realize that wheat which is not well worked up is very indigestible? Certainly wheat eaten this way has great potential if it has been concocted, nourishing the body very much and imparting notable 500 strength to those taking it.

8 On starch

This, which has the property of being emollient to roughened parts, is prepared from wheat. This action is common to all substances that, while dry in composition, have neither astringency nor bitterness nor any other manifest property. People call them, reasonably enough, neutral in quality, since this is how they are as regards sensation. Among moist substances water is like this. In property, starch is very like the light breads, providing less nutriment for the body than they do, and not being warming; just as they are not, while other breads are warming. For one ought not to compare it with wheat boiled in water, which is clearly warming and, if concocted, powerfully nourishing, although it is difficult to concoct, as I have said.

9 On barley 501

This seed also is of great service to men although it has not the same potential as wheat.* For while the latter is obviously warming, barley is not only far from warming (just as some foods are betwixt warming and cooling, such as starch and light bread) but it actually seems to be cooling in every way it is used, whether one has prepared bread from it or cooked a ptisane or made barley groats. And it is a far cry from the nature of wheat as regards the form of the juices which each produces. For wheat produces a thick, sticky juice but barley gives rise to one that is thin and cleansing. Barley never warms the body in any sort of preparation, but

when prepared in a variety of ways it is either moistening or drying. 502
For groats from roasted barley are manifestly drying; but a ptisane is
moistening when it has been made properly, that is to say, when it has
swollen to the greatest extent by boiling, and then has been made into
a liquor by long and gentle simmering. At that time, when it is fully
swollen, vinegar is mixed with it. When it has been cooked to a nicety,
one should add fine salt just before eating. And if right at the start you
were to add oil, you would do the boiling no harm. But you should not
mix in anything else except, at the beginning, a small amount of leek and
dill.

It is my observation that the ptisane is very badly prepared by all cooks.
For they break it up by grinding it in the mortar while raw, rather than
boiling it over a fire. And some also add starch so that the ptisane seems
to have been sufficiently converted to liquor by boiling. So, naturally, this
sort of ptisane is flatulent and excessively difficult to concoct.

But it is right to add what I said in the case of good preparation.
Having first soaked the uncooked ptisane in water for a short time and
then put it into a mortar, you should rub it with your hands while holding
something rough, like what is called broom, from which they plait shoes
for draught animals. Let the extent of the rubbing be such that it clears
away the adherent husk. For when barley is winnowed, the surrounding
thin coat is not all cleaned away. Hence it is first soaked and then rubbed
in the mortar. But if all the chaff-like material does not fall off, the cooked 503
ptisane is more cleansing but comes to no other harm.

The worst preparation of ptisane is when the cooks have ground the
uncooked barley in a mortar with water then, when they have boiled it
for a short time, they add a little of what is called must, and boiled-down
wine. Some also put honey and cumin in with this, making a potion rather
than a ptisane. But the well-made ptisane provides what Hippocrates said
was useful for healthy and ailing men alike. 'For', he said, 'its glutinous
quality is smooth, uniform and soothing; and slippery, moderately damp,
thirst-quenching and easily excreted (if there were also any need for this),
and with neither astringency nor bad palpitations; nor does it swell in
the stomach, since it has swollen during the boiling and has increased in
bulk to the greatest possible extent.'*

This is all that needed to be said about the property of ptisane in the 504
present treatise, which is not to do with therapeutics, but with explaining
the properties of foodstuffs alone. But during the course of the work some
of their therapeutic uses are also being taught.

10 On barley breads

It is time now to pass to the discussion of barley breads, which men make very much as they make wheaten ones. They are not only more friable than these, but also more friable than the ones made from emmer^o, and much more still, than breads from einkhorn, since there is no stickiness in them as there is with the wheaten breads.* It is very clear that they provide little nutriment for bodies, especially when they are from inferior barley, from which Hippocrates advised us not even to make ptisane;* for even when boiled it does not release much liquor from itself. The finest barleycorns are those which appear white after winnowing and have a certain thickness and weight, to the extent that barley can. And it is clear that those that are completely full, with a tight external appearance, are better than the hard, shrivelled ones. You should take this to be a common characteristic of all seeds, unless sometimes they have much more bulk 505 than is natural, and at the same time are softer and more spongy. For you must realize that these latter hold surplus moisture and are inferior to those mentioned previously. This is why it is not a good idea to use them after the harvest, but having laid them down in a dry place, to allow them more time to dissipate some of the excess moisture and become a little ripened, until on drying out they are moderately contracted. From all leaves, seeds and fruit, when they have been harvested and laid down, there falls away first the moist thin surplus contained within them, and after this, too, some of the natural moisture itself.* For whenever it has substance that is drier than it should be, while it is inferior to that which has reached peak condition nonetheless it is not now altogether bad; rather, it is even more useful for some conditions, namely those that need drying. But the grain laid away for the longest period is inferior in its properties. The measure of this is that when it is divided up it has what looks like fine dust falling out. Now understand that what has just been said in this one instance in regard to these things applies to all. For I get 506 no pleasure in saying the same things about the same subjects, unless on occasion it seems necessary to mention only the bare summary.

As for breads from barley, which is what the discussion was about, let me return to it and speak again, since there are differences among these comparable with the ones that were remarked on a little earlier in connection with wheaten breads. They are all far less nutritious than the wheaten breads; but while those obtained from the best barley suffer from this less, those from loose-textured and light barley are comparable with bran breads. And while the breads from this sort of barley pass down the gut best, the other barley breads also do this very well when compared with wheaten breads. As to matters concerning the finest and the worst, and those other preparations of barley bread in between them, these preparations are as was stated for wheaten breads.

11   On barley meal*

The best barley meal comes from young barleycorns that have been 507 moderately parched; but sometimes, when people are short of these, they make it from others. All well-prepared barley meal is sweet smelling, especially that from the best young barley with ears that are not very dry. Many healthy people are accustomed to sprinkle it with *siraion*,* sweet wine or honeyed wine diluted with water, and sometimes with water alone; and in summer to drink it two to three hours before their bath. They say that it gives the sensation of a thirst-quenching draught. But when drunk with a dry wine it dries the stomach.

In some countries they use barley meal for bread-making, as I saw in the countryside in Cyprus, and yet mostly they cultivate wheat.* The ancients also used to prepare barley meal for people on military service. But these days the Roman soldiery no longer uses barley meal, having formed a prejudice that it weakened them. For it gives the body a small amount of nutriment, sufficient for the ordinary individual who is not in training, but inadequate for those who are in any way in training. From barley meal, when it has been mixed with water, come barley-cakes, about which we shall speak next; since even Phylotimos, when he discussed barley meals at length in the first book of *On Food*, nonetheless 508 left undefined what is the most useful thing among them.

12   On barley-cake

Even before the defining trial, you should have been able to have drawn inferences about the property of each food from its nature. For to any intelligent man, would not the fine, white flour, free of all bran-like ma-terial, accurately indicate that it is changed in the stomach more quickly, and to a greater extent, and so is better concocted and more easily dis-tributed, and more readily nourishes, as if the whole is assimilated and applied to the bodies being nourished? But to the extent that there is bran-like and hard matter in it, just as outside the body it is obviously not dissolved in water, by the same reasoning it would not be dissolved

in the stomach when soaked, but remain completely undivided and unconcocted, as it was when it was eaten? For this can be neither well
concocted nor, because of its not completely matching the openings of
the veins reaching down* to the stomach and intestine, can it be well
distributed. From which it necessarily follows that there is more faecal
material from it, but that it passes very quickly, both because of its actual 509
weight due to the amount, and further, from the bran-like material as a
whole having a cleansing quality.

So it is clear, to anyone who has thought about these things, that
barley-cake is as inferior to barley bread in nourishing the body as the
latter is to wheaten bread. For although barley naturally already contains
a good deal of bran-like material, parched barley has the same in drier
and less breakable form; and the part of this which is stronger, from which
the body takes nourishment, is drier. So in virtue of this, barley-cake is
concocted less well than barley bread and makes the stomach more full
of wind, and if it stays in it for a longer time it produces disturbance.
But it passes through better when it has been mixed and kneaded for
a longer time. If one were to take honey with it, for this very reason it
would still more quickly stimulate gastric emptying.

Phylotimos believes that a thick, glutinous and cold humour, which 510
he himself, as well as his teacher Praxagoras, calls 'glassy',* is generated
from all barley-cakes. But this is not so, since barley meal has neither
stickiness, which occurs most in groats, nor nutrient value. But barley-
cake when it has been mixed further with sweet wine and *siraion* for a long
time deceives him. (He calls it *triptên* as the Athenians do.*) For the dough
from this, which is the equivalent of wheaten dough, can be drawn out
and is glutinous from having been softened for longer, and from thick
liquid having been mixed with the meal. Just as prolonged kneading with
thick liquid produces a kneaded flour which is sticky in appearance, even
flour from millet, for the same reason the liquor of ptisane appears sticky,
although in itself it contains nothing glutinous nor anything which makes
it adhesive; rather, it has a cleansing and cutting property, since even on
our skin it obviously removes dirt. Also, if you give it to somebody to
swallow and then produce vomiting, it will clean out the phlegm in the
stomach and expel everything, including itself, in the vomitus.

13 On einkhorn [*tiphê*], emmer [*olyra*] and emmer [*zeia*]

Mnesitheos placed einkhorn third after the naked wheats and barley. 511
Diocles discussed it rather superficially, since he preferred brevity in

writing to exactness in exposition. At any rate, that is how he wrote, abbreviating the discussion about wheat, barley and much else. Praxagoras and Mnesitheos wrote about them a little more fully than Diocles, but they also omitted some things. Phylotimos wrote at length about some but inadequately about others, and some, like emmer^z, he totally forgot. It is plain that his teacher Praxagoras did likewise. For while Phylotimos ignored nothing that Praxagoras spoke of, he works over it and adds much. One can wonder that the compiler of the Hippocratic *On Regimen*, whoever that ancient author was, did not even mention the name of *zeia*. For even if he believed that einkhorn is called emmer^z by some people, he should have made this plain. But perhaps it is better to attach their statements.

Now Diocles wrote as follows in the first book of *Health for Pleistarchos*, in which he also discusses the properties of foods: 512

coming after barley and the naked wheats in excellence are, particularly among the rest, emmer^o, einkhorn, emmer^z, foxtail millet and broom millet...

In some copies *zeia* goes completely without mention and, in some copies moreover, instead of 'excellence' is written 'use', in the following manner:

coming after barley and the naked wheats in use are, particularly among the rest, emmer^o, einkhorn, foxtail millet, broom millet

as though there was one particular grain, emmer^o; and another, einkhorn.

But Mnesitheos says that the two names relate to a single grain, when he writes thus:

and while, among the grains, barley and the naked wheats are the most naturally suited for food, next after these there follows that which is referred to in two ways, but is the same thing – some call it einkhorn, some emmer^o ...(and after this he goes on)...and after these come emmer^z, broom millet and foxtail millet.

Diocles contented himself with the remarks just quoted in connection with einkhorn and emmer^o. But Mnesitheos also discussed them later in a separate work when he wrote first about the naked wheats and barley, and then about einkhorn, under these same names, somewhat as follows:

While einkhorn is the best of the others, for it nourishes adequately and is   513
concocted without much trouble, nobody who eats his fill of bread from *zeia* would be healthy; nor would anybody unaccustomed to eating it even if he took it in extremely small quantity. For emmer^z is heavy and indigestible. But those living in an inhospitable region are forced to obtain their nourishment from

it, and to sow it, because it is the most resistant to cold. These people, indeed, usually first take a small amount, both because the food is not pleasant smelling and because of the scarcity of good harvests in such regions, but later, the fact that it is also their customary food makes its working up easier for their bodies. In general one should say that *zeia* is heavy and hard to concoct, but is strong and full of fibre.

In this passage Mnesitheos has shown very clearly what sort of seed grown in cold regions he is prepared to call emmer^z. But for myself, while I have not seen every cold region, I have not heard from anyone else who has done so that a particular cereal crop is called emmer^z [*zeia* 514 or *zea*] by the inhabitants (for one finds it written either way – in some the first syllable ends in *epsilon iota*, in some in *epsilon* alone). But when I reflected that it is possible that the Greeks name this seed in this way but that foreigners have applied a specific name to it, then having seen many fields of grain in Thrace and Macedon with not only the ear but even the entire plant very like what to us in Asia is einkhorn, I enquired what name it had among those people. They all told me that the plant as a whole, and its grain, is called rye [*briza*]* – the first syllable is written and spoken with three letters, *beta*, *rho* and *iota*; but the second is with *zeta* and *alpha* in the nominative, and *nu* is obviously the accusative ending. Bread from this grain is ill-smelling and black, and with a very fibrous substance, as Mnesitheos wrote. If he had in addition written that bread from this grain was also black, I should be more inclined to believe that it was this same one that he referred to as *zeia*.

In the most wintry parts of Bithynia, moreover, a particular grain is 515 called *zeopyros*, with the first syllable having no letter *iota* as it has in Homer: 'Wheat and *zeia* and broad-eared white barley…'*

Bread from it is much better than that in Macedon and Thrace. Roughly speaking, just as the name *zeopyros* is compounded of both names, *zea* and *pyros*, the substance is some average of both, since it has been blended from them. At any rate it is as inferior to naked wheat as it is superior to Thracian rye. The names of the cities in which this grain occurs are Nicaea, Prusa, Crateia, Claudiopolis and Iuliopolis; but Dorylaeum,* which is a city at the furthest extent of Asiatic Phrygia, also has this sort of grain produced in the region, as also do some other cities on its borders. One can also observe that bread from this grain is better than that from the *briza* of Thrace and Macedon as much as it is worse than wheaten bread.

In the seventh book of *On Plants* Theophrastus has made mention of 516 emmer^z, much as follows:

of grain resembling wheat and barley, such as emmer^z, einkhorn, emmer^o, oats and *aegilops*, emmer^z is the strongest and most depletes the soil; for it has many deep roots and many thick stalks. But its grain is very light and agreeable to all animals...

and again, following this:

einkhorn is the lightest of all. In fact it has a single thin stalk, which is why it seeks poor country and not, as emmer^z does, good rich land...

then after this, bringing it all together, he writes:

It is a fact that the two, emmer^z and einkhorn, are very like wheat.

Now that is what Theophrastus wrote.* Herodotus, in his second book, wrote as follows:

Many people live on wheat and barley, but it is a matter of the greatest reproach for any Egyptian who lives on these; instead, they make their food from emmer [*olyra*], which certain other people call *zeia*.*

Dioscorides in the second book of his *On the Materials of Medicine* writes this:

Zea is of two kinds; one is called single, the other two-grained, since it has the grain paired together in two husks. It is more nourishing and wholesome than barley, but when made into bread is less nourishing than wheat. A coarse meal, from which is made a porridge, and which comes from both emmer^z and wheat, is bulkier than flour when milled. It is quite nourishing and easily concocted, but that from *zea* is rather astringent to the stomach, especially when it has been previously roasted. Emmer^o belongs to the same group as emmer^z, but quantity for quantity is less nourishing. It too is made into bread, and *krimnon* similarly comes from it. Porridge is made from finely ground emmer^z. It is a porridge like gruel, suited to children; it also makes poultices. *Tragos* is more like groats in form, but is far less nourishing than emmer^z, because it has a lot of chaff-like material, which is why it is difficult to concoct and relaxes the stomach.* 517

Now this is enough about emmer^z.

It is a matter for wonder that Mnesitheos was unaware in what way emmer^o differs from einkhorn. For each occurs in quantity in Asia, 518 especially in the hinterland of Pergamon, since the country people always make bread from them because the wheat is taken down to the cities.

After wheaten breads the best are the ones from emmer^o when it is a good strain; and those from einkhorn are second. But the latter in no way fall short of the emmer breads when the emmer^o is of poor quality. When the einkhorn is very good quality, warm breads from it are much stronger than those from emmer^o, but when kept to the next day, they are inferior; for since they have a stickier dough they are very considerably condensed, especially when prepared carelessly. So that after one or two days (and much more on subsequent ones) a person eating this bread thinks that a lump of clay reposes in his stomach. But when still warm 519 it is eagerly sought by city-dwellers, who take it with some cheese of the country, which they call sour-milk cheese. This cheese should be soft, and the bread should still hold the heat from the oven. Bread eaten like this is highly regarded not only by country folk but by city-dwellers as well. But bread three or four days old is already distasteful even to the country people, is more difficult to concoct, and is slower to pass in the stomach – although warm bread does not give this symptom. While it is much inferior to barley bread in laxative effect it is not to be faulted in the same way as that from millet; and further, when warm it nourishes the body adequately, so that it is little inferior to wholemeal wheaten bread.

This grain from einkhorn has an external husk like emmer^o and barley, but when it has been pounded in a mortar, it is made into bread and put to a wide range of use. In fact when boiled in water, it is eaten in the same way as that which country people call *apothermos*, when what we call 'must', but others call *siraion*, is added. Sometimes it is also eaten boiled with salt, just as I myself said I have eaten wheat.

When they pound the best strain of emmer^o to the extent necessary, 520 they make what is called *tragos*,* which many people use by boiling it in water and, after decanting the water, pouring in must, sweet wine or honeyed wine. As well, they also put in pine nuts that have been soaked in water so that they have swollen as much as possible. Some say that this grain is of the same genus, but not the same species as emmer^o.

There are many other related grains but none has precisely the same form as the ones that have been discussed; some being between barley and einkhorn, some between emmer^o and einkhorn, and others between wheat and emmer^o. Some are very close in nature – those of emmer^o, barley, einkhorn or wheat; as are others – those of foxtail and broom millet; some bearing simple names like the Italian *sêtanion*; and others compound names, like the so-called 'naked barley' in Cappadocia, and *zeopyros* in Bithynia.

So it is better to abandon this sort of enquiry, not only about the names, but also about the seeds, and give a single account applying to all. Those 521 that contain the most substance in small bulk (and this substance both thick and tough) are all more productive of healthy humour, and more nutritious; however, they are not easily excreted. Those which are the opposite to these, which have a soft, porous substance and their parts bran-like, while they are excreted better, are less nourishing. And of these latter themselves, those that are ill-smelling and have on tasting a certain nauseating quality, clearly all produce unhealthy humours and are difficult to concoct. And when they are weighed in the scale, let the weight and the quantity of flour be your indication of the fact that there is most substance in small bulk. For with grain that has its substance condensed there is much from small bulk.

Before consuming them and taking them into the body you should look for differences in warmth and coolness manifested by colour and taste, and by their value when they are applied externally. After consuming them there is, on the part of those who eat them, an accurate diagnosis and a conscious sensation in the stomach that what has been taken is either warming or cooling, or that there is no clear effect either way.

White is the natural colour in barley and emmer^o, but the colour of   522 wheat is yellowish. Einkorn is paler than wheat. However, its body has been compressed into a dense state, and perhaps this contributes to the smallness of the grains. For in size they are a good deal smaller than wheat. Some include this grain, too, in the wheat family. And what was said in Homer about the horses, when Hector says to them '[Andromache] . . . set first before you delicious wheat . . .'* was said, they say, about the grains of einkorn for they are small wheat, and horses eat them without harm, but what is really wheat they do not eat without harm. One might persuasively name einkorn small wheat, since it has the appearance of wheat in colour, compactness and in its warm property.

14   On oats

This grain occurs in greatest quantity in Asia, especially in the part of Mysia lying beyond Pergamon, where much einkorn and emmer^o is also produced. It is food for draught animals, not for men, unless   523 perhaps at some time when, being at the extreme of hunger, they are forced to make bread from this grain. Famine aside, when it has been boiled with water it is eaten with sweet wine, boiled must or honeyed wine, the same as einkorn; and it is sufficiently warm, very much like that grain. However, it is not as hard as einkorn. This is why it provides less nutriment for the body, and the bread produced from it is unpleasant in other respects. Not that it checks or stimulates the bowel. Rather, in this respect it is situated at the halfway mark.

15 On broom millet and foxtail millet (which people also call *melinê*)

Sometimes bread is made from these when a lack of the above-mentioned cereal foods supervenes, but it is poorly nourishing and cold, and obviously friable and crumbly, as if it contained nothing fatty or glutinous. So, as you might expect, it is drying for a moist stomach. But in the country, after boiling the flour from this grain, they mix in pork fat or olive oil and eat it.

Broom millet is superior to foxtail millet in every respect. In fact it is more pleasant as food, easier to concoct, less constipating and more 524 nourishing. Sometimes country people eat the flour from these grains with milk, after boiling it, as they do with wheaten flour. It is clear that, in producing much healthy humour, and in everything else, this food is as much superior to the items when they are eaten on their own as milk is superior to the natural qualities of both, in the production of healthy humour and in everything else. By everything else I mean concoction, gastric emptying, distribution, and sweetness and pleasantness when eaten. For with these grains there is nothing pleasant, particularly with foxtail millet in our part of Asia. In other countries, just as in Italy, it is much better.

16 On pulse*

They call pulse those cereals from which bread is not produced – beans, peas, chickpeas, lentils, lupins, rice, bitter vetch, grasspea, wild chickling, birds' peas, calavance, fenugreek, dwarf chickling and any others like these. So I shall speak about the properties of all in turn, in the knowledge of which one might use them with less harm.

17 On rice   525

Everyone uses this grain for restraining the stomach, producing a boiled version like groats. But it is less digestible and less nourishing than groats, as it is also inferior to groats in its pleasantness as food.

18 On lentils

Neither does anyone make bread from these, for they are non-fatty and friable, with an astringent capsule, and the flesh-like part, which produces thick juice and is also earthy and small in amount, has a rough quality which the capsule shares to a great degree. Their juice, as stated previously, is the reverse of astringent. This is why if, after boiling them in water, one were to drink it seasoned with salt or fish sauce, and oil as well, the draught is aperient. But on boiling it twice, as described, the soup prepared from these lentils has the opposite property to the juice – drying up gastric fluxes and increasing the tone in the oesophagus, intestines and the stomach as a whole. This is why it is an appropriate food for those with gastric or dysenteric complaints. Soup made from lentils 526 that have been separated from the capsule loses its strongly costive effect and, of course, what goes with this; and it is more nourishing than soup from unwinnowed lentils, since it produces thick humour and is slow of passage. However, it does not dry up gastric fluxes like the unwinnowed one does. So it is likely that people who are excessive in their use of these foods have what is called elephantiasis* and ulcerating growths; for it is usual for thick, dry food to generate black bile.

Lentils are a beneficial food only in people with some dropsical disorder* of the flesh, just as they are very harmful in those with dried out and parched flesh. Similarly, while being excessively drying dims healthy vision, it helps vision that is the opposite of this. It is inappropriate during the menses when it makes the blood thick and sluggish, but is very useful in so-called female flux.* As regards this property, since ptisane has the opposite effect, a dish mixed from both, which men hereabouts call 527 'lentil-ptisane', is best when we do not mix them in equal parts but put in less of ptisane, on the grounds that when it is made into lentil-ptisane its bulk is greatly increased. But lentils swell only a little when cooked slowly.

Actually in this foodstuff the seasoning is the same as in ptisane, except that when savory and pennyroyal are added it becomes both more pleasant and more easily concocted, while ptisane does not go well with these but is content only with dill and leek. The worst preparation of lentils is that which cooks make for the wealthy, with boiled must. For it needs the admixture not of things that are thickening, but of liquids and things that dilute its thickness. Lentils that have been mixed with boiled must are also naturally disposed to produce obstructions in the liver. In this organ and in the spleen they cause increasing inflammation, and it is no better even if one takes some honey as well. It is clear that they also bring about hardening of both organs. If you want to boil them with pork, you will discover that fresh pork goes with ptisane, but pickled pork with lentils; just as what is between these, which they call 528 freshly salted, is useful in lentil-ptisane, both for pleasantness and for concoction.

Moreover the increase in thick humours occurs more with lentil dishes when they are eaten with pickled meats. In fact, these meats also give rise to blood that is thicker, and rather like black bile. That is why they should not be used to excess either, especially when one's body is either black-biled, thick humoured or, in general, has unhealthy humour. Regarding every food, you must also keep the same things in mind concerning regions, seasons and constitutions,* in autumn being sparing with foods that produce black bile and are drying, but using them in winter; just as in summer you should use moistening and cooling foods. But in spring, since it is of average mixture, one should consume foods that are average in their properties.

There is no one type of average food. For some are average because they have no part in the extreme positions at all; but others attain the mean position as a result of a mixture, equal in strength, of both extremes, 529 as when one mixes lentils with ptisane, as I was saying a little earlier. In this way Herakleides the Tarentine used to give beet and lentil dishes not only to healthy persons but also to those who were ill. For this food is also at the mean position, being compounded from opposites, which is why it is less laxative than beets but more aperient than lentils. And it is very clear that the humour that is distributed from it to the body is a mix of the properties of both the lentils and the beet.

19 On broad [or faba] beans

There is also much use made of these, since soups are prepared from them, the fluid one in pots and the thick one in pans. There is also a third preparation when it is mixed with ptisane. Our gladiators eat a great deal of this food every day, making the condition of their body fleshy – not compact, dense flesh like pork, but flesh that is somehow more flabby. The food is flatulent, even if it has been cooked for a very long time, and however it has been prepared, while ptisane gets rid of all flatulent effect during the period of cooking. But to those who pay attention and closely follow the disposition accompanying each foodstuff, a sensation of some 530 tension, like windy flatulence, occurs in the body as a whole, particularly when one is unaccustomed to this food or eats it when it is badly cooked.

Beans have a substance that is not dense and heavy, but spongy and light, with a little cleansing quality like ptisane. At any rate, the flour made from them appears to wipe dirt off the skin; having noticed which, slave-merchants use bean flour, and women use it every day when washing, as other women use both nitre and light nitre, and detergent substances generally. They also smear the face with bean flour much as they do with ptisane. It cleans off moles and so-called 'freckling' as well.* Because of this property there is no delay in its passage in the stomach, like those thick-juiced glutinous foods which have no cleansing power – such as, we said, groats, *tragos*, *semidalis* and starch.

While bean soup is flatulent, beans become still more so when one uses 531 them after boiling them whole. However, when roasted (in fact some eat them like this in place of sweetmeats) they avoid flatulence but become more difficult to concoct, slower to pass and distribute a thick humour as nutriment for the body. But the green ones, when eaten before they have been ripened and dried, have what is a common feature of all fruits that we eat before they have been fully developed, in that they provide the body with nutriment that is moister and so more productive of residue, not only in the intestine but in the system as a whole. So it is understandable that foods like this are less nourishing but more aperient. Most men eat unripe beans not only raw, but also boiled, with pork, like vegetables; and, in the country, with goat meat and mutton. Conscious of their flatulent quality, when they are making soup from them in a pan they mix in onions. But some use the onions with it raw, without cooking them all together. For, you see, in all foods the flatulent quality 532 is corrected by the addition of things that are heating and thinning.

20   On Egyptian beans

Just as the Egyptian bean differs greatly in size from the one in our part of the world, so it also has a nature that is moister and more productive of residue. If you think of what was said about concoction, excretion, distribution and nutrition with foods of the same class, but then think of them being moister in blend and so producing more residue, you no longer need to hear about this bean since you can transpose what you have learned about our local bean.

21   On peas

Peas, being rather close in their whole substance to beans, although eaten in the same manner deviate from them in the following two ways, namely, that they are not flatulent to the same degree as beans; and that they have no cleansing property. Consequently they are slower to pass in the intestine than beans.

22   On chickpeas

It is not very usual for people in the towns to make soup from chickpeas, 533
but in the country I have sometimes seen this take place, as indeed I have also seen chickpea flour cooked with milk. They do not suffer the same degree of fragmentation as beans, so that what is called 'bruised' chickpeas is made from them. In many countries people are accustomed to eating chickpeas after they have been boiled with water, some eating them bare, on their own; others seasoning them with a moderate amount of salt. Amongst us, people make something that resembles flour from dry cheese, and sprinkle the chickpeas with this. It is the case that the chickpea is less flatulent than beans, but it is more strongly nutritive than they are, and it has been believed to stimulate the sexual urge at the same time as being generative of semen; so that on account of this they also give them as food to stallions standing at stud. There is also a cleansing property in them to a greater extent than with beans, so that some of them clearly break up kidney stones. The chickpeas that do this are black and small, and especially produced in Bithynia, and are called 'rams'. It is better to drink their juice on its own after they have been boiled in water.

People use chickpeas even before they have ripened, while they are 534
still green, just as they use beans. The argument common to all unripe fruits was stated just now when we dealt with beans. Similarly you should consider that you have also learnt about roasted chickpeas from what was said about roasted beans. For all things that are roasted, though they avoid flatulence, are more difficult to concoct, more costive and give a thicker nutriment to the body.

23   On lupins

We know, of course, that this seed is multiply useful in one sense of the word multiple. For this is how we refer to what is appropriate for numerous conditions of the body; and also to what is useful for all or most men, even if they need it for a single specific use. In terms of this second meaning, at least, the lupin is a multiply useful legume. For when boiled, then steeped in sweet water until the water has removed all innate unpleasant features, it is eaten in this way with fish sauce and fish sauce

with vinegar, and aside from these, moderately seasoned with salt – unlike
barley and the other grains that are prepared in a variety of ways. In its 535
substance it is hard and earthy, so that it is difficult to concoct and gives
rise to a thick humour from which, if it is not satisfactorily worked up
in the veins, what is specifically called crude humour accumulates. But
since, having lost in its preparation what bitterness it naturally contained,
it becomes like foods that are quality-free as regards sensation, it is likely
to be suitable neither for excretion nor for checking a gastric flux, as
astringent foods are, but to be slow of passage, hard to remove by purging
and difficult to excrete. For this is how physicians refer to these sorts
of foods, which have no outstanding quality as regards their ability to
stimulate excretion in the bowel, or to prevent it.

Now these qualities are not present in them *qua* foods but *qua* drugs.
Those that clearly have no such quality are with good reason called in- 536
ert by physicians, but taking into account the differences in moistness,
dryness, thickness and viscidity it follows that they are different in being
either fast or slow of passage, or at the mean of these states – the moist
and slippery passing rapidly; the dry and hard, like the lupin, being the
opposite. Those between these in the above differentiae produce neither
conspicuous rapidity nor slowness of excretion. So just as by common
consent it is proper to understand this regarding all foods, by the same
token it is also proper to understand the following: all foods that are
moister in composition deliver to the body little nutriment, which also
rapidly evaporates and is dispersed, so that in no time it again needs
further nutriment; but the hard, earthy foods deliver more stable, less
dispersible nutriment. And if it contains anything glutinous it accom-
plishes all this much more obviously. It is clear that it is not easy for foods
like these to be concocted, just as they do not easily convert to blood nor
assimilate to the solid parts of the animal; and if this is so, neither do
they rapidly provide nourishment. But when indeed they are mastered
and worked up, they deliver a great deal of nutriment to the body.

24   On fenugreek   537

Some call this seed not only fenugreek but also ox-horn and goat-horn.
It is clearly one of the warming foods, providing, as food, the same service
for people that lupins do. For they take it with fish sauce in order to move
the bowels, and it is more suitable for this than lupins, since in its own
substance it contains nothing hard to pass. Like lupins, it is also eaten with
vinegar and fish sauce. Many also eat fenugreek and lupins with wine,

fish sauce and oil, and some, with bread as well; and for them this last becomes a dish in its own right, moving the bowels less, neither affecting the head, as fenugreek with fish sauce affects some people, nor upsetting the oesophagus; for with some people fenugreek also has this effect. Some people use calavance and birds' peas, done in the same fashion, as food; in respect of which I shall in a moment add an argument with common application to all foods like this.

Fenugreek is eaten by some people, even before the plant has borne 538 seed, by dipping it in vinegar and fish sauce. Some pour oil over it and take it with bread as a relish, and others, with vinegar and fish sauce. When taken in quantity this affects the head, and even more so if one takes it without bread. In some persons it also affects the oesophagus.

The liquor of fenugreek that has been boiled, when taken with honey, is good for removing all troublesome fluids in the intestines, since from its slipperiness it is gentle, but from its warmth it is soothing. Because it has a cleansing property it promotes excretion by the intestine. The honey mixed in it should be small in amount, lest it becomes irritant in some way. In the case of pains persisting in the chest in the absence of fever you should boil plump dates with it and, having expressed the liquid and mixed it with plenty of honey and boiled it on the coals again until it is moderately thick, you should use it well before meals.

25   On cowpeas and birds' peas

Men also eat these seeds before the rest of their food, as they eat fenugreek, for moving the bowels, soaking the seeds in water until the root 539 sprouts before dipping them in fish sauce. They have a nutritious chyme when it has been distributed, for it is concocted better than fenugreek.

I know that a certain young man, who practises the art of medicine in Alexandria, for four years every day used these alone as seasoning – I mean fenugreek, cowpeas, birds' peas and lupins. Sometimes he also used oils from Memphis, vegetables and a few fruits that are eaten uncooked; for it has been his policy not even to light a fire. So, in all those years this man has stayed healthy and maintained his bodily condition not a whit worse than it was at the outset. He ate them with fish sauce, that is to say, sometimes adding oil alone to it, sometimes also wine, and on occasion also vinegar; but at other times, as with lupins, he ate them with salt alone.

Now there has been extended discussion about the healthy regimen in my work *On Hygiene*, and it will be restated in summary in this book. 540

But for the present let me also add this to what I have already said about birds' peas and cowpeas. In a way these foods are an average of foods that produce healthy humours and foods that produce unhealthy ones; of those that are easily and those that are with difficulty concocted; of those that are slow and those that are speedy in passage; of those that are and those that are not flatulent; and of those that give little nutriment and those that give much. For they do not have any active quality at all, as other foods have sharp, astringent, salty, sweet or bitter juices.

26   On grasspeas [chickling vetch]

In substance grasspeas are very like birds' peas and cowpeas, and once again the countryfolk in our part of Asia, and especially in Mysia and Phrygia, use them in great quantity; not only as people in Alexandria and many other cities use birds' peas and cowpeas, but also preparing them like a lentil-ptisane. They have a liquor which is close to these in property, but thicker in consistency, and for this very reason they are somehow more nourishing.

27   On wild chickling [*arakos*]   541

We find that the final syllable of the name of *arakos* is written with a *kappa* in *The Merchant Ships* of Aristophanes,* where he speaks of 'wild chickling, wheats, ptisane, emmer, darnel and *semidalis*'. The seed is very like the seed of the grasspea, and indeed some think that they are of the same family. In fact its every use and property are close to those of grasspea, except to the extent that it is harder and more difficult to cook; and consequently it is more difficult to concoct than grasspea is. People in our region call the wild one that is spherical, hard, smaller than bitter vetch, and found among cereals, *arachos*, pronouncing the final syllable with a *chi* and not a *kappa**; and they pick it out and throw it away as they do axeweed.

28   On *dolichos* [? calavance]

The name *dolichos* was included in the writings of Diocles, together with the names of other seeds that nourish us, and also in the *On Regimen* of 542 Hippocrates, which work I have already discussed. I think that they were speaking in this way about the seed of a cultivated plant which nowadays is referred to by most people in the plural, in two ways. For some call them *loboi* [pods] but others *phaséoloi*, producing a word with four syllables and in this way making a name different from *phasélos*, with its three. Some say that *phasélos* [cowpea] is the same as *lathyros* [grasspea], but others say that it is a species of it.

One might indeed infer from what Theophrastus said about them in the eighth book of *Enquiry into Plants* that the plants we now cultivate are those he called *dolichos*. The statement went as follows:

and some have straight stalks like wheat, barley and cereals and summer grains in general; but some are spreading, more like chickpea, bitter vetch and lentil; and others have a prostrate form like birds' pea, pea and grasspea. *Dolichos*, if one stakes it with a long wooden stake, climbs and becomes fruitful; but if one does not it is poor and prone to mildew...*

From his recommendation to drive long wooden stakes alongside it, and 543 the remark that when this is not done they are made prone to mildew, one might infer that his statement is concerned with what are now called both *phaséoloi* and *loboi*. He himself gives the name *loboi* [pods] to what surrounds the seed of legumes like these, such as the lentil, bitter vetch, pea, bean and lupin. For just as ears embrace the seeds of cereals, so pods surround those seeds just mentioned, and indeed pods also surround the *dolichos* seeds themselves. I think that for this reason people call the total product 'pods', just as the cereal product as a whole is called 'ears'. We know many other things also, which are in great use by men, that have taken over the name of the family as a whole, like the reed with which we write, and the ink.*

In the *On Regimen* of Hippocrates* it is written as follows: 'Peas are less flatulent but pass more easily; birds' pea and *dolichoi* pass more easily than they do, and are less flatulent, but nourishing'. In this passage he compares peas with beans, which he has said previously are a flatulent food, but by writing about *dolichos* and birds' pea straight after this he indicates that *dolichos* belongs to the same family of aforementioned seeds, and is especially akin to birds' pea. Since he does not mention grasspea 544 and cowpea at all, there is some suspicion that one of those seeds might have been called *dolichos*. But even if one includes cowpeas in the class of grasspea, it is inescapable that in the passage before us grasspea could not have been called *dolichos*.*

In the *Catalogue of Legumes* Diocles, speaking first about broad beans, and then peas, next writes word for word as follows: '*Dolichoi* are just as nourishing as peas, are similarly non-flatulent, but are not so pleasant and pass less easily.' This author also, by going on to mention birds' peas,

peas, lentils, chickpeas and bitter vetch, but ignoring the name grasspea, produced the same ambiguity. One can say that all these – birds' peas, grasspeas and cowpeas – while they constitute one kind of thing, go under more than one name, like pillar and column do perhaps; or maybe in 545 virtue of certain specific differences they display. But the fact that *dolichoi* are no less nourishing than peas and are similarly non-flatulent indicates that Diocles is referring in this way to what are now called *phaséoloi*. For it is a fact that grasspeas are no less flatulent than peas, just as birds' peas and cowpeas are not either, whether these constitute one class, as I said, or particular variations within one class.

Phylotimos and Praxagoras mentioned no such foodstuffs, except only broad beans and peas, so that with these authors we have nothing to provide an answer to the question about the name *dolichoi*, as to which item it has been assigned to. Accordingly let everyone refer as they please to what are now called by many people both *phaséoloi* and *loboi*, but let them be aware that their property is the same as Diocles described for *dolichoi*.

The author of the Hippocratic *On Regimen* comes close to Diocles' view when he says that birds' peas and *dolichoi* pass more easily than peas, but 546 are less flatulent; but he testifies that they are also nourishing. And in fact this is so, with the proviso that men eat them whole, together with their pods, while they are still green, generally with oil and fish sauce. Some also add wine. But they do not use them for storage as they do with peas, for since they are moister in nature they are usually ruined. Whoever wants to store them safely, as my father used to, must dry them thoroughly. In this way they will remain free from decay and imperishable throughout a whole winter, providing the same value as the pea. One of my friends who lives in Rome used to say that in Caria, in his own city which is called Ceramos,* *dolichoi* are planted in cultivated land like the rest of the legumes, and have a more elongated shape than grasspeas.

29   On bitter vetch

With ourselves and many other countries, cattle eat bitter vetch which has first been sweetened with water, but people absolutely avoid this seed; for it is distasteful and produces unhealthy humour. But sometimes in a severe famine, as Hippocrates wrote, from force of necessity they come to it.* We ourselves use bitter vetch with honey as a drug for getting rid 547 of thick fluids in the chest and lungs, first preparing it as we do lupins. The white ones among them have less pharmacological activity than those that tend more to golden or yellowish. The ones that have been boiled twice and frequently sweetened with water, while they avoid the unpleasant taste, at the same time also do away with the cleansing and cutting properties, so that the earthiness of their substance is left behind, which, in the absence of obvious sharpness, becomes a rather drying foodstuff.

30 On sesame and rocket

Sesame seed is greasy, which is also why it very quickly becomes oily on storage. For this reason it quickly fills up those who eat it, and disturbs the oesophagus and is concocted slowly; and it delivers greasy nutriment to the body. So it is obvious that it cannot impart tone and strength to the parts of the alimentary tract, just as no other oily thing does. But since it produces thick juice, neither does it pass through rapidly. People do 548 not eat it on its own very much, but with boiled honey, fashioning what many call 'sesamids'. They also sprinkle the seed on bread.

Just as foxtail millet (which we stated is also called *melinê*), while similar in a way to broom millet, is in every respect inferior to it, so also rocket, although in a sense of the same class as regards substance, is inferior to sesame since it is more distasteful to eat, provides less nutriment to the body, and is worse in every respect. But in their mixtures both are warm, which is why they excite thirst.

31 On poppyseed

Like sesame seeds, the seed of the cultivated poppy is useful sprinkled on bread as seasoning. The whiter seed is better than the darker and has a cooling property, and so is also hypnotic; and if taken in greater quantity it produces lethargy, is difficult to concoct and, further, it inhibits the coughing up of material from the lung and the chest. However, it benefits those suffering from catarrhs from the head which are accompanied by a thin discharge. But for the body it produces no nutriment worth talking about.

32 On the seed of flax [*linon*] (which they also call by the compound name, linseed) 549

Some roast this, as they do prepared salts, and use it as a relish with fish sauce, but others use it kneaded with honey. Some sprinkle it on bread, although it is bad for the stomach and difficult to concoct, and produces little nutriment for the body. As an aperient you would neither praise nor fault it. It has, however, some slight diuretic property which becomes more evident when it is eaten after it has been roasted. In this case it somehow steadies the stomach more. Country people frequently use it after roasting, pounding it finely and mixing it with honey.

33   On sage

This they use by roasting it and then pounding it finely so that it becomes meal; and they also mix honey with it. It contains little nutriment in itself, being in its nature between rocket and cumin.

34   On the seed of Indian hemp   550

It is not the case that since the Indian hemp plant itself resembles the chaste tree, its seed is somehow similar in property to that seed. Rather, it is completely different from it, being difficult to concoct and unwholesome, and produces headaches and unhealthy humours. Nevertheless some people roast and eat it with other sweetmeats. (Clearly, I am calling things that are eaten after dinner for pleasure while drinking, sweetmeats.) The seeds are quite warming, and consequently when they are taken in quantity over a short period they affect the head, sending up to it a vapour that is both warm and like a drug.

35   On the seed of the chaste tree

This is also eaten on its own and roasted, having been believed to keep the sexual urge in check; it gives little nutriment to the body (and this both drying and cooling), but is quite non-flatulent. So it is suitable in every respect for those who wish to abstain from sexual activity. They say that this is why the name has been applied to the plant. It does not affect the head as Indian hemp does.

36   On tare and vetch

The shape of these seeds is not round like that of beans, but rather flattened, like that of lentils. Farmers store them, together with the pods 551 themselves and the plants as a whole, for stock feed. Just the same, I am aware that some people eat them in time of food shortage, especially in the spring while they are still green; just as they commonly eat chick-peas and beans. Not only is the taste unpleasant but they are also difficult to concoct and costive. It is obvious that, being of such a nature, the nutriment distributed from them is thick and unwholesome, being fit for the generation of blood that is black-biled, as has been stated previously about lentils. But while lentils have many virtues, none of their virtues exist in these foods.

The name vetch [*bikos*] is certainly usual in our region, and it is referred to only in this way, but among the Athenians it was equally called wild chickling [*arakos*] and grasspea [*lathyros*].

37 On the different species and hybrids contained in each class of seeds

A lot of darnel is frequently found in wheat. It also occurs in barley, 552 although in small amount, but much *aegilops* is found among the barley whenever the latter comes to grief in the early stages of its growth, or its germination.

My own father, having become keen on farming in his later years, once sowed wheat and barley after he had painstakingly picked out from them all seed of a different class that had been mixed with them, in order to understand* clearly whether darnel and *aigilops* originate in a change from wheat and barley, or whether these seeds also have a specific nature. Together with the pure seeds, as it turned out, a great deal of darnel was generated amongst the wheat, but little amongst the barley; rather, there was an abundance of *aegilops*. He also made trial of other seeds in the same manner. He also discovered that the hard, round seeds of wild chickling, and axeweed seeds, which are inedible, are produced among the lentils by transition from these plants; as well as cleavers, which is not only inedible but, on being sprouted, becomes entangled with the lentil plants and strangles and chokes them, and pulls them down like dodder does bitter vetch. So these are very troublesome seeds. So-called black wheat is itself also generated from wheat, but falls a long 553 way short of the bad features in darnel.

He also found some such changes occurring with other seeds, which is why he instructed those using them, so that they might be healthy when used, to pick out everything harmful whenever the seeds are brought and not to ignore them as the public millers do.

Mark you, once, when it had been a bad year, a great deal of darnel had been generated in the wheat, which neither the farmers properly cleaned out with the appropriate sieves (for the total of wheat cultivated was small), nor did the bakers for the same reason, and at once many headaches occurred and, with the onset of summer, skin ulcers, or some other occurrence indicating an unhealthy humoral state, arose in those people eating it.

And so we should not neglect to clean all seeds being prepared for food, in the knowledge that even if because of its insignificance on a day to day basis we experience no sense of harm, the cumulative effect from it over a longer time will some day become apparent.

BOOK II

1   Although we receive nourishment from both plants and animals, 554 since everybody before me began their instruction about foodstuffs with the so-called 'seeds of Demeter'* because the food from bread is the most valuable, this is why I also examined wheat, barley, einkhorn and emmer^o when I discussed foods in book 1; and as well as these the so-called legumes and pulses. In this book it is appropriate to move next to 555 the other foodstuffs we have from plants, and then to those from animals, which are more valuable for men. This seems to be a logical approach. Some writers too, while they did not discuss all foods of the same class, nor give instruction about all foods from plants straight after dealing with the cereals, always wrote first about those that were more useful to man. At any rate, it is clear that pork, the meat of goats and kids, and veal, beef and mutton (and no less than these, the meat of animals that huntsmen catch in the mountains) provide much value for man, as also do many winged and aquatic creatures. Then, when I reflected on the impossibility of encompassing each class in a single book, I assumed that, as regards the foodstuffs that remain in addition to those already described, it made no great difference to go through the foods from plants in this second book, and those from animals in the third. For anyone who wishes to select the book in which the properties of foods he particularly wants to use have been set out can at one time go to the first, and at another to the second or the third. So in order that the whole discussion of plants 556 will be completed in the first two books, having made this introduction I shall come to the ones that were omitted from what has already been spoken about.

The foods in the first book were all seeds of plants. But this time I shall start with the fruits after I have first distinguished their seeds, particularly because many thought that it made no difference whether they said fruit or seed. Now, the seeds already discussed differ slightly from fruits, but those to be discussed now are a long way removed from them. Thus, the fig is the fruit of the fig tree but the pip within the fruit is the seed of the fig tree; just as also, while the whole berry is the fruit of the vine, the grape-stone alone is the vine's seed. In the same way the fruits of the pear tree and the apple tree are the pear and the apple, but the seed is the three or four pips in their middle. What should one say in the case of colocynths and cucumbers, both ripe and unripe, and all others of the same sort? For in these the whole fruit is completely different from the 557 seed. But in the broad bean, the lupin, the *dolichos* and the lentil, and others with a pod enclosing the seeds, the fruit is what comprises both seed and pod, but the greatest portion of their total substance is in the seeds. Of virtually all the others that I discussed in book I only the seed is eaten. Only with *dolichoi* is the fruit as a whole eaten, when they are still green. For when they have been dried, the pods surrounding the seeds are useless for man. But the pod of the broad bean is not even edible when it is still green, and neither is that of the chickpea, nor that of those others that Theophrastus used to call 'podded ones'. So, I said, it is with good reason that those which some call *phaséoloi* are by many called 'pods', since their pod alone is edible. But I have earlier spoken about the property of these, as also of the fact that I believe that some of the ancients apply the name *dolichos* to them. There are also fruits from trees and from cultivated vegetables, amongst which some physicians include gourds, melons and colocynths, from which I shall commence my instruction in this section. 558

2 On so-called seasonal fruits

The Greeks give the name 'season of the year' to that period in the middle of which the rising of the Dog Star* takes place. The duration is about forty days. At any rate what are called 'seasonal fruits' occur during this time – some already past their best and some just beginning; others at their peak, or just before or after it. They call them seasonal, not only because they occur at the specific time but, I believe, because they want to distinguish them from fruit suitable for storage. For wheat, barley and all those I discussed in the previous book have an annual, summer production, but are not quickly spoiled like colocynths, mulberries, melons and apple-melons, peaches and other such fruits. Some people, in point of fact, dry these latter and store them away, keeping them for winter, 559 and in this way they all change their original nature towards its opposite.

At all events, some people remove the seeds of the colocynths and then store the dried flesh-like component until winter, and use the seed very much as they do the colocynths themselves. These become juiceless and dry, more like leather than like any edible fruit. However, in the case of wheat, barley and other cereal seeds the nature of the stored material is certainly not changed to its opposite. For all such are stable in their substance from their first reaching full maturity in summer.

It is clear that fruits with a dry body formation, since they are in a stable state, are thus solid and earthy, and consequently nutritious. But those that are moist in composition are spoilt and so have nutriment that is small in amount and easily expelled from the body. For the same reason fruits like the latter are excreted in the bowel better than solid ones, especially when they have any alkaline or detergent quality. I shall show that some seasonal fruits have this property to a remarkable degree, the ones we also say are more unwholesome than those that have no 560 perceptible quality of flavour, just as the best water also has none. So all like these, and much more so those that we eat before they are fully ripe, are flatulent, but are evacuated more quickly, just as those with thin juice are distributed more quickly. These latter are all unwholesome, and one would only use them with benefit when worn out during very long walking or by excessive stifling heat. For at this time they are beneficial, moistening the dryness of the body and being moderately cooling if, that is, one were to take them cold. Now while they can moisten at all times, when taken warm by those in that condition they will not be able to cool. For they are not so cold in their specific mixtures that they cool the stomach even if they have been taken warmed. Accordingly there is need of acquired cold, acting in opposition to the warmth in the parts near the stomach and liver, which it meets first.

Now that this has been understood in a general sense concerning all foods of this kind, I shall pass to the specific properties of each food.

3   On the colocynth*   561

When raw it tastes bitter, is extremely bad for the stomach, and is indigestible. So that if anyone through lack of other food were to force himself to eat colocynth, as indeed in the past people have forced themselves to do, he would feel a cold heaviness pressing in the stomach, and would be disturbed in the *stomachos* and start vomiting, only this being able to give relief from the oppressive symptoms. Everyone, at any rate, is accustomed to eating this and many other seasonal fruits after boiling – either straight away, or when they have fried or roasted them. Please keep in mind this statement, which happens to be common to everything that needs alteration by heat.

The colocynth, which the discussion is about, when it has been properly cooked has no distinct quality of flavour, unless one were to say that even something like this, which is neither bitter, salty, astringent nor pungent, nor anything else of the sort, is a flavour. In the same way water 562 also is not a flavour. But, since everyone is accustomed to call such things 'bland', let me refer to them in this way for the sake of clear instruction. Given that it is like this, the colocynth admits of many styles of preparation, standing as it were at the mid-point of all extremes and so able to move, equally and evenly, towards one or the other. For no fruit that possesses whatsoever innate extreme is, in its preparation, easily taken to the other extreme.

Now, this in itself gives the body a nutriment that is moist and cold and for this reason it is also scanty, as was remarked a little earlier in connection with all those fruits that have thin, watery juice. But it passes easily in the stomach, both from the slipperiness of its substance and from the common fashion of all moist foods, that is to say, those like these that have no astringency. When it has not previously been spoilt, it is quite well concocted. It experiences this spoiling through bad preparation and whenever any unsound fluid has accumulated in the stomach; but sometimes it is also due to delay there, which usually happens with all the other seasonal fruits that are moist in blend. For it undergoes corruption 563 in the stomach unless it has previously been quickly eliminated.

Just as the colocynth in itself has a chyme, bland as regards sensation, that is distributed as nutriment to the body as a whole, similarly, when it has been mixed with anything with a strong property, it is easily made like it. If it is taken with mustard, it makes the humour distributed from both of them obviously warm and, by the same reasoning, if taken with some salt, as some people prepare it in a pan with pickled fish, it will generate a salty humour in the body. What is prepared in this way is a very pleasant food if the pickled fish is one of those they call *myllos*, from the Pontic region. When it has been cooked with quinces and appropriately seasoned, it will possess a harsh juice that is dominant in the distribution. But when boiled or fried, it gets rid of most of its own particular moisture, and what remains of it acquires no additional strong property, just as it does not do so when prepared in a simple sauce. But because of the innate watery quality* that exists in it, it is reasonable for it to accept oregano. For all such foods need to be mixed with bitter, harsh or salty 564 juices if they are not to be unpleasant to take, or nauseating to those who take them.

4 On gourds

The whole nature of these is rather cool, with abundant moisture. But they have some cleansing capacity, which is why they also stimulate the flow of urine and are more aperient than colocynths and apple-melons. You can learn that they are cleansing by rubbing dirty skin with them. That is why even if someone has freckling, moles on the face or superficial white patches, they also clean these off. The seeds clean better than the fleshy part, so that the gourd is also suitable for dealing with kidney-stone formation; but it produces a defective humour in the body, more so when it has not been well concocted. Under these circumstances it commonly brings on choleraic symptoms. In fact even before it has been corrupted it is useful for producing vomiting, and when a greater quantity has been eaten, unless one has consumed some wholesome foods with it, it will 565 stimulate it in every case.

It is very clear, in the case of this fruit too, that men have coined the name as they did with writing ink. For, you see, the word gourd [*pepôn*] points to what has, so to speak, become ripe [*pepanon*], a state that exists in other fruits which have matured. For the bunch of grapes can also be called *pepôn* when it has become fully ripe [*pepeiros*], just as what is not yet ripe is not called *pepôn* but 'raw' and 'unripe'. By the same reasoning all seasonal fruits, pears and colocynths, are usually referred to as 'ripened' [*pepeiroi*], just as the name melon [*mêlopepôn*] includes within itself 'ripe' [*pepôn*]. Whence some physicians think it wrong to speak simply of gourds [*pepones*] but say that this group as a whole should be referred to as ripe cucumber [*sikyopepôn*]. But in the present work I am not concerned about such things, since they would contribute nothing to medicine. It is far better to provide a clear explanation than, with this sort of over-elaboration, produce instruction that is obscure. Using names that are the most usual for most people, while at the same time 566 one retains their meaning, is the best way to attain clarity.

5 On melons

Melons are less moist and less unwholesome than gourds, and less diuretic and aperient. But they do not stimulate vomiting as much as gourds, just as neither are they quickly corrupted in the stomach like gourds whenever any troublesome fluid has collected in it, or when any other corruptive influence supervenes. While greatly inferior to the seasonal fruits in the degree to which they are good for the stomach, they are not as bad for that organ as the gourds are. For they do not stimulate vomiting as the latter do. Although people do not eat the inside of the flesh of gourds, where the seed is, they eat that part of melons, and this brings about purgation. But those who eat only the flesh-like part of the melons excrete it less easily than they do that of the gourds.

6 On cucumbers 567

These also have some diuretic property like gourds, but not so much, because their substance is less moist. Consequently they are not easily corrupted in the stomach to the same extent as gourds. Some people concoct them, as they concoct certain other things that most people cannot, due to a natural affinity with them, as I explained in my treatise *On Mixtures*, and more still in that *On Drugs*, when I showed that, by virtue of the specific character of their substances, foods are peculiar to each species of animal – chaff, grass, barley and the like to donkeys and horses; raw animal flesh to lions; and to man, cooked flesh and bread made from cereals, as was stated. Furthermore, quail eat hellebore, as starlings also eat hemlock, and come to no harm when they eat them, just as neither do oxen when they eat bitter vetch.

So, for each individual, one must distinguish foods that are well concocted and those that are poorly concocted, by testing either in terms of 568 the specific character of the substance of the food, or in respect of some symptom. The sort of thing I mean by 'in respect of some symptom' has been made clear in book 1. For with people who accumulate in the stomach either bile or, in general, any harmful residue whatever, those foods that by their nature can be well concocted are easily corrupted, as happens with some individuals who have innate warmth that is neither moist nor well-blended, but parched and fiery. In fact, the foods that with other people are best concocted are also easily altered and corrupted by these persons, and generally speaking a greasy belching occurs with them.

But please always bear this in mind, that even if one concocts whatever is difficult for most people to concoct, the humour from it has the same nature when distributed to the body. For it is not possible for the humour from the gourd to become thick and earthy, even if it has been perfectly concocted, just as it is impossible for the humour from the lentil, or from beef, to be watery and moist, that is to say thin in composition. The

value of this is particularly in the maintenance of health and the cure of 569
disease, as has been shown elsewhere and will now be stated again, in
summary, as the discussion continues.

So when those people who concoct cucumbers well gorge themselves
to satiety from confidence in this same ability, over a lengthy period
it happens that a cold, moderately thick humour accumulates in the
veins,* since it is not easily altered into useful blood during concoction
there. This is why I advise avoiding all unwholesome foods, even if some
people concoct them easily. For defective humour from them escapes
notice when it accumulates in the veins over a longer period, a humour
which, when it takes hold of a small pretext for putrefaction, produces
malignant fevers.

7   On fruit from trees

That is to say, pears, apples, figs, peaches and pomegranates, and all such
fruits that are useful to people as food, since there are other fruits that they 570
do not eat, about which I do not propose to speak at present. Generally
speaking, then, you should understand, as a general principle regarding
fruits edible for man, that the nutriment the moist ones produce and
deliver to the body is moist and thin. From which it follows, absolutely,
that such nutriment passes through the system and goes rapidly through
the body as a whole, being quickly evacuated both in the urine and
through the skin. This is why all such foods have been properly described
by physicians as poorly nutritive. As against that, the contribution to the
body in nutrient value of fruits that are solid in composition is greater,
and the evacuations are slower, especially when the fruits contain within
themselves any fluid, be it thick, viscid or astringent.

8   On figs

Figs possess the feature that is common not only to all late-summer fruits,
but also to those called 'seasonal', since not even they can avoid producing
unhealthy humour. However, they do so less than all the other seasonal
fruits. But there are benefits associated with them, both the fact that they 571
have a rapid passage through the stomach, and that they move easily
through the body as a whole. They also have some notable cleansing
ability, as a result of which, after meals of them, much sandy material
is excreted in the case of patients with kidney complaints. And while all
the late-summer fruits give little nutriment to the body, this is least of all

so with figs; however, they do not produce firm, strong flesh like bread and pork do, but a spongy flesh, as the broad bean does. Furthermore they also fill the stomach with wind, and in this way they would be quite distressing had they not also quick excretion; but having acquired this, due to the speed of their passage they produce a short-lived flatus. In this they are usually less harmful than other late-summer fruit.

The superiority of ripened figs, when compared with the unripe, is considerable, and this is apparent with all other fruits, although there is less difference than with figs. For indeed the fully ripe fig is close to causing no harm at all, in this resembling dried figs, which have many useful features, but one harmful one for those who use them to excess. For they generate blood of little value, which is why a large quantity of lice* 572 accompanies their use. But they have a cutting and thinning property, because of which they stimulate gastric emptying and clear out the kidneys. They are harmful to the inflamed liver and spleen, and like undried figs, in common with all sweet foods and drinks, they are without any singular, specific property; but while in themselves they produce nothing either beneficial or harmful in people with obstructive or indurated conditions, when they are mixed with cutting, thinning and cleansing drugs there is marked benefit. For this reason some physicians administer them in the above-mentioned conditions of the liver and spleen, well before food, in conjunction with thyme, pepper, ginger, pennyroyal, savory, catmint, oregano or hyssop. So too, if the administration of dried figs takes place together with anything else that has a bitter or, in general, a thinning and cutting property, it not only benefits those who suffer in this way, but 573 healthy people, too. For not only in patients but in healthy people, it is safest for the nutrient passages in the liver to have been opened up.

At any rate, many physicians who have discovered their value empirically also offer figs in this way, together with preparations of thinning salts, and vinegar and fish sauce. It is also likely that, when a particular physician has recommended others to do likewise, the knowledge has been extended to many. But people who eat figs or dried figs with any of the thickening foods are greatly harmed.

9 On grapes

Figs and grapes are, so to speak, the head of the late-summer fruits. For they are more nutritious than all the seasonal fruits and more wholesome, especially when fully ripe. The people who look after the produce of the vineyard are the best evidence for their being nourishing, since all the 574 time in the two months when they are tending them they eat only figs with grapes, perhaps including a little bread, but remain quite plump. However, the flesh that is generated from them is not strong and compact, like that generated from meat, but loose and flabby. This is why it is rapidly reduced when they cease the food.

Grapes are less nourishing than figs, and their greatest benefit is that they are quickly excreted. Consequently, if they are ever retained, they are quite harmful, while ripe figs do not have this characteristic. In fact if the latter are not passed through in a noteworthy fashion, but are well concocted in the stomach, they deliver a harmless nutriment to the body. But neither situation applies to grapes. For they are not even well concocted when they have been retained, and on distribution to the liver and veins they give rise to a crude humour that is not easily converted into blood. For, you see, the substance of the berries is compounded from their flesh-like material and the moisture interspersed in it from which wine arises; and as well as these, from the pips and the membranous covering that surrounds all of these things externally. But while the substance of the pips is somehow dry and astringent, it is passed through all the intestines 575 with no perceptible alteration, much the same as fig seeds. For each pip is analogous to that of other fruit, being the seed of the plant as a whole, but passing through unaltered, unliquefied and unchanged. There is also an analogy in the coverings surrounding each fruit, supplying the same sort of service for them as the skin does for animals. Very little change of this covering occurs in the stomach, and some spit it out as valueless after sucking out all the contents, including the seeds. Some try to spit these out also, especially when the berries are large (it is difficult to do so with small ones).

It is very clear that the laxative effect is greater when only the flesh of the berries has been swallowed with the juice, without the pips and the skin; and it is still more so when the juice itself is expressed and drunk 576 on its own. People call it 'must' [*gleukos*], and unless it passes through quickly it fills the stomach with wind. There is some nutriment from it for the body, but there is more from the fleshy substance, and so while some grapes are more nourishing than they are easily excreted, others are more easily excreted than they are nourishing.

They call 'noble' the sorts of grapes in which the berries have little liquid substance but a lot of solid substance, which I said was the flesh of the berry. People store them in late summer and use them in a variety of ways. In fact they put them into must, and they are also stored in pressings [*stemphyla*], filling new vessels. By pressings I mean the solid remnants of the grape when all their juice has been expressed in the wine-vats. Men place these remnants in pithoi, pressing and compacting them strongly, naming this same thing that I called pressings, *tryx*. (The same people give the name *stemphylon* to the stalk of berries that sprouts from 577 the branches.) Into this *tryx* they put new vessels full of grapes, closing them accurately with covers so that air is not let in from anywhere, and they smear pitch over where the lid meets the container, excluding all passage of air. The vessel itself must be made of sweet-smelling clay, and thoroughly baked. This sort of grape gives tone to a relaxed stomach, and stimulates eating in people without appetite; however, it does not cause purgation, and if eaten in greater quantity it affects the head. The grape stored in must brings on headache even more than this does. However, the grape that has been hung to dry does not affect the head at all, and neither constipates nor promotes excretion. It is the same as regards appetite, neither arousing the feeble nor weakening the robust. It is better concocted than the other grapes which, as I said, men store in must and pressings for the whole of the following year, until the next vintage. But the grapes that have been hung become useless when dried, some immediately in spring, the others, certainly, during the summer. 578

There is great variation among grapes in respect of sweetness, harshness or acidity, or the lack of any marked quality. They call the last vinous. Sweet grapes have juice that is warmer, which is why they are thirst-producing. The harsh and the acid ones are colder, and the vinous are midway between warm and cold. The sweet ones, especially when juicy, are aperient, and juicy vinous grapes are next to these. Acid and harsh grapes are not only unsatisfactory in this respect, but also as regards concoction in the stomach, distribution and nutrition.

Acid grapes, even when hung on the vine until fully ripened, do not even become sweet in this way, but some of the harsh ones change to a sweeter condition when hung for a longer time. But as with the acid ones, even if they are hung for a very long time sour grapes cannot change to sweet. This is why it is always a good idea to take care when eating 579 them. The safest use of all is when the grapes have a fleshy constitution and one eats them in moderation when they are fully ripe, whether they have been ripened on the vine to the greatest extent, or from being hung have added what was lacking. Next to the juicy grapes that are quality-free one can consume the acid or harsh ones liberally, for purgation. Some also drink must for the same purpose, especially the very sweet sort; for this is very aperient. But the must from harsh or acid grapes is the worst in all respects.

I myself use the names that people use nowadays, since I think that it is better to teach things clearly than to Atticize in the old-fashioned way. But those for whom the latter is worth more than clear instruction call the solid parts of the grape, after the juice has been expressed, *brytia*; and they call the solid parts of the olive, when they have expressed the oil, *stemphyla*. Moreover, the Atticizers similarly call the thick dregs from most wines *tryx*. So that there is no uniformity among them, as there is among the others who refer to *brytia* as *tryx*. Moreover, there is also a 580 third meaning of the word *tryx* in the vernacular of today's Greeks. For they refer to an infusion of pressings as *tryx*, while the Atticizers, on the other hand, call it 'seconds' [*deuterias*].*

When they put the pressings into small jars, they also pour on water so that it all becomes saturated, and when they consider that this has been acted on sufficiently, they open the aperture at the bottom of the jar, so that the infusion of the pressings is delivered, and they drink this instead of wine. It is clear that they pour on the water in line with their experience so that the seconds are neither very watery nor very strong. Next they pour different water on to the same pressings (but less than formerly), so that this becomes in proper proportion for a beverage which itself some Atticizers also call seconds, although it is not what was previously so called. Each of them causes headache when drunk unless it is very watery, although the former one affects the head more. The fact that it is rapidly diuretic is a benefit of this sort of drink, although there is a great 581 difference according to the species of grape from which the pressings come. When they are sweet, the draught is far more pleasant and more quickly diuretic; when sour and acid, it is less pleasant and less diuretic. This infusion becomes stronger and more vinous when the *tryx* is kept into spring or even into summer. When people use it in winter, just as it affects the head less, so also is it less diuretic.

10   On raisins

Raisins bear the same relationship to grapes that dried figs do to figs. Many are sweet, a few are completely sour, but most are a mixture of sweet and harsh. However, the sweet raisins also have a faint harsh quality, and the harsh raisins a sweet one. Now the harsh ones are colder in blending, just as the sweet are warmer. The harsh ones strengthen the *stomachos* and check gastric emptying, and it is clear that the astringent ones do this more than the harsh. Sweet raisins produce in these organs a condition that is about average, neither clearly relaxing the *stomachos* nor provoking gastric emptying. However, in sweet raisins there is always astringency,* as also a moderate cleansing capacity; so that as a consequence of both properties they dull minor irritations at the mouth of the stomach (which they also call the *stomachos*), since it is obvious that more 582 severe irritation demands more intense remedies.

Among the raisins, the plumper ones and those with, in a manner of speaking, 'bark' that is thin are better. Some people make them satisfactorily from large sweet grapes such as the *Skybelitides*, removing the seeds before eating them. When aged these also have skin that is hard and thick, and one must first soak them in water. In fact the seed is also more readily removed in this way. Against these, some others are harsh and small with no seed at all. These, with yellowish skin, are produced in Cilicia, but the *Skybelitides* and those that are black in colour are produced in Pamphylia. As I said, the latter are the largest, and the tawny ones from Cilicia are the smallest, although other sweet black ones of average size are also produced in Cilicia, as also in many other countries, particularly Libya. A diverse range of raisins is produced in Asia; in fact there are 583 yellowish, black, sweet and rather harsh ones. In cold regions, however, grapes are not even ripened fully; much less are there any raisins, which is why they add resin to the wine, so that it does not quickly become acid.

Now, difference in colour among raisins has no effect as regards their property, as neither does difference in size. But difference in tasting quality is absolutely influential, and by paying attention to this alone you will discover in which people and at what time you should use them, as stated previously.

Nutriment that is distributed to the body from raisins is close in quality to that from the grapes themselves – sweet from sweet ones, harsh from harsh ones, and mixed from those with both qualities. It is greater in amount from those that are full and sweet, but less so from those that are harsh and not full. If you put a mass of full, sweet seeded raisins beside an 584 equal bulk of grapes, you will find that the raisins are more nourishing. Raisins like these have both less aperient and less cleansing properties than dried figs, but are the better ones for the stomach.

11 On mulberries [*sykamina*], which they also call *mora**

This is not written for those who prefer to Atticize in their speech (for perhaps someone who is disdainful of a healthy body, as also of a healthy

soul, will not even want to read about it). Rather, it is written especially
for physicians who are not greatly concerned with Attic style, and also
for those others who live as rational beings, preferring to give heed to
their body and soul ahead of reward, reputation, wealth and political
power. For these people, I am well aware, believe that the speech of the
Athenians is not inherently more dignified than the speech of other men.
But they consider that the health of the body is a matter most worthy of
attention by one who is eager to live in conformity with nature. Since it is
likely that the clearer language will be of greater benefit to these people,
I write names that they recognize, even if they were not usual among the
Greeks of old.

Well now, the name mulberry is, I dare say, familiar to most people
if for no other reason than that the medicament for mouth complaints 585
that they call 'the mulberry cure' contains their juice. But most men are
ignorant of how the Athenians of over six hundred years ago named
some of the late-summer fruits that will be successively referred to. For
they observe that today's Athenians name each fruit no differently from
other Greeks; but also, that they now refer to *mora* as *sykamina* just as often
as *mora*, and they speak of peaches, nuts, apricots and the rest with single
names, as is customary with the rest of the Greeks. They will certainly not
come to any harm if, while ignorant of the ancient names, they know
their properties. For, of the foodstuffs that stimulate excretion, rather
than having recognized their names, it is better to be aware that one
should take the slower passing ones later, but should take first of all those
that are rapidly aperient but are destroyed if they delay in the stomach. 586
However, I do not think that people are totally ignorant about the order
of what they eat. At any rate I see that they take care about it in the case of
most foods. Certainly they first take radishes, oil and fenugreek without
fish sauce, and following these mallow, beets and other such vegetables
with fish sauce. For long experience becomes the instructor about the
property of what they prepare daily for food, even if they have limited
intelligence. But those foods that need a longer period of trial are closely
observed and retained in memory only by careful people.

Accordingly, mulberries that have been taken first and fallen upon
an empty stomach pass through very quickly and precede other foods.
When they are taken second after other foods or have also found bad fluid
in the stomach, they are very rapidly spoilt, sustaining a certain strange,
indistinct corruption, as happens with colocynths. For the latter are the 587
most harmless of the seasonal foodstuffs, but when they do not pass
through quickly after being concocted, they undergo bad corruption,

like melons. However, those too, when they pass quickly, do no great harm.

As with melons so also with mulberries; the proper time of use is when the body of the stomach becomes dry and hot. For it is inevitable that at this time the liver also is somewhat the same. Now the colocynth and cucumber, both when already ripe and prior to ripening, and with them the apple-melon, do not possess an astringent quality. But in mulberries, and especially when they are not very ripe, this sort of quality is obvious; and further, in the less ripe ones there is also acidity. Some people strip these from the trees, dry them, and store them as a medicament which will be good for the cure of dysentery and of chronic diarrhoea.

But I do not propose at present to discuss pharmacological properties. So let me repeat the effects of mulberries as food. It has been stated that they pass easily, due perhaps only to the moistness and slipperiness of their substance, but perhaps also due to the admixture of some sharper 588 quality that is sufficient to provoke excretion, since the astringent quality on its own does not assist excretion, but is naturally constipating. The fact that many bodies partake of contrary properties you have learnt in my work *On the Properties of Simple Drugs*. Accordingly, I conjecture that mulberries have within themselves in a small degree the sort of property that exists in cathartics in a large degree, through which not only do they cause easy evacuation but, when delayed in the stomach, they are also corrupted. And as I said, when uncorrupted they are absolutely moistening but in no way cooling unless they have been taken cold. They provide very little nutriment for the body, much like melons, but unlike melons they have no emetic effect, nor are they bad for the stomach.

12 On cherries

Some cherries are like mulberries, with very little astringency; but others are like blackberries, being more obviously astringent, and some are 589 even more astringent than these. So you can draw inferences about the property of each of the aforesaid types from what is said about mulberries and blackberries.

13 On the fruit of brambles

People in our part of the world call the fruit of brambles [*batoi*] blackberries [*batina*], just as they call the fruit of the mulberry tree [*morea*;

sykaminea] mulberries [*mora*; *sykamina*] – they refer to these in either way. Blackberries are more astringent than mulberries and if one takes them in quantity they will produce headache. Some people also suffer distress in the gullet. For this reason one should wash this fruit well before attempting to eat it, which is also no less necessary to do in the case of mulberries. However, blackberries do not move the bowels; rather, they are constipating, and if one stores the unripe fruit after drying it, it becomes much more so. Furthermore, all those drugs that are prepared from mulberry juice are more active in property when they are prepared from blackberries.

14   On the fruit of dog roses

The fruit of dog roses is a little more astringent than that of blackberries, and for this reason restrains the stomach more. Certainly country folk 590 often eat it although it affords the body little nourishment. They call the fruit 'rose hips'.

15   On the fruit of the juniper

People call the fruit of the juniper 'juniper berry'. It is quite bitter, with little sweetness and still less astringency. It is also rather aromatic. So it is clear that it is also warming because of the pungency (for everything pungent has been shown to be warming), but not least also on account of its smell and taste, which are aromatic; for all aromatics are warm. It also clears out material in the liver and kidneys, and it is plain that it thins thick, viscid humours. This is why it is mixed with drugs that promote health. But it contributes little nutriment to the human body. If one takes a lot of them, they irritate the *stomachos* and heat the head, and in this connection they sometimes bring about fullness in the head and produce pain there. In the bowel they neither inhibit nor promote excretion. However, they produce urine flow to a moderate extent.

16   On the fruit of cedars   591

The fruit of the cedar, which they call 'cedar berry', is the same as juniper berries in size and form – for they are yellowish and round, too – but they differ in terms of pungency. Actually, this fruit runs close to being a drug, since it gives no nutriment to the body unless one has first soaked it in water. For this is a common feature of all pungent foods, that when their pungency has been released they contribute insignificant nutriment to the body. Furthermore, the fruit of cedars is harder and drier than that of junipers, just as it is also without doubt smaller, nor is it to the same extent aromatic. So it is obvious that it is quite irritating to the *stomachos* and productive of headache, unless one takes it in small amount.

17 On the fruit of pine cones

Pine-cone fruit is wholesome, thick-juiced and nourishing, but not easily concocted. Greeks of today do not call them cones [*kônoi*], but spinning tops [*strobiloi*].

18 On the fruit of myrtles   592

Greeks name this fruit myrtle-berry. Like the juniper berry, it is devoid of nutriment, but it has the opposite property. For it is exceedingly astringent and as a result is constipating. Nevertheless it is not cold in property in proportion to its astringency, because not only has it astringency but some pungency has also been mixed with it. In common with all foods that have any very strong pharmacological property, whenever it loses this by boiling, roasting or wetting, it contributes a small amount of nutriment to the body where formerly it gave none at all. The same thing also happens with onions and leeks.

19 On peaches

Whether you are disposed to call this fruit persian apples [*mêla persika*] or, as do most Greeks today, simply peaches [*persika*], or you want to seek some ancient name in addition to these, you can do so at your leisure. But for now you ought to know what is more useful than the name, namely that the juice and the fleshy material are easily corrupted 593 and are troublesome in every way. So that you should not, as some do, take them last of all other food, for as they float on the surface they are corrupted. And you should remember what is common to all foods, that this is why you should eat before all other foods those which, although unwholesome, are moist, slippery and able to pass easily; for in this fashion they quickly lead the way for the others. But those that are taken last corrupt the others at the same time.

20   On apricots and *praikokkia**

These are also of the peach family, with some advantage over them. For
they are not corrupted in the stomach in the same way, nor do they become acid. To most people they seem more pleasant,* and so are better
for the stomach. This is the case with all foods that are pleasant and in
other respects the same, just as with unpleasant foods it is the case that
they upset and disturb the stomach, and stimulate it to vomiting because it
desires to reject, as quickly as possible, that which is distressing. Moreover,
it also does this in relation to the weight of the distressing foods. For those
that sink downwards it expels downwards, but those that float on top it
gets rid of through vomiting, doing the same thing also in the case of trou-   594
blesome fluids that run down into it from the body as a whole. For such
of these fluids as flow together into the upper alimentary tract are evacuated by vomiting; but those that flow into the lower bring on diarrhoea.

That the nutriment from all such fruits is scanty has been remarked
earlier. What are called *praikokkia* are superior to apricots. Those people
who avoid the term *praikokkia* call both of them apricots [Armenian
apples, *armeniaka mêla*], but some refer to *armenia*, with four syllables, not
five.

21   On apples

There is no single family of these, just as there is no single family of
pears and pomegranates. For some have harsh juice, others acid, or sweet,
and there are those that have a mixture of these qualities, since they seem
at the same time to be both sweet and astringent; and some others with
sweetness clearly appear acid; and as well as these there are others that   595
are sour with acidity. Sometimes you might also find some which clearly
share three juices, since they appear acid and sweet, and also have some
sourness. It is plain that these three words – astringent, harsh and sour –
describe a single quality of juice. The fact that sour things differ from
the harsh by being more astringent, but that astringency is general in the
group, you learnt in the fourth book of *On the Properties of Simple Drugs*, in
which the discussion concerns the essence and properties of the juices. So,
bearing these facts in mind, you must understand that those apples that
are astringent have a cold, earthy juice, but those that appear acid have
juice that is cold and with a fine substance. But the sweet ones, inclining
towards the warmer, are of average blend, just as the completely bland,
watery ones incline towards the colder.

For that reason you will use them according to the properties of the dominant juices – the harsh apples when the stomach is relaxed, whether because of a warm ill-blending or great moistness; the sour ones whenever these features are sufficiently increased; and the acid apples when you suspect that some thick, but not very cold, fluid has accumulated in the stomach. Since fluid that is cold does not need acid things but 596 bitter ones; for while both the acid and the bitter ones cut the thickness of fluids, they differ in the manner of doing this, in the one case being accompanied by chilling, in the other by warmth. It is clear, from what has often already been stated, that while astringent things, to the extent that they are on their own, always restrain evacuation, acid ones, on finding thick fluid in the stomach, by cutting this bring about its downward passage and so moisten the stools. But when they find the stomach clear, they restrain it more. The sweet juice, to the extent that it is on its own, if absolutely on its own without bitterness and thickness, is better distributed; but when it holds bitterness or thickness it is more aperient.

There is another class of juice, not only in apples but also in everything else, which they call watery and bland, as I said earlier, of very little use for the stomach but, like water itself, an average of the properties which I discussed just now. This sort of juice is a defect in an apple, for those who have recourse to it for food do so either for benefit or for pleasure. So when apples like these are neither pleasurable to eat nor put strength into the stomach as the astringent ones do, nor check looseness, quite 597 reasonably they are held in little esteem, just as among ourselves, in many places in Asia, they throw them to the pigs, calling them *platanistina*, since in a way they are close in taste to the soft leaves of the plane tree [*platanos*].

One must be cautious about even the best apples in the group until they have ripened on the trees. For they are difficult to concoct, slow to pass and unwholesome, and also have juice that is cold and slightly thick. Those that are well ripened, which they keep into the winter and the following spring, are often very beneficial in illness, either plastered all round with dough and baked moderately in hot ash, or steamed well over boiling water. One should give them immediately following food, sometimes with bread, to strengthen the stomach and *stomachos* in people with anorexia and slow concoction, and in those who are prone to vomiting and suffering from diarrhoea, and liable to dysentery. Sour apples are suitable for such use, for when prepared as I have just described they have a proper degree of astringency, whereas in this sort of preparation 598 the moderately harsh apples have got rid of all their astringency and so are much like those that are watery from the beginning.

22   What is the reason that in some people the consumption of astringent apples and pears empties the bowel?*

Since I heard some saying that they experience purgation following the consumption of astringent items, I thought it better to discuss in this book, at length and once and for all, what I have frequently recognized through both a theoretical and a practical approach.

When I heard a certain Protos, an orator and fellow-citizen, say that his bowels are evacuated after eating harsh pears and apples, I considered what was occurring and tested it by a trial, after which I then approached the same trial in others with greater confidence. For I asked the fellow to join me at meals, if only for one day, so that I might observe when he took astringent items, and in what quantity. At the start, on the first day, I invited him to eat as he had become accustomed, changing absolutely none of the items in his diet. Following his bath, he first drank a little water, then took fenugreek and radishes and those things that many people eat before tasting anything else. Subsequently, having drunk a 599 moderate amount of sweet wine, he ate mallows with oil and fish sauce, with a little wine, and following this, some fish, pork and poultry. Then when he had had one, maybe two, drinks, after a short interval he ate harsh pears. Then, when we had been for a stroll, after he had walked about a little, his bowel evacuated in a remarkable fashion.

Having observed this, on the following day I agreed with my friend to trust me, in turn, with the items in the diet. Since he was readily prevailed upon, after the bath I first of all gave him pears to eat, then the rest in succession as he had been accustomed. When this had taken place, his bowel did not even evacuate moderately, let alone remarkably. He was understandably amazed at what occurred and asked me the reason for it, and I had the following discussion with him:

'For', I said, 'since fish sauce, together with what is taken with it at the same time, naturally promotes gastric emptying and has already prepared the way, astringent items, when taken last and particularly in those with an atonic *stomachos*, become the cause of purgation, strengthening 600 the stomach and impelling emptying of its contents. And you would be the better persuaded of this on the following day', I said, 'by taking the astringent things first of all, the meat dishes next after them, and last of all the foods taken with oil and fish sauce.'

'Don't say that!' he said, 'For I should vomit on the spot when I eat mallows last with oil and fish sauce.'

'You are right,' I said, 'for while these upset the stomach and especially its mouth (what is now usually called the *stomachos* by everyone), astringent foods strengthen them and increase their tone. This is why, even if some other fluid upsets the stomach, as yellow bile commonly does in some people when it accumulates in greater quantity, once having tasted some astringent substance the person so affected very quickly excretes the offending fluid.'

Next I showed him a certain young man who had taken scammony juice as a purgative a few days previously and who said, when five hours had passed since taking it and no evacuation had followed, that his 601 *stomachos* was oppressed and his belly swollen and weighed down. As a result he had become pale and was puzzled, and was consulting me in regard to the symptoms that had taken hold of him.

'Hear from the young man himself', I said, 'how I treated him.' And I actually provided him with the young man in person, who explained that I had told him to eat a little bit of astringent apple or pomegranate or pear; and that, as soon as he swallowed it, he was at once relieved of the distressing symptoms when his bowel all of a sudden expelled a great quantity. 'Accordingly,' I said to the orator, 'you must understand that, because of relaxation of the bowel as a whole and of the *stomachos*, this also happens in your case when you eat astringent foods last.'

'Yes, indeed,' he said, 'and you've spoken the truth. My *stomachos* is naturally like that, and is easily upset after all manner of things,* and sometimes, when I feel that it has become quite relaxed and is now reaching the point of nausea, then I take more harsh items after food.'

Let this story about the orator be sufficient for you to understand why, in people who have an atonic *stomachos*, the bowel empties itself whenever they consume something astringent.

23 On Cydonian and Strouthian apples [quinces]*   602

In contrast to the other apples, something remarkable exists in these, since they have acquired more astringency and have a juice that is stable if, after boiling it in honey, one wants to preserve it. The juice of the other apples becomes acid on storage since it contains much cold moisture. I also once found out that the drug from the juice of Strouthian apples, which is very suitable for people with anorexia, when it chanced to have been stored out of sight, had suffered no alteration in quality after a seven-year interval. It had developed a thick crust at the mouth of the vessel like that which often coagulates in honey and some other things. When you want to maintain the drug or honey unchanged as much as possible you must keep the crust on top. Now I have spoken of this as a side issue, but I shall take up again the reason why I mentioned the drug's not deteriorating over a lengthy period.

When it has been prepared well, the juice of Strouthian apples, like that of the Cydonian ones, is stable, but this juice is less sweet and 603 more astringent than the latter. So that sometimes this might also be of service for strengthening an excessively relaxed stomach. In Syria they also make the so-called quince-cake, a food so stable that new contain- ers filled with it are carried to Rome. It is compounded from honey and quince flesh that has been made smooth by boiling with the honey. My own medication, which I make for people with anorexia, does not consist of honey and quince juice alone, but also contains some white pepper, ginger and vinegar. But the present is not the right occasion for instruction about it, since it has been fully discussed elsewhere.

24   On pears and pomegranates

If you transfer to pears and pomegranates everything that I have said about apples, you will need no further statement about them. For some of them also appear harsh only, or sour, just as others appear acid, others 604 sweet, and others are composed of a mixture of these qualities; and some have absolutely no such dominating quality, and so are watery and harmless. The use of pears is in every way like that of apples.

But the pomegranates, although alike in other respects, are never baked with dough, boiled in water or steamed. They have more juice than apples and pears, and as well as this are sweeter to the taste than these are. They are sometimes more useful than those fruits for certain other conditions, and for what was described by Hippocrates* in the second book of *Epidemics* as follows: 'a woman was suffering from heartburn and nothing settled it. By sprinkling fine barley meal into pomegranate juice and making one meal of it a day she warded off the heartburn, and did not vomit up what Charion did...'

So it is clear that when bad fluid soaked the area round the mouth of the stomach (which they also call the cardia), the woman was nauseated and had heartburn. The expression 'having heartburn'* means nothing other than the symptom that occurs in the case of irritation of the *stomachos*. 605 So that while the barley meal dried up this fluid, the pomegranate juice taken with it strengthened the stomach, so that it was able to rub off the fluid contained in its coats.

All in all, pomegranates provide very little nutriment for the body, so that we never need them for food, but only as a medication. But pears, especially the large ones (people hereabouts call them *mnaiai*), do contain some nourishment, so they cut them into very thin circular slices and dry and store them, and when they have boiled them, they eat them in winter and spring in the capacity of low-nutriment foods.

Athenians more commonly say the first syllable of pomegranate [*rhoia*] without the *iota*, but the Ionians with it. The distinction means nothing of value for human life, just as with sorb-apples [*oua*], which all Greeks these days pronounce thus, although the Atticizers do not agree to say their name with the *upsilon*.

So, abandoning consideration of the letters to those people, I shall discuss the properties of the fruit.

25 On medlars and sorb-apples 606

The same statement relates to these that has been made previously. Both are astringent, medlars much more so than sorb-apples. This is why it is a very useful food for looseness of the bowels. Sorb-apples are the more pleasant of the two for eating. To begin with, unlike medlars they do not even have any sourness; rather, the juice in them is harsh without being sour. It is clear that it is right to eat small amounts of all such foods, not great quantities as one does with figs and grapes. For we do not need them as foods, but more as medicaments.

This is more useful for you than to know that the first syllable of the name of the sorb-apple [*oua*] was written and spoken by the Athenians of old with the letter *omicron* alone.

26 On the fruit of date palms

Whether you wish to call their fruit acorns of date palms [*balanai phoinikôn*] or give them the same name as the date-palm tree as a whole [*phoinix*], as is now usual with all Greeks, in neither case will you do any harm, nor be of any benefit, in the investigation of their properties.

But there are great differences among them. Some, such as the Egyptian variety, are dry and astringent; others, like the so-called *karyôtoi*, 607 are soft, moist and sweet, and these are produced best in Palestinian Syria, in Hierichous.* All other dates lie between the above-mentioned varieties, some more, some less, moist and dry, sweet and astringent. But when the extremes have been established it will then be very easy for you to detect everything that lies in between. At any rate there is none that does not hold some sweetness and astringency. In fact the *karyôtos* partakes of a little astringency, and the Theban variety a faint sweetness. But the sweet juice has been shown to be nutritious, while harsh juice is good for the stomach and checks looseness of the bowels.

All dates are difficult to concoct, and when eaten in great quantity cause headache. Some produce a certain gnawing sensation at the mouth of the stomach; these produce headache more. (I have often said that physicians call the mouth of the stomach *stomachos*.) The humour distributed from them to the body is in general thick, but it also has some stickiness when the date is oily (as is the *karyôtos*); but when there is 608 sweetness mixed with such humour, the liver is very quickly obstructed by it* and damaged, being inflamed and extremely cicatrized by their consumption. Following the liver, the spleen is also obstructed and damaged. But fresh dates, indeed, are much more harmful in all respects when eaten only a little to excess. It is obvious that the sweet dates have warmer juice and the astringent ones colder juice. But the fresh ones also fill with wind, like figs; for figs bear the same relationship to dried figs that fresh dates do to the others. In the cooler regions dates do not ripen completely so as to become valuable for storage and, for this reason, when people are forced to consume them unripe, they become full of crude humours and are overcome by rigors which are difficult to warm, and they develop obstructions in the liver.

27   On olives

These give very little nutriment to the body, especially the very ripe ones. People eat them more often with bread, but without bread they eat the 609 salted ones and so-called 'swimming' olives, together with fish sauce, before meals, in order to purge the intestine. Just as the very ripe ones have the most oily juice, so the latter have the most astringent. This is why they strengthen the *stomachos* and stimulate the appetite. The ones that have been stored in vinegar are best for this.

People who practise the culinary arts (of which activity I expect the physician not to be completely ignorant) prepare olives in a variety of ways. For among things that are equally healthy, the more pleasant is better for concoction. But now is not the time to discuss either the theory of culinary practice, or cooking as an art. For another, specific, account will be devoted to these aspects.

28 On walnuts

These, which now are generally called walnuts by everyone, some persons call 'royal' nuts; and certain others, which some people refer to as Pontic, far smaller than those, are also called 'thin-shelled nuts'. Much use is made of both of them, although they do not give much nutriment to 610 the body; however, there is more in the so-called Pontic variety than in the royal nut. For the substance of the former is also more compressed and less oily, whereas the substance of the royal nut is more porous and contains more oil. It also has to a slight extent an astringent quality that diminishes with the passage of time as its substance as a whole changes into oily juice, so that, because the oiliness in it appears very like old olive oil, it becomes completely inedible. But the fresh and still moist nut does not obviously have either an astringent or an oily quality, but is somehow blander, what we usually call watery, as I said.

The 'royal' walnut is concocted better than the thin-shelled variety, and is more wholesome (and even more so when eaten with dried figs). Many physicians have written that if both of these are taken with rue before other foods the person will not suffer any great injury from lethal drugs. It is clear that the nut that is still moist is better for excretion, but 611 the dry one is less so. Not a few take it with fish sauce to move the bowels. For this purpose the fresh nut is more suitable, since it has less astringent quality. But when those that are already dry are soaked in water, as is done by some people, their property is very much the same as the fresh ones.

29 On almonds

Generally speaking, these do not have an astringent quality. Amongst them only the cleansing and thinning property is predominant, as a result of which they clean out the internal organs and bring about the expectoration of moist material from the lungs and chest. In some of them the property of cutting thick and viscid material is so dominant that because of their pungency they cannot even be eaten. However, they have an oleaginous, fatty quality like walnuts, due to which they themselves become oily with the passage of time, as those nuts do. This quality is scarcer among them than it is among walnuts, which is why it takes longer for them than for walnuts to become visibly oily. It is plain from 612 this that they are of no value for purgation, and they give little nutriment to the body. But those with a sufficiently dominant pungent quality are most useful for the expectoration of purulent material, and thick viscid fluids, from the lungs and chest.

Some of those who call themselves Atticizers, who have practised no skill of value for life, think it right to refer to this fruit in the feminine, *amygdalê*, but others of them in the neuter, *amygdalon*, not realizing, about this very matter that they take so seriously, that the Athenians wrote both names.

30   On pistachios

These are also grown in Great Alexandria,* but much more in Beroia,* in Syria. While they have very little nutriment they are valuable for strengthening the liver and at the same time for clearing out fluids causing obstructions in its passages. They have a somewhat bitter and rather astringent aromatic quality. I also know many other such items that are very useful for the liver, as I demonstrated in my treatise *On Simple Drugs*. But I cannot testify that they result in either benefit or noteworthy harm to the oesophagus; just as I am unable to confirm that they result in either looseness or constipation.

31   On plums

When it has properly ripened, you seldom find that this fruit is either 613 harsh or acid or, in general, that it has any disagreeable feature. Until they have reached this point, just about all of them show something, in some cases acidity, in others bitterness and pungency. The body gets very little nutriment from this fruit, but it is useful for those who choose to moisten and cool the stomach moderately. Because of their moisture and viscidity plums are also laxative, like some of the fruit mentioned earlier. It is also the case with them that they are valuable when dried, like figs, and the ones produced in Damascus in Syria have a great reputation of being the best of all. Next to these are those that take their names from Iberia and Spain. But while the latter do not exhibit any astringency, some Damascenes have a great deal.

Those moderately astringent ones that are large with loose pulp are 614 the best. The small, hard bitter ones are bad both as food and for gastric emptying, a feature which is particularly associated with those from Iberia. But when boiled in a *melikrat* which has a higher proportion of honey, eaten on their own they empty the stomach adequately, and even more so if one drinks the honey-wine as well. It is also clear that drinking a little sweet wine after consuming them, then waiting for a time without having a second meal straight afterwards, contributes to gastric emptying. But this is a common feature of everything that empties the stomach, and, just like other features that are common to many other species, should be remembered so that you do not need frequent reminding about them.

32   On so-called jujubes

I am unable to give any information about these, either as a preservative of health or a cure of disease. For it is a meal for women and children at play that is poorly nutritious and difficult to concoct, and at the same time bad for the stomach. It is clear that the fruits themselves give little nutriment to the body.

33   On carobs

615

Carobs [*keratia*], which have the third syllable spoken and written with the letter *tau*, are nothing like cherries [*kerasia*], with the letter *sigma*. They are a food that is unwholesome and woody, and necessarily difficult to concoct for nothing woody is easy. But the fact that they also are not excreted quickly is a considerable defect with them. So that it would be better for us not even to import them from the eastern regions where they are produced.

34   On capers

The caper is a shrubby plant that grows in great quantity in Cyprus. In property it is of fine substance, and because of this it distributes very little nutriment to the body of those who eat it, like everything else that has fine substance. We use the fruit of the plant more as a medicament than as food. Because it rots when stored on its own, it is exported to us after being sprinkled with salt. It is apparent that it holds more nutriment while still green, before it has been salted. The nutriment is completely destroyed by salting, and unless the salt has been washed away, the fruit 616 becomes in every respect without nutritive value; but it is aperient. But when it has been well washed and soaked until it has finally got rid of the property of the salt, although as a food it is very lacking in nutritive value, it is useful as a relish and as a drug to stimulate a poor appetite; and it washes away and gets rid of phlegm in the stomach, and clears out blockages in the liver and spleen. In these conditions it is a good idea to use it before any other food, with oxymel or oil and vinegar. People also eat the tender branches of this plant in the same way that they eat those of the terebinth, packing them while still green in brine-vinegar and ordinary wine, as they do with the latter.

35   On sycamore fruit

In Alexandria I saw the sycamore tree, with fruit resembling a small, white fig. This fruit has slight sweetness but no bitterness, and is rather moist and somewhat more cooling in property, as mulberries are too. Rather, one might reasonably place it between mulberries [*mora*] and 617 figs [*syka*]. It seems to me that its name also derives from this. For those who say that this is why this fruit has been named sycamore [*sykomoron*], namely because it resembles insipid figs [*syka môra*], are ridiculous. Its origin is very different in comparison with other tree fruits, for it does not sprout from the twigs and shoots, but from the branches and trunks.

36   On the fruit of the *persea**

I also saw this plant in Alexandria, it being one of the large trees. They record that in Persia the fruit of the tree is so harmful that it kills those who eat it; but that it became edible when imported into Egypt, and is consumed much like pears and apples, which it also resembles in size.

37   On the citron

Those who prefer that nobody should know what they are saying also call this 'Medean apple', and yet they place clarity among the virtues of speech. It would have been better to have enquired about the property 618 of the parts of the citron tree, and what use they have for man, than to waste time with such things. So I shall do so, saying that the fruit has three parts, the acid part in the middle, the flesh, so to speak, that surrounds this, and the third part, the external covering lying around it. This fruit is fragrant and aromatic, not only to smell, but also to taste. As might be expected, it is difficult to digest since it is hard and knobbly. But if one uses it as a medicament it helps concoction, as do many other things with a bitter quality. For the same reason it also strengthens the oesophagus when a small quantity is taken, so that they customarily pound it and express the juice, and mix it in medicinal pills, those that are purgative, or those that cleanse the body as a whole. But for some other things they use the acid, inedible part of the fruit that contains the seed; and often they put it into weakened vinegar for the sake of making it more bitter. The part between both, which in fact gives nutriment to the body, while having neither an acid nor a bitter quality, is difficult to concoct because 619 of its hardness. This is why everyone takes it with vinegar and fish sauce, since they want to enliven the dull taste. Perhaps they know, having learnt from experience or having heard from physicians, that when consumed in this way it is concocted better.

38   On the fruit from wild plants, among which are included the mast* [*balanoi*] from oaks

Everyone usually refers to as 'wild' the plants which spring up in the countryside without any agricultural attention; and indeed they also call wild those vines that no vineyard worker takes care of by digging or hoeing around, or by pruning, or by doing anything like that.

Among these plants are the Valonian oak, the common oak, the Holm oak, the Cornelian cherry, the strawberry tree and other trees like these; as also certain shrubs, like the bramble and the dog rose, the wild pear and its relative, and the wild plum, which people hereabouts call *proumna*, 620 and the shrub that bears medlar pears. In Italy they call the fruit of this last shrub 'unedo'; it is bad for the stomach and causes headache, and is quite sour, with some slight sweetness.

People in the country regularly eat wild pears, blackberries, mast and *mimaikyla* (as the fruit of the strawberry tree is called), but the fruit of the other trees and shrubs is not eaten very much. However, once when famine took hold of our land and there was an abundance of mast and medlars, the country folk, who had stored them in pits, had them in place of cereals for the whole winter and into early spring. Before that, mast like this was pig food, but on this occasion they gave up keeping the pigs through winter as they had been accustomed to doing previously. At the start of winter they slaughtered the pigs first and ate them; after that they opened the pits and, having suitably prepared the mast in various

ways, they ate it. Sometimes, after boiling it in water, they covered it with
hot ash and baked it moderately. Again, on occasion they would make a
soup from it, after crushing and pounding it smooth, sometimes pouring
in honey, or boiling it with milk.   621

The nutriment from it is abundant, like nothing that has been mentioned in this work up to the present in this section of the book. For mast
is just as nourishing as many cereal foods. Of old, so they say, men supported life with it alone – the Arcadians for a very long time – although
all present-day Greeks use cereals. But the food from it is slow to pass
and has a thick juice, from which it follows that it is also difficult to
concoct. The fruit of the strawberry tree is in every respect inferior to
the acorn from the common oak, just as the latter is inferior to what are
called chestnuts, for these are the finest of the mast, and some call them
'easily peeled'. Alone of the wild fruits, these give noteworthy nutriment
to the body. For Cornelian cherries, wild plums, blackberries, dog roses,
sloes, the fruit of the strawberry tree, jujubes, the fruit of the nettle tree,
winter cherries, terebinth fruit and the fruit of the wild pear, and others 622
like these have little nutritive value, are all unwholesome, and some of
them are bad for the stomach and distasteful – being food for pigs; not
the domesticated ones so much as those that live in the mountains. The
former, at any rate, are very nutritious.

39   On the food from the plants themselves

Not only do we eat the seeds and fruits of plants, but also the plants themselves, often whole, but often only the roots, branches or young shoots, according as there is a pressing need for each. At all events, men in my part
of the world, who usually reject the stems and leaves of turnips [*gongylidai*],
which they also call *bouniadai*,* also eat these when they lack better foods;
and in this circumstance also eat radishes and what, in our local vernacular, is called *rhapys*. One might say that this plant is wild radish. And under the compulsion of famine, people often eat pellitory, water-parsnips, 623
alexanders and fennel; and wild chervil, pimpernel, gum succory, French
carrot, wild carrot and, after boiling them, the tender shoots of most trees
and shrubs. But some eat them even in the absence of famine, just as
some eat the top of the date palm,* which they call its brain.

Why must I go on to speak about tender thistles? Because, famine
aside, these are really a reasonable meal when eaten with vinegar and
fish sauce. Some people also add olive oil to them, especially after having

boiled them in water (for they use them in two ways, often raw, but some-times boiled). I am speaking of the spiny plants – golden thistle, spindle thistle, eryngo, safflower, *atrakis** and so-called 'white' thistle; and as well, one or the other chameleon, some of which they store in brine or vin- 624 egar, just as they do turnips, the onions that are called wild leeks, pelli-tory and others like that. *Kibôria* and *kolokasia** are in a way the same, also what is called *abaton*.* It is clear that, as well as giving little nutriment to the body, these are all unwholesome except, as I said, the spiny plants that have just emerged from the ground. Those of them that they put into brine or vinegar and keep in storage for the whole succeeding year acquire from the preparation, if one tastes them in moderation, some-thing stimulating to the appetite, just as with the shoots of the chaste tree or the terebinth.

Now they reckon these among the wild plants, and it is sufficient to know about them, in a general way, that they are all unwholesome. But with cultivated plants it is much better to understand the specific property of each, not in a general statement; especially of those in repeated use, which are also highly regarded on this account, and because by long experience they have been proved to be better than the rest. Accordingly I shall speak about them forthwith, one after the other, commencing with the garden vegetables.

40   On lettuce

Many physicians prefer this vegetable to all the others, just as they do figs among the autumnal fruits. For it is more wholesome than they are. And the feature of it that some find fault with carries the greatest 625 commendation. If it were really true, lettuce would be second to none, not only of vegetables but of all the most wholesome and nutritious food-stuffs. For they say that it generates blood. And some do not simply say blood, but they add 'much', asserting that lettuce generates much blood. But these people, even if they make the allegation more intelligently, are further from the truth than the others. And indeed one could not reasonably disapprove of it being said merely that it produces much blood, for it is clear that this sort would be the most wholesome of all foods if in fact it naturally produced much blood but none of the other humours. But if they assert that a large quantity of blood is collected from lettuce, and find fault with this, the charge is very easily countered, since those who consume it, while they eat a small quantity, are able to

work harder. Now I have said enough about those who have wrongly
criticized this vegetable.

You should understand that while all vegetables produce a very small
quantity of blood, and that unwholesome, there is not much unwhole-   626
some blood from lettuce, although it is not completely wholesome. For
the most part people eat it uncooked, but when it runs to seed in summer
they boil it in sweet water and eat it with oil, fish sauce and vinegar, or
with one of the piquant sauces, especially those prepared with cheese.
But many use it even before it sends up a stalk, by boiling it in water,
as I myself have started to do since I have been troubled by my teeth.
For one of my friends, knowing that for a long time it had been my custom to eat lettuce, but that chewing was now painful, introduced me to
boiling it.

In my youth I used to use lettuce for cooling when my upper intestine
was continually full of bile, but when I reached middle age this vegetable
alone was the cure for my insomnia – since my concern about sleeping
was the opposite to when I was young. For, although accustomed to
staying awake voluntarily in my youth, together with the fact that the
age of those past their prime is conducive to insomnia, when against my
will I was unable to sleep I became distressed, and the only antidote to
insomnia was, for me, a lettuce eaten in the evening.

By lettuce [*thridakinê*] I mean nothing other than what everybody
nowadays calls lettuce [*thridax*] hereabouts, since there is another wild   627
vegetable called lettuce [*thridakinê*] which grows in quantity beside roads
and on the banks of ditches, and also in what are called 'soaks', and in
many uncultivated places. This vegetable is small, like the newly shooting
cultivated lettuce, and reveals a slight pungency, even more so during its
growth; and when it is putting out a stalk it has very distinctly pungent
juice.

There is also a wild vegetable like this lettuce that they call gum
succory, which is quick to put forth its stalk, more distinctly pungent
and with some sticky, white juice, like that of the spurges but less bitter,
which we sometimes use for glueing up the eyelashes.* These are called
wild vegetables to distinguish them from cultivated ones. There has been
a general statement about them a little earlier.

As a reminder, I take up again the matter of the cultivated lettuce
that is customarily eaten by everyone – the *thridax*, so called – and shall   628
say, in summary, that it has moist, cold juice but that nonetheless it is
not unwholesome. Because of this, neither is it unconcocted like other

vegetables nor does it inhibit bowel action (just as neither does it promote it). It has this effect with good reason since it has neither harshness nor sourness, which for the most part are what restrain the bowel; just as it is stimulated to excretion by salty and bitter substances and, generally speaking, by things with some detergent quality – none of which even exists in the lettuce.

41 Concerning chicory

I cannot say precisely whether the earlier Athenians gave the name chicory to what among the Romans is called endive, or to some other wild vegetable plants. Chicory has a property very much like the lettuce, while being inferior to it in flavour and the other features previously mentioned concerning lettuce.

42 On mallow

The wild variety of this also differs from the cultivated one, just as the wild lettuce differs from the cultivated lettuce. Among plants of the same class, the wild one is always different by virtue of its dryness, the cultivated 629 one by virtue of its moistness. The mallow also has some viscidity in its juice, while the lettuce does not. It is far from being cooling, as one can appreciate even before its use as food, after poulticing one of the warm affections like erysipelas with both vegetables in turn, as people do when they have carefully rubbed the soft leaves until they become very smooth. In this way you will realize that, while the lettuce is obviously cooling, the mallow has a certain moderate and, so to speak, lukewarm heat. This vegetable brings about easy passage of stools, not only because of its moistness but also because of its viscidity, especially when one swallows it with plenty of oil and fish sauce. It is moderate as regards concoction. If you compare the juice of these three vegetables, that of the beet is thinner and more detergent, that of the mallow is thicker and more viscid, and that of the lettuce is midway between them.

43 On beet

I said that mallows are not only domesticated, but some are also wild, 630 as are lettuces, too. But there is no wild beet, unless one wants to speak of monk's rhubarb in this way. It appears that beet juice is moderately detergent, since it stimulates excretion and sometimes irritates the *stomachos*, especially in those in whom this is naturally very sensitive; and this is why, for these people, when eaten in greater quantity it is food that is bad for the stomach.

The nutriment from it is slight, as from the other vegetables; but it is more useful than mallow for obstructions in the liver, and even more so when eaten with mustard, or at any rate with vinegar. When eaten in the same way by those with splenic conditions, it becomes a good drug. For one might reasonably refer to it as a drug, rather than a food, when it is eaten in this way. I notice that nearly all such things are eaten in the manner of a relish, not food, as also sometimes are leeks, pennyroyal, thyme, savory and oregano; and onion, garlic and cardamon too, and other such items.

44   On cabbage

The majority of people eat this as a relish too, but physicians use it as   631
a drying drug. Some things have already been said about it, both in *On the Properties of Simple Drugs* and in the preceding chapter, but it will now also be stated, in summary, that while its juice has some cleansing action, because of its drying action it constipates the body more than it stimulates it to excretion. Whenever we want to move the bowels, while the pot in which cabbage has been boiled is lying nearby we must draw up the cabbage together with the water and immediately put it into vessels in which oil has been prepared with fish sauce. (It makes no difference if it is taken with salt instead of fish sauce.) When we wish to dry a moist stomach, after the cabbage appears to have been moderately boiled we at once pour off the first water and put it into different hot water, and then boil it again in that water so that it becomes tender. We do not boil it when it is taken for purgation. For we do not want to remove all its juice that is specific for such a purpose, but to preserve it as much as possible. Nothing boiled can preserve the specific juice completely, but the more it has been boiled the more it gets rid of it.   632

Indeed, I also said that one should prepare lentils in the same way as cabbage, and that they can bring about both purgation and constipation. Cabbage and lentils prepared like this are called 'twice-cooked'. You must also prepare in this way onion, leek and, particularly, wild leek and garlic, bearing this in mind before everything, that what is twice-cooked must not come into contact with air or water that is cold; for it no longer becomes nicely tender even if you boil it to the greatest extent. Rather, as I said just now, having hot water ready, you must take it from the first water and at once transfer it into the hot.

Now, lentils and cabbage are drying to about the same degree as each other, and because of this they dull the vision unless it sometimes happens that the whole eye is unnaturally moist. But while lentils give much nutriment to the body, and this both thick and black-biled, cabbage has scant nutriment and this moister than that from lentils, since 633 it is not solid food but a vegetable. Moreover cabbage is certainly not a wholesome food like lettuce, but has bad, ill-smelling juice. I can say that neither evident benefit for the passage of urine, nor evident harm, results from it.

Those who practise the accursed pseudo-education think it right to call this vegetable *rhaphanos*,* as though we were speaking to Athenians of six hundred years ago, and not to today's Greeks, all of whom are accustomed to ascribe the name *rhaphanos* to another plant.

45   On blite and orach

These are the most watery of vegetables and, as one might say, the most bland in quality. They are more, certainly no less, nourishing than the colocynth; that is to say, when they have been cooked. For among vegetables like these, only lettuce is eaten both raw and cooked. Anyone who has observed the quality of orach and blite through their taste and then recalled that of cabbage will agree that the lettuce is half-way between these vegetables and cabbage, since while the latter is quite drying, the former are absolutely watery. For this reason they eat them by adding vinegar more than they eat them dipped in oil and fish sauce alone. When 634 taken in other ways they are bad for the stomach.

It has been said that vegetables like these in some way lead to easy defecation, especially when they have some lubricity with their moistness. However, they do not have a strong tendency this way, because there is no quality in them, either acrid or alkaline, to stimulate excretion. And it is clear that in themselves they contribute little nutriment to the body.

46   On purslane

As food it holds little nutriment, and this moist, cold and viscid; but as a drug it cures inflammation of the gums through its non-irritant viscidity, regarding which quality there is discussion at length in my treatise *On Readily Available Medicines*.*

47   On monk's rhubarb [or sorrel; *lapathon*]*

One can say, as I said earlier, that this is wild beet, since it is very like the cultivated beet, not only in taste, but also in property. But since the beet is   635 more pleasant everybody prefers to eat it. Consequently I shall need no specific discussion about monk's rhubarb, since I have previously stated all that is necessary under beet.

48   On curled dock [*oxylapathon*]

The name also reveals the quality and property of this plant, for it is acid [*oxy-*] sorrel [*lapathon*]. Now one would not eat raw monk's rhubarb, just as one would not eat raw beet; but in country areas pregnant women with strange cravings, and sometimes curious children, eat curled dock. It is clear that, much more so than monk's rhubarb, it is one of the non-nutritious vegetables.

49   On nightshade [*strychnon*]*

I know of no edible vegetable with as much astringency as nightshade. So that we seldom use it as a food, but frequently as a drug. It is efficacious to the extent that there is need for astringent coldness, but it has very little nutriment.

50   On thorny plants

When newly emerged from the ground and before their leaves have   636 attained thorns, many people eat such plants not only raw, but also boiled in water, dipping the raw ones in fish sauce and vinegar, and pouring oil over the cooked ones as well as this. The fact that all vegetables have very little nutriment, and that what there is, is watery and thin, has been stated earlier; but, just the same, the thorny plants are moderately good for the stomach. Among these plants are the golden and spindle thistles and the so-called white thistle; the teasel, safflower, tragacanth and *atrakis*; and the over-valued artichoke [*kinara*]. Those who in every way avoid customary usage refer to this by spelling the first syllable not with *kappa* and *iota*, but with *kappa* and *upsilon*. It is unwholesome food, especially when already rather hard. In fact at this time it contains within itself more biliary humour, and its whole substance is more woody, so that while from this substance black bile is generated, from its juice a thin, bitter bile is produced. So it is preferable to boil it down and eat it in this way, adding coriander if one is taking it with oil and fish sauce, but without coriander if one prepares it in a pan or fries it. Many people also eat the heads, which they call 'whorls'.*   637

51 On celeries, alexanders, water-parsnips and Cretan alexanders

These are all diuretic. The celeries are the most commonly used because they are pleasant and more wholesome. The alexander and the water-parsnip are less common. The Cretan alexander is not uncommon; at any rate, a good deal of it is sold in Rome. It is more bitter and far warmer than celery, and also is somewhat aromatic. It is more diuretic than celery, alexander and water-parsnip, and in women brings on menstruation. In spring it makes a stalk which can be eaten raw, just like the leaves that exist alone on the plant during winter before the stalk grows, as is the case with celery too. Later, when the stalk occurs as well, the whole plant is tastier, even if one eats it raw and, if cooked, whether you want it with oil and fish sauce or add some wine and vinegar. But some eat it 638 with vinegar and fish sauce alone, as with the celeries. Some add a small amount of oil to them.

People eat alexanders and water-parsnip boiled, for each seems unpleasant when raw. But some eat celery and Cretan alexander by mixing them with lettuce leaves. For since the lettuce is a blander vegetable, and further, has a cold juice, when taken with some bitter vegetables as an addition, it becomes more pleasant and at the same time more beneficial. At any rate, in this respect some mix the leaves of rocket and leeks with it; and there are also others who mix it with basil leaves. In Rome now, everybody usually calls this vegetable *olisathron*, not *smyrnion*. One might perhaps think that in the first place it is not right to reckon it among foods, just as it is also not right in the case of alexanders, the water-parsnip and celery itself. For all such are food flavourings, just like onions, garlic, leeks, wild leeks and, in general, all bitter vegetables. Also among this class are rue, hyssop, oregano, fennel and coriander, regarding which there has been discussion in the compilations on cookery which in a way are common to both physicians and cooks, but have a specific aim and purpose. For we physicians aim at benefits from foods, not at pleasure. 639 But since the unpleasantness of some foods contributes largely to poor concoction, in this regard it is better that they are moderately tasty. But for cooks, tastiness* for the most part makes use of harmful seasonings, so that poor rather than good concoction accompanies them.

52 On rocket

This vegetable is obviously heating, so that it is not easy to eat on its own without mixing some lettuce leaves with it. But it has also been believed to generate semen, and to stimulate the sexual drive. It produces headache, the more so if one eats it on its own.

53 On the stinging nettle [*akalêphê*], which they also call *knidê*

This, which has substance with a fine property, is also one of the wild herbs. So it is reasonable that nobody uses it as food, except under the pressure of very great hunger. But it is useful both as flavouring and as a purgative drug.

54 On cress and wild chervil   640

A great deal of cress grows in Syria, and it is eaten much as wild chervil is with us. It is good for the stomach, whether you want to eat it raw or boiled. It does not tolerate lengthy cooking. Some people take it with oil and fish sauce, but others also add wine or vinegar. When eaten with vinegar it is much better for the stomach and stimulates those who have no appetite. It is plain that this herb is a drug rather than a food; for it has considerable astringency, as well as obvious pungency.

55 On basil

Many use this as a relish, taking it with oil and fish sauce, but it is most unwholesome and for this reason some falsely say of it that if it has been pounded and put into a fresh pan, in a few days it quickly generates 641 many scorpions, especially when one warms the pan in the sun each day. But while this is false, you can truthfully say that it is an unwholesome vegetable, bad for the stomach and difficult to concoct.

56 On fennel

Sometimes this sprouts of its own accord, like dill, but people also sow it in gardens and, while they most often use dill as a dressing, they also use fennel for a relish. In fact, among our people, they store it much as they do pellitory and terebinth, so that it is useful throughout the whole year like onions, turnips and other such things. Some is combined with vinegar alone, some with brine-vinegar.

57 On *asparagoi**

I do not intend at the present time to examine whether you want to say the second syllable of the *asparagoi* with a *phi*, or with a *pi* like everyone else. For this is not being written for those who Atticize in their speech, but for those who want to be healthy, even if, as Plato said, they understand neither letters nor how to swim.* So since just about all modern Greeks call the soft stalks (when they are increasing to the stage of throwing out fruit and seed) *asparagoi* with a *pi*, we shall now discuss their properties, 642 allowing those who use them to call them what they like.

Now, many vegetables, and many plants in general, produce shoots like these, but people do not eat all of them. Consequently my discussion will concern the more usual ones, as has been the case with what has gone before.

The stalk of the cabbage, which some call *kyma* (a contraction, I think, of the name *kyêma*, spoken with three syllables) is less drying than the cabbage itself. However, the stem of other vegetables is for the most part drier in blending than the leaves, especially when close to coming into seed. By other vegetables I mean such ones as lettuce, orach, blite, beet and mallow. On the other hand it happens that the *asparagos* is moister than radish, turnip, mustard, nose smart, pellitory and almost all things bitter and warm. But purse-tassels, celery, water-parsnip, rocket, basil, curled dock and monks' rhubarb, and almost all vegetable herbs, develop a stem like this before any of them go to seed. When they have gone to 643 seed, they become dry and valueless for human food. People eat all such, after they have been boiled in water, with oil and fish sauce, adding a little vinegar. For in this way they become more tasty and better for the stomach. However, they deliver to the body little nutriment and that unwholesome.

There is another class of *asparagos* that occurs in shrubby plants, butchers' broom, periwinkle and fiery thorn; and ones that are different from these – royal and so-called 'marsh' – just as the shoot of bryony is different from the latter two. All are good for the stomach and are diuretic, with little nutriment. However, if shoots like these have been well concocted, they are more nourishing than the *asparagoi* on vegetables to the same extent that they are also drier. There is a certain likeness to, but not identity

with, the shoots of shrubs and trees. For the shoots of trees are more   644
woody, and this is why one must next speak about them, specifically.

58   On shoots

The shoots of trees and shrubs are analogous to the *asparagoi* on vegetables. For they, too, are the sprouts of the plant when it is embarking upon
the production of fruit. But they differ in that the tree trunk, which is the
analogue of the stems of vegetables and herbs, always persists; whereas
in their case the stem arises each year.

When they have been boiled in water, all shoots of trees and shrubs
can be eaten, unless any of them are unpleasant or poisonous. However,
people do not eat them because of the abundance of other, better foods.
But in famine, of necessity they tackle the consumption of them; for
even they are nourishing in a way if they have been well concocted. The
better ones of them are the shoots of the terebinth, the chaste plant, the
vine, mastic, the bramble and the dog rose. In our country, people store
terebinth shoots by packing them in vinegar or brine-vinegar.

59   On the differences between the parts of edible plants   645

I could have wished that the account by Mnesitheos, which he wrote in
his *On Foodstuffs*, had been true. For universal definitions, in a few words,
are greatly instructive when true; just as they do great harm when false.
What follows is what Mnesitheos said, in a general way, about the parts
of plants:

First, all roots are difficult to concoct and upsetting; I mean, such as radishes,
garlic, onions, turnips and this whole class. For all of these in which the root
and what grows beneath the ground are edible are allocated to the indigestible
group. For it happens that the nutriments from the roots are sent up to every
part of the growing plants. The roots collect much moisture in themselves and
retain this unconcocted for the most part, since it is impossible for all of it
to have been concocted. For what has been concocted appears to have been
completely dealt with, but the moisture in the roots must get the completion   646
of its concoction somewhere else, after it has been delivered to the parts of the
growing plant, for everything receives its nourishment from the root. This is
why it is inevitable that the liquids at this point are unconcocted. For although
they have collected here, they await the completion of concoction further up.
So it is reasonable that within the roots most of the moisture is unconcocted,
and it is likely that the nutriment from them also stays liquid in our bodies, and
is a cause of disturbance.

This statement of Mnesitheos, persuasive so far as the argument goes, you will judge from experience to be false. At any rate radishes have a root that is much more bitter than the stem and leaves, and similarly with the onion, wild leek, leek and garlic. If you like to compare the root of beet, mallow and turnip with their leaves you will discover that its property is more powerful, as also is that of marsh mallow (which seems to be a particular wild mallow). At any rate its root also reveals its property, as does that of the beet, by dispersing many inflammatory masses; however, its leaves cannot adequately do so. Moreover, the leaves of medicinal plants with roots like the above are also weaker, that is, of cyclamen, squill, Egyptian arum, edder-wort and very many others. For 647 just as in other plants most of the substance is in the stems and trunks, so in the case of these it is in the root, and their nature particularly augments and nourishes this, and what has not been concocted in the roots it separates off into the leaves and the stems. For these plants keep a large root through the winter, but they put out the stem in spring when they set out to fruit. And just as Aristotle said in the case of animals, Nature seems sometimes to make use of what is superfluous from the whole substance of the animal, for the generation of certain unnecessary parts – as in the case of deer, the horns; and in some other animals the number or size of spines or hairs.*

Accordingly it is safer to consider each plant in its own right, by taste and smell first, and then by trying it as food. For smell and taste, while teaching what sort of flavour and odour the part of the plant possesses, 648 immediately indicate, together with these, its total blending. But through trial, if one makes this with the appropriate criteria, the properties are discovered precisely, and sometimes the composition of the plant together with the juice within it are jointly indicated along with them. For while some have moist and watery juice, others have juice that is thick and viscid, plants which it is proper to taste again, specifically. For some of them are bitter, or acid, or sharp; others are weakly or strongly salty; just as some are harsh, others astringent, and others watery or sweet.

Therefore you should not, under the influence of Mnesitheos, trust that the statement is universally sound, rather, you should make individual trial of each part in the plant.

60   On the turnip

Whether you want to call this plant *gongylis* or *bounias*, the part of it projecting from the ground is like a vegetable, and the root contained 649 in the ground is hard and inedible before it has been cooked; but when boiled in water I should be surprised if it were less nourishing than any plant of the same group. People prepare it in a variety of ways, even to the extent of storing it brine and vinegar so as to be able to use it for the whole year. It distributes a humour to the body that is disproportionately thick. This is why, if one eats it to excess, especially if he inadequately concocts it in the stomach, he will accumulate what is called 'crude' humour. One might say that turnip neither restrains nor brings about bowel evacuation, especially when it has been well cooked. For it requires very long cooking, and is best when it has been boiled twice, as was described previously for such a preparation. If it is eaten in more raw form, it is difficult to concoct, flatulent and causes loss of appetite, and sometimes gnawing sensations in the stomach.

61   On the Egyptian arum [or cuckoopint]

The root of this plant is eaten much the same as that of the turnip, but in certain regions it grows somewhat more bitter, so that it is very like the root of the edder-wort. In cooking, one should pour off its first water 650 and add more hot water, as was described in the cases of cabbage and lentils. But in Cyrene the plant is the reverse of what it is in our country. For in those parts the arum has very little pharmacological activity and very little bitterness, so that it is more useful than turnips. Because of this they also export the root to Italy, on the grounds that it can keep for a very long time without rotting or sprouting. It is clear that this sort is better as nutriment, but if one wants to cough up any of the thick, viscid fluids that accumulate in the chest and lung, the more bitter and more pharmacologically active root is better.

When boiled in water, it is eaten with mustard or with oil, vinegar and fish sauce, and of course with other mashed dishes, especially those prepared with cheese. But it is plain that the humour distributed from it to the liver and the body as a whole, from which animals are nourished, is somehow thicker, as was mentioned in the case of turnips. This is especially the case when the roots, like those from Cyrene, have no pharmacological activity. With us in Asia, many arums are more bitter and have a medicinal property.

62   On edder-wort   651

When we have also boiled the root of this plant two, perhaps three, times, so that what is poisonous has been got rid of, we sometimes give it as food, as we also do the roots of arums, when the viscid thick material contained in the chest and lungs demands a stronger property. But you should keep in mind what applies to all foodstuffs, namely, that bitter, sharp foods in a meal give less nutriment to the body; and the bland ones, and more than these the sweet foods, give much nutriment; and still more so if they have a compacted substance so that they are neither moist nor porous in composition. So, having always borne these things in mind and, further, considering whether everything being put to the test gets rid of strong properties in the boiling, roasting or frying, you will have no need to hear from me about each one separately but, as I did in the case of the others, I shall especially expound on the ones that are eaten frequently.

63 On asphodel   652

In size, shape and pungency the root of asphodel is rather like squill. However, like lupins, it gets rid of most of the pungency in preparation, and in this way it differs from squill. For the quality of the latter is almost impossible to wash out. Hesiod* seemed to be praising asphodel when he said 'nor how much good there is in mallow and asphodel', and I am myself aware that, through hunger, some country-dwellers have made it just edible by further boiling, and soaking in sweet water. Just the same the property of this root is obstruction-clearing and thinning, like edder-wort. This is why some give the shoot to people with jaundice,* on the grounds that it is the best remedy.

64 On grape-hyacinth [purse-tassels]

Purse-tassels are from the same class as the above-mentioned. For their root is eaten apart from the leaves, but sometimes the shoot is also eaten in spring. In itself it has an obvious sharp, harsh property, due to which it somehow stimulates appetite in the relaxed *stomachos*. Nor is it un-favourable for those who need to cough anything up from the chest and 653 lung, even though the substance of the material is rather thick and viscid. Its pungency counteracts the thickness, since it naturally cuts viscid, thick things, as was stated in my *On Drugs*. So that if they are twice-boiled they are more nutritious, but are now no use for those who need to cough material up, since they have got rid of everything pungent. In this case it is better to eat them with vinegar, together with oil and fish sauce. For in this way they also become tastier, less flatulent, more nourish-ing and more easily concocted. But some men who had eaten them to excess clearly noticed that they had more semen and an increased sexual appetite.

Men also prepare these in a variety of ways. For not only do they boil them, as I said, but they also create dishes from them with a variety 654 of dressings. Others eat them fried, while many take them roasted on a brazier. But they do not withstand prolonged boiling; and very little suffices for them. Some people do not even cook them beforehand at all, since they enjoy their retained pungency and harshness, for it stimulates them more to food. If, since it does stimulate, they were to use up to two or three, there would be greater benefit for them. But if they are excessive in the use of what has been prepared in this way – especially when they take them in more raw form, as they are used to – they will experience poorer concoction. Indeed, some poorly concocted purse-tassels also bring on flatulence and colic.

The nutriment from what is eaten like this is not wholesome, but when boiled for a longer period (or even twice, as has been stated) the juice somehow becomes thicker, but in other respects better, and more nutritious.

65   On carrot, wild carrot and caraway

The roots of these plants are also eaten and, like those of the Cyrenian arum, they hold less nutriment than the turnip; but they are clearly warming and also are obviously a little aromatic. Their difficulty of concoction is the same as in other roots. They are diuretic and, if one uses 655 them to excess, they are moderately unwholesome. However, the caraway is more wholesome than the carrot. Some call the wild carrot *daukos*; while more diuretic it is actually more poisonous and needs protracted boiling if one intends to eat it.

66   On truffles

Although they have no obvious quality, one must also number these amongst the roots and bulbs. For that very reason those who use them do so as a base for seasonings, in the way that they use others which they call bland, harmless and watery in taste. It is a common feature of all these that not even the nutriment being distributed to the body has any singular property but, while it is rather cool, it is itself similar in thickness to what has been eaten – thicker from truffles, but moister and thinner from the colocynth, and along the same lines with the others.

67 On fungi

Among the fungi the field mushrooms, when boiled well in water, come close to the bland foods. However, people do not use them alone in this 656 fashion, but prepare and season them in various ways as they do other foods that have no special quality. The nutriment from them is apt to produce phlegm and it is clear that it is also cold and, if one uses it to excess, unwholesome.

Now, these are the least harmful of all the fungi, and the *amanitai* are second to them. It is safer not even to touch the rest at all, for many people have died from them. I myself know someone who, having eaten excessively of field mushrooms (the very ones that seem to be most harmless) when they had not been properly cooked, was afflicted at the mouth of the stomach, felt oppressed and suffered from cramps, had difficulty in breathing and felt faint, and experienced cold sweats; and was saved with difficulty through taking agents that cut thick humours, such as oxymel, both alone and with hyssop and oregano boiled in it to a moderate degree. In fact the fellow also took these too, after sprinkling them with *aphronitron;** following which he vomited the mushrooms that had been eaten, which now were somehow changed into an excessively cold, thick mucus.

68 On radish

For the most part city-dwellers eat this on its own raw, with fish sauce, as a purgative, but a few people also pour vinegar on it. Country people also 657 frequently take it with bread, much as with other wild relishes, amongst which are yellow oregano, nose-smart, thyme, savory, pennyroyal and tufted thyme; and wild mint, catmint, pellitory and rocket. For all of these food items, which are herbaceous plants, act as food relishes. Of necessity rather than voluntarily they also eat the stem and leaves of the radish. However, the root is something that is customarily eaten as a relish rather than as food, since it manifestly has a thinning property and is obviously warming; for the bitter quality in it is predominant.

In the spring it usually produces a stalk which rises to a height, like other plants which are about to bear fruit; which stalk, as that of the turnip, mustard and lettuce, they eat boiled with oil, fish sauce and 658 vinegar. It is clear that this stalk is more nutritious than raw radish, since it loses its bitterness in the water. Nevertheless it has very scanty nutriment in itself.

Some people eat not only the stem but also the radishes, after boiling them as they do turnips. One can but wonder at those physicians and laymen who eat them raw after meals for the sake of good concoction. For while they themselves allege that they had made sufficient test of this, everybody who has imitated them suffered harm.

69 On onions, garlic, leeks and wild leeks

People most often eat the roots of these plants, but very seldom the stem and leaves. In proportion to the root the latter have an extremely bitter property and are heating to the body and thin its thick humours, and cut the viscid ones. Yet, when they have been boiled twice or even three times, they lose the bitterness. However, they are still thinning and give very little nutriment to the body. But up to the time they were boiled they gave none at all.

Furthermore, garlic is eaten not only as a relish but also as a health-giving medication, since it has the ability to remove and disperse 659 obstructions. On being boiled for a short while to remove the bitterness it becomes weaker in its property, but it no longer preserves an unhealthy humoral state, and the same applies to leeks and onions when one boils them twice.

Wild leeks differ from leeks to the same degree that wild vegetables of similar class differ from cultivated ones. Some store them for the whole of the following year. Just as they pack onions in vinegar, so they do with wild leeks, which improve as food and are less unwholesome.

One should be sparing in the regular consumption of all bitter foods, especially when the person taking them is rather bilious by nature. For foods like these are suitable only for those who have accumulated mucus, or crude, thick, viscid humour.

BOOK III

It remains to discuss food from animals, since it has many different pro- 660 perties both in respect of the parts of the animals, and what is contained within them or is produced by them, amongst which are eggs, milk, blood, cheese and butter.

1 On food from terrestrial animals

Not all parts of animals have the same property. Flesh, when well concocted, produces the best blood, especially in the case of animals 661 such as the pig family, which produce healthy humour. But the sinewy parts produce blood that is more full of mucus.

Pork is the most nutritious of all foods, and athletes provide a very visible test of this. For when, after identical exercises, they take the same amount of a different food on one day, straightway on the following day they appear not only weaker but also obviously less well fed. You can make the same test of the statement in the case of youths being worked hard in the wrestling school, and in people carrying out any forceful and energetic activity whatsoever, like that of ditch-diggers.

Beef itself gives a nutriment that is neither small in quantity nor easily dispersed; yet it produces blood that is inappropriately thick. If anyone has more black bile in his natural blending, when he has been excessive in his consumption of beef he will be seized by one of the afflictions of people who are prone to black bile.* Such are: cancer [*karkinos*], elephantiasis [*elephas*], the itch [*psóra*], 'leprosy' [*lepra*], quartan fever* and what is called, specifically, 'melancholia'.* In some people, because of this sort 662 of humour, the spleen is increased in size, often accompanied by wasting [*kachexia*]* and dropsy.

Pork is as more glutinous than beef as beef, in its whole substance, is thicker than pork. But pork is much better for concoction – that of mature animals for people in their prime who are strong and hardworking; but for other people, that from animals that are still growing is better. But just as among pigs it is the mature ones that are appropriate for fit young men, oxen are so before maturity. For the ox is drier by far in its blending than the pig, just as an adult man is drier than a boy.

So it is likely that those animals that naturally have a drier blending are helped by youth to a well-proportioned blending. Those with moister blending also acquire, as a result of maturity, what they lack for well-proportioned blending. Not only do calves have flesh that is better for concoction than that of grown oxen, but kids, too, are better than goats. 663 For the goat is less dry in blending than the ox, but much drier than man and the pig.

One can observe the similarity of the flesh of pigs to that of man from the fact that, as regards both taste and smell, some people who have eaten it have had no suspicion that human flesh had been eaten as pork. For from time to time this has been found to have occurred with rascally innkeepers and others. So it is natural that young porkers, to the extent that they are moister than large pigs, give us nutriment that produces more residues. It is also natural that it is less nourishing, for moister food is more quickly distributed and dispersed.

Lambs also have flesh that is very moist and productive of mucus. But that of adult sheep is more productive of residues and more unwholesome. The flesh of goats is unwholesome too, with bitterness. But the flesh of male goats is the worst, both for the production of healthy humour and for concoction. Next is that of rams; then that of bulls. In all these, the meat of the castrated animal is better. But aged animals are the worst for concoction, the production of healthy humour and nutrition; 664 so that among pigs themselves, although they are moist in blending, the very old ones are fibrous and dry and for this reason have flesh that is difficult to concoct.

The flesh of the hare, while productive of rather thick blood, is better for the production of healthy humour than that of oxen or sheep. The flesh of deer is no less unwholesome than the latter, and is also hard and difficult to concoct.

The flesh of wild asses that are young and in good condition comes close to that of the deer. However, some people also eat the flesh of very old donkeys, which is most unwholesome, very difficult to concoct, bad for the stomach and, still more, is distasteful as food, like horse and camel meat; which latter meats men who are asinine and camel-like in body and soul also eat!

Some people even eat bear meat, and that of lions and leopards, which is worse still, boiling it either once only, or twice. I have said earlier what twice-boiled is like.

As to dogs, what must I also say? That in some parts very many people eat young plump dogs, especially ones that have been castrated. And as well as these, many eat panther meat, as they also eat that of asses, when 665 they are in good condition, as wild animals are. Indeed, not only do they eat them, but some physicians hold them in high regard. And amongst ourselves, huntsmen often eat the meat of foxes in the autumn, for they are being fattened by grapes.

Of the other animals, those that have an abundance of their proper food are at their best for eating, just as those that do not are at their worst. And those that eat herbage that comes up from the soil, or even the tips or shoots of trees, in whatever season has these in abundance, are in better condition, and become fat, and in every way are more suitable for our food. And consequently, animals that need to graze on lush grass become thin and unwholesome in winter and the beginning and middle of spring, like oxen, which clearly are more wholesome and fatter with the passage of time, when the herbage is increased in size, becomes thick, and forms seed. But animals that can be nourished by sparse grass, like sheep, are better in the commencement and middle of spring; and goats 666 are better in the beginning and middle of summer when the shoots of the shrubs they usually eat occur in greatest quantity.

So, when you hear me comparing species of animals with one another, examine and judge the statement and put it to the test, not comparing what is well-nourished and plump with what is withered and ill-nourished, nor the young with the old, for this is a faulty and unjust judgement; but comparing the one that is best disposed in each species (or genus, or whatever you want to call them) with another just like it. At any rate I shall no longer need lengthy statements to discuss all indigenous animals in all countries, such as the small animal in Spain which resembles the hare, which they also call 'rabbit'; and the one in Lucania in Italy that lies somewhere between bear and pig; as also the one eaten in the same area of Italy and in many other places that is halfway between the so-called *eleios** and fieldmice or dormice.

For you must test by experience those animals that are well nourished 667 and obviously plump, hearing and learning from the locals the various ways of preparing them. But you can already learn from me the sort of property that belongs to each of them. Those items that they boil or fry and eat give a rather dry nutriment to the body; those that they have first boiled in water, a moister one; and those that they season in pans are midway between these. And among these last themselves, there is a considerable difference according to the manner of seasoning. Those prepared with plenty of wine and fish sauce are drier than those prepared without them. But those items with rather less of such seasonings are far moister than the last-mentioned foods if the seasonings contain more boiled new wine [*siraion*], which some call *hepsēma*, or have been boiled in what is referred to as simple, unadorned white sauce. But those boiled in water alone are still moister than these.

The greatest difference is in the preparation, and in the properties of the things that are added to them, all of them being to a greater or lesser extent drying. These are the seeds of dill, parsley, caraway, 668 *libystikon,** cumin and some others like them; and among the plants themselves, leeks, onions, dill, thyme, savory, pennyroyal, sweet-smelling mint, oregano and others of the same sort, which belong to the study of cookery, which I do not propose to discuss at this time.

So just as I said earlier that comparison of the differences in animals should be made between those in best condition, now also let the comparison be between what have been prepared best.

This is all you need to know about the flesh of terrestrial animals. But as to their other parts, what properties they possess, you will hear in turn following the section on snails.

2   On the snail

It is quite clear that we should count this animal among neither the winged nor the aquatic creatures. But if we do not include it among terrestrial animals either,* we shall be saying absolutely nothing about the food from it. Nor again is it sensible to ignore it as we ignore woodworms, 669 vipers and other reptiles that they eat in Egypt and some other countries. For none of those people will read this, and we ourselves would never eat any of what to them are foods. But all Greeks eat snails on a daily basis, although they have hard flesh, which for this reason is difficult to concoct; however, if indeed it has been concocted it is very nutritious.

Like the molluscs their juice is aperient, and for this reason some people dress them with oil and fish sauce and use the resultant sauce for the evacuation of bowel contents. If you wish to use this animal's flesh only as a nutritious food, having first boiled it in water you will transfer it to different water and boil it again, and only then will you dress it and boil it a third time until the flesh becomes perfectly tender. When prepared in this way, it will keep the stomach in check and impart adequate nutriment to the body.

3   On the peripheral parts of terrestrial animals

People eat the peripheral structures of terrestrial animals – the feet, snouts and ears – and for the most part take them, when they have boiled them in water, with vinegar and fish sauce, and sometimes with mustard, too. 670 But others take them with oil and fish sauce, pouring on wine as well. And there are those who eat them with vegetables, either boiled in water or seasoned in pans. The feet of young porkers are most useful when added to a ptisane while it is being cooked, to make it stronger, and they themselves become softer and so are better for working up in the mouth and the stomach.

Now, there is great difference according to the manner of preparation, not only among the peripheral parts of the animals but among all other parts also, which I shall speak of at greater length in the works on cooking. But so far as the structures themselves are concerned, only general differences are made clear in this present treatise, where the parts are being compared with one another as if they had been prepared in the same manner that has previously been described. For such a comparison is valid.

The distal structures of the body have very little fat, and very little of fleshy nature, but what look like nerve and skin predominate – not the sort of nerve and skin in the body as a whole, since in the extremities they 671 have been subjected to more activity. As a result they are more glutinous (in fact, all skin and nerve arrive at this sort of nature when boiled). So it is natural that while they give less nutriment to the body, because of their glutinous condition they pass through more easily. The feet of pigs are better than the snout, just as the snout is better than the ears. For the last are constructed from cartilage and skin alone. In the mature animal, cartilage is totally indigestible, but in the growing animal it is concocted when it has been well chewed, and gives a small amount of nutriment to the body. And in the case of other animals, by way of analogy, take note of the statement that has just been made. For in them the peripheral parts are worse than those in pigs to the same extent that their flesh is worse than that of pigs in the excellence of its nutriment.

It is clear that I am calling the parts in the feet nerve-like structures in virtue of their similarity to what is properly called nerve, which takes its origin from the brain and spinal cord. But the nerve-like structures 672 in the peripheral parts, while they are so called from this similarity, are ligaments of bones, without sensation, and certain tendons attached to them.

4 On the tongue in terrestrial animals

A peculiarity of substance in this structure is flesh that is rather spongy and more full of blood.* Flesh, strictly speaking, is muscle, and of the muscles themselves, especially the middle parts. For many muscles terminate at their extremities in significant tendons, which most physicians call their 'aponeuroses'. The muscles reaching the extremities of limbs produce the largest of these. But some muscles also have heads that are tendinous.

Of the tongue itself, which cooks remove from pigs and boil, the body proper is spongy flesh, as I said; however, they do not remove it alone nor boil it on its own. Rather, they boil it complete with the attached muscles, generally with the epiglottis and larynx, and with the glands at this site that produce the saliva, which are specific to the tongue itself, and with those adjacent to the tonsils and the larynx. The presence of 673 arteries, veins and nerves is common to the tongue and other flesh. For they are also eaten with the flesh, except that in the structure under discussion the three types of vessel are larger, and in greater number, than in a comparable bulk of other flesh. What the properties are of the food from the glandular bodies comes next.

5   On glands

The substance of glands is as different from that of the tongue as the latter is from flesh. But not all glands differ to the same extent. Rather, those lying beside and touching the tongue are somewhat similar to those in the breasts when they are not yet full of milk. The glands in the breast do not perform their task continuously as just about all other glands do, including the glands of the tongue. For the glands of the tongue have been prepared by nature for the production of saliva, but those in the breast, while loose-textured, spongy and full of milk in pregnancy, are contracted and thickened during the time when the animals are without milk, bearing the same difference one to another that soaked sponges do to 'withered' sponges (for people refer in this way to those sponges which, when they have squeezed out every bit of moisture, they would   674 tighten and contract the whole body of the sponge by tying it up).

There are some glands like this in the pharynx, as there are in the mesentery too, but while these are small and so are missed by most people, the tonsils and those by the larynx are large and distinct. There are also other small glands in many parts of the body, supporting the bifurcations* of vessels. Nor is the so-called thymus gland small, rather it is very large in newborn animals and becomes smaller and harder as they grow.

It is a common characteristic of all of them that they appear pleasant to the taste, and friable, on eating; and the glands in the breasts, when they hold milk, also reveal a little of the sweetness of milk. As a result, when these glands have become full of milk they are a food that is eagerly sought after by gourmets, especially the milk glands of pigs. The nutriment from them, when well concocted, is rather close to the nutriment in flesh; but when they have been less adequately worked up they produce a crude humour, or mucus – mucus from the moister glands, crude humour from   675 the harder ones – about which there has been earlier discussion.

While the testes belong to the class of glands, they are not wholesome in the same way as those in the breasts, but are somewhat foul-smelling, revealing the nature of the semen they produce, just as the kidneys reveal the nature of the urine. The testes of terrestrial animals, moreover, are much worse concocted, for those of grain-fed cockerels are most pleasant and provide useful nutriment for the body. The glands lying beside the neck of the bladder* are close to the testes in nature.

Some people also reckon the kidneys among the glands, for they think that they also have a glandular structure. But they are manifestly unwholesome and difficult to concoct, like the testes of animals that have been growing for a long time, when people cut them out and eat them. Those of younger animals are better, but the testes of bulls, male goats and rams are distasteful, difficult to concoct and unwholesome.

6 On testes

In our part of the world people cut out the testicles of young pigs and oxen, but not for the same purpose; rather, those of pigs for the sake of 676 eating (for the flesh of castrated pigs is also more tasty, more nutritious and better concocted), and those of oxen for their usefulness in farming (for bulls are difficult for them to manage). But they remove the testicles of goats and sheep for both reasons.

The testicles of all the above animals are difficult to concoct and unwholesome, but nourishing when well concocted. Their defects and virtues parallel what was said about flesh. For just as the flesh of sheep is superior in all respects, so too are their testes, to the same extent. Only cockerels' testes are the best in every respect, especially the testes of grain-fed ones.

7 On brain

All brain produces more mucus and thick humour, and is slow to pass and difficult to concoct; and not least, it is also bad for the stomach. Some physicians administer it to patients, being deceived by its softness, 677 although as well as its other features it is also nauseating. Whenever you want someone to vomit following food, it is better to give this part in an oily dressing to take at the conclusion of the meal. But be careful in the case of those with anorexia, whom the old physicians called 'poor eaters' [*apositoi*].

It is understandable that one does not eat it even after other foods, since all have learned from experience how nauseating it is. But people, sensibly, also take it with oregano, just as some eat it with a variety of salty dressings. Because it produces thick humour and is full of residues, it is in every way better when prepared with things that are cutting and warming. However, if it has been well concocted, it gives noteworthy nutriment to the body.

8   On bone marrow

The marrow found in bones is both sweeter and tastier, and more fatty than brain, such that if one were to taste them by way of comparison he would consider the brain also had a certain harshness. As with brain, marrow also is nauseating food when taken in quantity. Nevertheless it, too, is nutritious when well concocted.

9   On the spinal marrow [cord]

The spinal marrow is of the same class as the brain, and is wrongly called 678 marrow. For not only is marrow moister, softer and more fatty than the spinal 'marrow', but also than the brain itself. But since it is surrounded by the bones of the spine and approximates the marrow in colour, they call it 'marrow'; just as some similarly refer to the brain itself. The spinal marrow, while in continuity with the brain and of the same nature as it, is a good deal harder, especially at the lower extremity of the spine. For it becomes harder the more distant it is from the brain. It has less fattiness and therefore avoids nausea; and if well concocted it provides much nutriment to the body.

10   On soft and hard fat

Both are oily, but they differ from one another in moistness and dry-ness. Soft fat is a rather moist substance, very similar to olive oil that has become thickened with age. Hard fat is much drier than the soft 679 variety and so, even if you pour it after warming it, it readily congeals and thickens. Both are weakly nourishing – dressings for the meats that nourish us rather than nutriments in themselves.

11   On the entrails of terrestrial animals

The liver of all animals produces thick humour, is difficult to concoct and slow to pass. Among livers, the one called 'fig-fed'* not only tastes better but is also better in other respects – it chanced upon this name since, when the animal is intended for slaughter, it produces such a liver with a diet of plenty of dried figs. They do this especially with pigs because the entrails of this animal are naturally more tasty than those from other animals. And even these improve when the animal eats a lot of dried figs. But I do not think that it is sensible for people to go beyond what is naturally better and have recourse to inferior things.

Amongst the other entrails the spleen is not completely pleasant to the taste, for it possesses obvious astringency. It is also, with reason, believed 680 to be unwholesome, producing blood that contains black bile.

The lung, to the extent that it is more loose-textured, is more easily concocted than both liver and spleen; however, it is by a long way less nutritious than liver, and what nutriment it does give to the body contains more mucus.

The heart, in substance, is fibrous, hard flesh, and so is difficult to concoct and slow to pass; but if it is well concocted, it delivers much wholesome nutriment to the body.

There has been earlier comment about the kidneys* (for some people also include them among the entrails).

12   On the stomach, uterus and intestines in quadrupeds

These structures are harder than flesh, which is why, even if well con-cocted, they do not produce absolutely perfect blood, but blood that is colder and cruder. So they require a longer time to be well worked up and become useful.

13   On the differences between domesticated and wild animals

The blending of domesticated animals is moister than that of wild ones, 681 because of the moistness of the air in which they spend their time and because of their easy life. Animals in the mountains endure hardship and toil mightily, and pass their time in drier air. Because of this their flesh is firmer and they have absolutely no fat, or very little. Mind you, in this way the flesh remains less liable to decomposition for longer than does the flesh of animals that are domesticated and have led an idle life. It is also clear that the food from them is freer from residue, just as that from idle, domesticated animals produces residue. It is inevitable that such food is more nourishing and much more wholesome than the other.

14   On milk

This also is one of the nutriments from animals, and while it varies greatly with the seasons, the variation in terms of the animals themselves* is even greater. For cows' milk is very thick and fatty, while milk from the camel is very liquid and much less fatty; and next to the latter animal is that from mares, and following this, ass's milk. Goat's milk is well proportioned 682 in its composition, but ewe's milk is thicker. As to the seasons of the year, while the milk after parturition is very liquid, as time goes on it becomes continually thicker. In midsummer it reaches the mid-point of its natural state. After this time little by little it becomes thickened until finally the milk ceases. Just as it is most liquid in spring, so also is it in greatest amount. The fact that milk differs with the species of animal, as has been said, is at once apparent to the observer, and becomes more obvious from the cheese made from each of them. For the most liquid milk has the most whey, and the thickest milk the most cheese. For this reason, naturally, the more liquid milk moves the bowels more, and the thicker less. On the other hand, the thicker is more nourishing and the thinner less so. But if, by first boiling down the milk one exhausts the whey, it 683 does not even move the bowels at all. And when such a quantity of red-hot pebbles* has been added that they have used up all the whey, the resultant preparation, as well as no longer moving the bowels, actually has the opposite effect. Indeed, we also give it to those people with gastric irritation due to bitter residues. When red-hot iron discs are added, they have the same effect, no less than the pebbles do, rather, even more so. Certainly milk prepared in this way is easily curdled in the stomach. This is why we also mix honey and salt with it, but it is safer to pour in water as well, as many physicians do. Do not be surprised if, when they have used up the whey, they pour some water in again. For they are not avoiding the moistness of the whey but its bitterness, in virtue of which, whole milk, being a mixture of opposing substance, cheese and whey, moves the bowels.

As well as these components* milk also has, as has been said, a third, fatty juice, the greatest amount occurring in cows' milk. This is why they make from it what is called butter, regarding which, when you have but tasted and seen it, you will clearly recognize how much fattiness it contains. If you smear it on some part of the body and rub it in you will see the skin becoming greasy just as with olive oil. Even if you rub the skin of a dead animal with it, you will see the same effect. Furthermore, 684 people in many cold regions where they lack olive oil use butter for washing themselves. If you pour it onto hot coals, it is seen to produce flames as soft fat does. However, we often also use it as we use hard fat, by mixing it in poultices and other medicaments.

Cows' milk, as I said, is the most fatty. That of sheep and goats has some fat, but much less, and asses' milk has least of this sort of fluid.

This is why milk drunk warm, straight from the teats, is seldom curdled in the stomach by anyone. And if one takes salt and honey with it there is no possibility of it thickening and curdling in the stomach. For the same reason its excretion in the stools, since it contains much whey from which whole milk takes its excretory property, is just as great as the costive property of milk that is due to the cheesy material it contains.

For the production of healthy humour, whey is as inferior to the natural constituents of the rest of milk as it is superior to everything else for emptying the bowel. This is why, I think, the old physicians most often 685 used this drink as an aperient. One should add to it so much of the best honey as will sweeten it without upsetting the stomach, and likewise you should also add salt to the extent that it does not cause a troublesome taste. But if you want it to be more aperient you should add as much salt as possible.

Now this has been related at greater length than is needed for the present work. For it was proposed to discuss those things in milk that happen to possess benefits as nutriment. But since the matter of the purgative effect has been mixed up with the benefits, the argument has suffered a digression from this association. So let us bring the discussion back to what was proposed at the outset and speak about things that have not yet been stated about the properties in milk, among the greatest of which is this, namely, that the best milk is just about the most wholesome of any of the foods we consume. But do not miss what is additional in that statement. I did not say simply that all milk is the most wholesome; rather, I added 'the best'. For unwholesome milk is so far from producing healthy humour that even when people with healthy humour use it, it makes them full of unhealthy humour. Indeed in an infant, when the 686 first nurse had died, and another who was full of unhealthy humour was providing the milk for him, his whole body was obviously infected with numerous ulcers. When famine had taken hold in the spring, the second nurse had lived on wild herbs in the field. So she and some others in the same country who had lived in the same way were filled with such ulcers. We observed this in many other women who were nursing children* at that time. But even if, when a goat or some other animal has been pastured on scammony or spurge, one takes its milk as part of one's food, the stomach is in an absolute flux from it.

As with all other foods, so it is also with milk. You should understand that the properties are not described as applying to every specimen but only to that one that is best. The specimen in each class that falls short of the best must to the same extent fall short in its benefit to us.

The milk with the most whey is free from danger even if one uses it 687
continually. But milk with little such fluid and much cheesy thickness is
unsafe for people who use it to excess. For it will also damage those kidneys
with a propensity to stone formation, and it produces impactions* in the
liver of people with the potential to suffer this easily. These are the sort
of people in whom the distal parts of the vessels that transfer nutriment
from the concave to the convex parts of the organ are narrow.

All milk is good for the parts in the chest and lung, but is unsuitable
for the head unless one has a very strong one, just as it is no good for
organs in the hypochondrium that are easily made flatulent. For in very
many people it generates wind in the stomach, so that there are very
few who do not suffer from this. But when it has been boiled as much as
possible with any of the foods with thick juice, it gets rid of flatulence but
becomes more obstructive in the liver and more productive of stones in
the kidneys. Such foods were written about in book 1. They are: starch,
semidalis, groats, *tragos*, rice, vegetables, pour-cakes and bread that has
been neither well baked, nor first prepared with much kneading and
plenty of salt, nor has a proper proportion of leaven.   688

As with these last, so also with other foods that people mix with milk
and eat. The property of the foods being mixed will either reinforce or
diminish one of the properties in milk. But for now, dealing with the
property of milk in isolation, I am saying that it is wholesome and nutritious since it is composed of opposing substances and properties –
both aperient and costive; both prone to obstruct and conducive to thinning. For on the one hand its whey-like component thins the thickness of
the humours and moves the bowels; and on the other hand the cheesy
component checks the bowels and thickens the humours, which, as I
said, produce blockages in the liver and stones in the kidney.

Its continued use also harms the teeth, together with the flesh surrounding them, which they call 'gums'. For it makes these flabby, and
makes the teeth liable to decay and easily eaten away. Accordingly one
should rinse the mouth with diluted wine after consuming milk, and
it is better if you put honey in it. For in this way everything that has 689
been plastered around the teeth and gums from the cheesy component
is washed away. If one can use it in this way, without adding water to the
wine, it is better for the teeth and gums, provided that it does not affect
the head. Honey mixed with the wine and water certainly improves the
mixture. But the best usage for the protection of teeth so that they come
to no harm from milk is first, to rinse with *melikrat* after taking milk, and
second, to rinse with astringent wine.

15 **On** *oxygala* **[curds; cottage cheese]**

So-called *oxygala** is not harmful to normal teeth, and only those that are colder than need be, whether as a result of innate ill-blending or some acquired disposition, are damaged. In the same way that they are damaged by other cold things, so also are they damaged by this one. Sometimes the symptom due to cold things is what is called 'setting the teeth on edge', the same sort of symptom that commonly occurs with out-of-season mulberries and other astringent, acid foods. It is clear that a stomach that is rather cold for whatever reason does not concoct it 690 well, and while it is difficult for a well-balanced stomach to concoct, nevertheless it is not totally so. Those stomachs that are abnormally warm, whether innately or brought to such a blending from some secondary cause, in addition to suffering no harm enjoy some benefit from foods like these. These same stomachs also tolerate *oxygala* without harm when it has been surrounded with snow, just as they also tolerate other such foods and, it is clear, water that has been treated in the same way.

As a result of this I have been amazed at the number of physicians who give advice about each food in simplified terms – of one food that it is good for us; of another that it is harmful; that it is easily concocted or concocted with difficulty; wholesome or unwholesome; nutritious or lacking in nutriment; good or bad for the stomach; aperient or constipating; or having some other virtue or harmful effect. For while everyone can say about some foods that this particular one is unwholesome, or difficult to concoct or bad for the stomach, about most it is impossible to speak with truth in a single unqualified sentence. And since the whole statement 691 will necessarily be lengthy if I write for each food about criteria relating to natural blendings and acquired dispositions, it seems better, generally speaking, to reveal the method of enquiry at the outset of the instruction, as I did in the first of these books. But sometimes it seems better to recall them separately, especially those whose nature is not simple, as is the case with milk, of course, since it is composed of opposing substances and properties, while appearing uniform to the senses. For even if it is the best milk, it happens that in line with the differences between stomachs it sometimes becomes acid, and at another time, again, sends up a greasy eructation, despite the fact that it is the opposite dispositions which make unconcocted material in the stomach become acid or greasy. For lack of warmth naturally acidifies it, but excess of heat makes it greasy. Both of these conditions occur with milk because it has not only a whey-like nature within itself, but also an oily and a cheesy one.

At any rate unconcocted cottage cheese never becomes greasy for this reason, even if it falls on a very bilious or very inflamed stomach. For 692 within itself it has neither the warm, bitter quality which milk has because of the whey, nor the oily, moderately warm one which it has acquired through the oiliness in itself. The cheesy character alone remains in this sort of preparation, and even this is not like what originally existed, but has been altered towards what is colder.

Accordingly it is sufficient to say about cottage cheese that it is cold and produces thick humour. It follows from this that a disposition with a well-balanced blending does not concoct it easily. For often in all my works I have thought it right to refer back to that blending whenever I am propounding something in simple terms. Moreover it is probable that so-called crude humour, whose nature I have previously discussed elsewhere and have explained in book 11, is generated from such foodstuffs. It is not unreasonable that this foodstuff is valuable for warmer stomachs, just as absolutely the reverse for colder ones.

However, it is not necessary to write this about each food, but to mention only in the case of some that this sort of humour – the sort that 693 comes from cottage cheese, cheese and everything that produces thick humour – naturally produces kidney-stones whenever the kidneys are warmer than is needful (whether from innate ill-blending or from some other later disposition that has arisen), but do not have passages that are wide in proportion to the warmth. For, you see, the most diseased states of bodies are composites of structures that are opposites in blending, so it may be that while a stomach is quite warm the brain is cold. So also, sometimes the lung and the whole thorax are cold, on top of a warm stomach. Often too, to the contrary, while everything else is warmer than is needful, the stomach alone is colder, and at times the whole head is colder but the liver warmer, and so too with other parts.

This is why right at the outset I indicated that instruction about the properties in foodstuffs is most helpful when teachers expound the vari- 694 ation in moistness, dryness, warmth and coldness; and further, the vis-cidity or thickness of the substance of the foodstuffs; and as well as this, whether the substance is uniform, or composed of items that are oppo-site in blending, like milk. And I said that we are guided to the diagnosis of these properties by smell and taste, and as well, by the other features that I discussed at the beginning of this treatise; just as I am now doing in the case of milk, indicating its nature from the features it possesses – whether it is warmed, or thickened by rennet, or whether its components are separated in any way whatsoever.

In fact, what is called 'curdling' also produces this thickening without rennet when after sufficiently preheating the milk we sprinkle it with cold oxymel.* We also produce the same effect with honey-wine; and sometimes, apart from sprinkling its substance, we produce curdling by lowering into it a vessel containing very cold water.* Also, the milk obtained following parturition curdles immediately without rennet when heated briefly on hot ashes. The old comic writers usually called milk set like this *pyriatê*; in our part of Asia we call it *pyriephthon*. Now this is 695 milk in the strictest sense, devoid of any other substance. When they mix honey with it and set it with rennet, by this action the thin, watery part is separated. Some eat only its curdled part that results from joining the cheesy part of the milk and the hot, fiery property in the rennet, and the honey that is mixed with them. But others drink the whey together with the curdled component, either all of both in the same degree, or more of one component than the other. It is clear that the bowels are moved more in some people and less in others in proportion to the amount of whey. It is also clear that the whole body will be nourished more in those people who have consumed only the curd, and less in those who have also drunk with it some of the whey; and still less so, in those who have consumed a little curd but much whey. So too, with milk curdled after parturition, there will be a great difference according to whether it is curdled with or without honey. For when it does not have honey as well, it is more difficult to concoct, more productive of thick humour and, further, it is slower to be evacuated. However, in both instances there is abundant nourishment for the body as a whole. 696

This is sufficient to understand about milk in the present work. To what extent it is useful in disease, or for those wasting from whatever cause, or for those with ulceration of the lung, properly belongs to the study of therapeutics.

16   On cheese

There has already been discussion about the properties of cheese* in the chapter on milk, but it is better that I now assign a specific chapter to it, in its turn. In its preparation it gains additional sharpness from the rennet that is put into it, and gets rid of all moistness, particularly when it has aged, when it also becomes sharper and obviously both warmer in itself and more heating. Because of this it turns out to be more thirst-provoking, more difficult to concoct and produces more un-healthy humour. Therefore, with foods that produce thick humours, because of these same factors, not even the benefit that they acquire when mixed with foods with sharp and thinning properties is had without damage. For the harm to the individual that results from the unhealthy humoral state and the burning heat is greater than the benefit that re- 697 sults from thinning the thick humour. In the individual, indeed, such humour is even more harmful in terms of stone production in the kidneys, for these have been shown to be generated in those bodies in which thickness of the humours meets with fiery heat. So among the cheeses one should especially avoid this sort, since it holds absolutely no advantage, whether for concoction or distribution, or the passage of urine, or moving the bowels, just as it also holds none for a healthy humoral state.

Next, one must regard as bad, but less so, cheese that is neither old nor sharp, while young cheese is the best of all, namely, the sort which here in Pergamum (and in Mysia beyond Pergamum) is called by the inhabitants sour-milk cheese, being most pleasant as food, harmless to the oesophagus, and less difficult to concoct and to excrete than all other cheeses. Moreover it is neither unwholesome nor very markedly productive of thick humour, a common charge against all cheeses. A very fine cheese is the one highly regarded by the wealthy in Rome (its name is *bathysikos*), as well as some others in other regions.

Although there is a very great difference among them individually, in terms of the natures of the animals, the types of preparation and, still 698 more, the ages of the cheeses themselves, I shall myself try at this point to define their properties with a few markers, by paying attention to which one will most easily diagnose which is better and which inferior. The markers are of two types, one in the sort of composition of the substance of the cheese, in virtue of which it is softer or harder, denser or more loose-textured, more glutinous or more crumbly; the other in the taste, regarding which, while acidity dominates in some, in others there is sharpness or oiliness or sweetness, whether some of these characteristics or, so to speak, equal shares of all.

As to the specific differences among the above-mentioned types, the softer cheese is better than the harder, the spongy, loose-textured cheese is better than the cheese that is very dense and compressed. But while the cheese that is quite glutinous and the one that is friable to the point of roughness are bad, the one that is average in respect of these features is better.

As to diagnosis by taste, best of all is the one without any strong quality, with a sweetness that to a small extent surpasses the others; but 699 the tastier cheese is also better than the distasteful one, and the one with moderate salt is better than cheese with a lot of it or cheese with none at all. Moreover, after eating it one can identify, even from the eructation, which cheese is better and which worse. For the one with a quality that gradually diminishes is better, but the one with a persistent quality is worse. It is clear that it is hard for the latter to undergo change and difficult to alter it, and so it is also difficult to concoct. For with food, concoction is necessarily accompanied by an alteration from all its previous qualities.

17   On the blood of terrestrial animals

All blood is difficult to concoct, especially when it is thick and full of black bile, like ox blood. Hares' blood has been highly regarded as being tastier, and it is customary for many people to cook it with the liver; but for some people, with other entrails too. Some also eat the blood of young pigs, but others eat the blood of older pigs that have been castrated. They never attempt boars' blood since it is both unpleasant and difficult to concoct. Homer also knew that goats' blood was eaten by some people on the grounds that it is tasty.*   700

18   On the food from winged animals

While the ancients used the word bird [*ornis*] for all winged, two-footed animals, it has now become usual for present-day Greeks to restrict the use of the word to what those folk called hen [*alektoris*] (and similarly, the males among them cock [*alektryón*]).

The family of all winged animals is poorly nutritious when compared with that of terrestrial animals, especially pigs: you would find no flesh more nutritious than theirs. However, the flesh of winged animals is more easily concocted, particularly the flesh of the partridge, the francolin, and both the hen and cock pigeon. The flesh of thrushes, blackbirds and little birds, among which are the so-called 'house sparrows', is harder than these, and harder again is the flesh of the turtle-dove, the wood pigeon and the duck. The flesh of pheasants is like that of hens in concoction 701 and as nutriment, while being superior in its pleasant taste on eating. The flesh of peacocks is harder, more difficult to concoct and more fibrous than these.

One should recognize what is a common feature of all winged animals, as it is also of quadrupeds, namely, that the flesh of growing animals is much superior to that of animals that are past their prime; that the flesh of young adults is midway between both of these; and that the flesh of extremely young animals is also bad, but in the opposite direction to that of aged ones. For the flesh of the latter is hard, dry and sinewy and so it is poorly concocted and gives little nourishment to the body. But the bodies of extremely young animals are slimy and wet and for just this reason are full of residues and more readily move the bowels. Please bear this in mind as a general statement to do with all animals. For in the differentiae according to age it is the same with them all.

Also common to all animals is the manner of preparation in relation to health, which I have already discussed earlier, and perhaps shall speak of again in summary. But for the present I shall speak only about the 702 properties, namely that while foods that have been roasted and fried are drier, those that have been boiled in sweet water provide a moister nutriment for the body. And there has been enough said earlier about dishes in white sauce and various seasonings, as also about domesticated and wild animals.

There is a great difference also between animals that pass their days in swampy, marshy or muddy regions and those in mountains and dry places. For according to the region animal flesh is rather dry, free from residue and more easily concocted; or moist, full of residue and more difficult to concoct.

19   On geese and ostriches

The name geese is usual even with the old people, but that of ostrich [lit. 'camel-sparrow'] is unusual, for they call them large sparrows. Once, while still a youth, I heard one of the professors who discuss this sort of problem arguing both sides and proving that sometimes these animals were birds, but sometimes they were not. It is better not to enquire into this but rather into what sort of property the food from them has. So when you have heard this from me, you will learn at leisure from someone else 703 whether you should call such animals birds or not.

Well then, their flesh is full of residue and very much more difficult to concoct than that of the previously mentioned winged animals. However, the wings do not have flesh that is worse than the others. For in many winged animals, and particularly in those that are small with hard flesh, the nature of the wings is fibrous and hard; and with some of them the flesh is hard in its entirety, such as the flesh of cranes, which people also eat after first keeping it for several days. But somewhere between the flesh of cranes and that of geese is the flesh of what are called *otidai* or *ótidai* [bustards], for they both pronounce and write the first syllable in either way, with the letter *omicron* or *omega*.

20   On the differences between the parts of winged animals

The entrails in winged animals bear the same relation to the flesh as they were said to bear in terrestrial animals. The intestines of all of them are 704 absolutely inedible; however, their stomachs are not comparable with the intestines. For they are both edible and nutritious, and some are very tasty, such as the goose's, and following it, that of fattened roosters. And just as in pigs people sweeten the liver in the living animal beforehand with a diet of dried figs, they do likewise with geese, by steeping their food in milk whey, so that it becomes not only more tasty but also more nutritious, more wholesome and is excreted without difficulty. And it is the same as regards concoction in the stomach.

The wings of geese also, and more so than these, of hens, are suitable for concoction and nutrition, and while there is quite a lot of difference in the flesh of very old animals as opposed to those more obviously young, the difference is far greater with their wings; and similarly with the thin as opposed to the plump ones. The wings of well-nourished young birds are best, but those of thin, very old birds are worst. The feet of all birds are almost inedible.

One can neither praise nor fault the wattles and combs of roosters.

The testicles, especially of fattened roosters, are very good, and still more so, of those that have been eating foods with milk whey. For they 705 are wholesome, nutritious and very easily concocted, and they neither promote nor inhibit excretion.

Winged animals have brains that are small, nevertheless they are much better than those in terrestrial animals, to the same extent that they are also drier. Among birds themselves, mountain birds have better brains than marsh birds, to the same extent as all the other parts.

Some people mistakenly praise the stomach of the ostrich on the grounds that it is a medicament that promotes concoction. But others praise the stomach of the shearwater much more. But neither are they easily concocted themselves, nor are they medicaments promoting concoction of other foods, as are ginger and pepper and, in another way, both wine and vinegar. If I were to try to say what everyone knows about the tongues and beaks of birds, I should of course be assumed to be just chattering.

21 On eggs

These are also among the foods from birds, varying from one another according to three differentiae: one, in virtue of the specific substance 706 (for hen and pheasant eggs are better, but goose and ostrich eggs are worse); another, whereby some have been laid for a longer time but others more recently; and the third, whereby some have been boiled for longer, some until they are moderately firm, and others have only been warmed. As regards the last differentia, the first are called 'hard boiled', the second 'soft boiled' and the third 'sucking' eggs.

Now of these, the soft-boiled eggs are the best for body nutrition but the sucking ones, although less nourishing, pass more easily and smooth away roughness of the pharynx. The hard-boiled eggs are difficult to concoct and slow to pass, and distribute thick nutriment for the body. And eggs that have been baked in hot ashes are still slower to pass than these last, and produce more thick humour. But eggs that have been thickened in frypans and so are called fried have a nutriment that is the worst for everything. For during concoction it also becomes greasy, and as well as producing thick humour it also contains juice that is harmful and liable to form residues.

What are called stifled eggs* are better than both the boiled and the 707 baked ones. They are prepared in the following manner. When cooks have soaked them in olive oil, fish sauce and a little wine, they put the container in a three-legged pot holding hot water. Then, when they have entirely closed the pot, they apply heat underneath it until the eggs are of medium consistency. For eggs that have been thickened for longer become very like those that have been boiled or baked, but those that have been removed at a moderate degree of thickening are better for being concocted than the hard ones, and provide better nutriment for the body. So one should aim for the same moderate degree of consistency in eggs that are poured onto pans, in no way permitting these to be completely thickened, but removing the vessel from the fire while they are still runny.

Among eggs the superiority of fresh to stale ones is marked. For the very fresh are the best, and the very old are the worst; and those in between differ from one another in goodness and badness in proportion to their distance from these extremes.

22   On the blood of winged animals

Some people eat the blood of hens and pigeons, especially the grain-   708
fed ones, since it is no worse than pigs' blood either for tastiness or
for being concocted; but it is very much inferior to the blood of hares.
Nevertheless, however one prepares it, all blood is difficult to concoct
and full of residues.

23   On the food from aquatic animals

There are very many families of animals that dwell in water, and very
many varieties, or species, of these. But for the present, as with those
animals that have been dealt with previously, I shall speak of the similar-
ities among them that relate to their medical use. In the present context
there will be no difference whether we say 'medical' or 'health-related'.
So, as with the others there will be discussion about the most important,
namely, those that are eaten regularly.

24   On grey mullet

The grey mullet belongs to the family of scaly fish that grows not only in
the sea but also in pools and rivers. This is why the various grey mullet   709
differ greatly from one another, so that the class of sea mullet appears to
be another one from that in the pools, rivers or swamps, or in the drains
that clean out the city latrines. The flesh of those that spend their time
in muddy, dirty water is full of residue and quite slimy, but the flesh of
those in the clean sea is very good, and more so when the sea is subject
to winds. For, to the extent that they get less exercise, the flesh of fish
in a calm sheltered sea is worse, and worse than this still in so-called
lagoons; and worse again in pools. If any of these pools are small ones
that neither receive large rivers, nor possess springs, nor have an ample
run-off, then they are a great deal worse. If there is no run-off at all and
the water is stagnant, they are exceedingly bad. There was discussion at
the beginning about fish in marshes and swamps and suchlike places; for
the ones that spend their time in spots like these have flesh that is bad
in the extreme. But of those that grow in rivers, the ones in the sorts of
river in which the flow is brisk and large are better. In rivers that form
stagnant pools they are not good.   710
   They are better or worse according to their food. For while some have
plenty of weed and valuable roots and so are superior, others eat muddy

weed and unwholesome roots. And some of them that dwell in rivers running through a large town, eating human dung and certain other such bad foods, are worst of all, as I said; so that even if they remain for a very short time after death, they straight away become putrid and smell most unpleasantly. These are all unpleasant to eat and concoct, and contain little useful nutriment but much residue. Accordingly it is not surprising if they produce an accumulation of unhealthy humours in the body of those who eat them on a daily basis.

Although these are among the worst, against that is the fact that, as I said, the finest of all grey mullet are the ones in the clearest sea, especially where neither muddy nor smooth beaches surround it, 711 but sandy or rough ones. If the beaches are open to the north wind, so much the better. For while in all animals proper exercises contribute in no small degree to a healthy humoral state, the purity of the wind mingling with the water further augments the excellence of their substance.

It is also clear from what has been said that, for this reason too, one sea is better than another so far as it is either completely clear or receives many large rivers like the Pontus. For in such a sea the fish are as superior to those living in pools as they are inferior to those in the open sea. There are also certain pools of this sort, people call some of them lagoons, where a large river forms a stagnant pool connected to the sea. But also, apart from the river forming pools, wherever it first mingles with the sea the water is a mixture of salt and fresh, and the flesh of the fish that live in it lies between the flesh of river fish and sea fish.

You may take this as a general statement about other fish produced 712 in rivers and marshes and in the sea. The great number of them are unambiguous, since the sea fish avoid river water and the river or pool fish avoid sea water. But grey mullet, most of all fish, make use of both waters, and can by their nature travel the current to the upper reaches of the river as far as possible from the sea. Now this mullet, like any other sea fish, does not possess many small spines. But the mullet that enters the sea from rivers and marshes is full of such spines, much the same as other fish from the same source. For the flesh from just about all fish produced in marshes and rivers is found to be full of fine spines while the sea fish do not have them. Wherever the mouth of the river joins with the sea, some river fish are caught in the sea and some sea fish in the river – recognized from the fact of having respectively many, or absolutely none, of the aforementioned spines. Now few river fish enter the sea, but all sea fish enjoy rivers.

When you eat it, the taste immediately indicates to you the better grey 713
mullet. For its flesh is sharper, more tasty and free from oiliness. The
ones that are oily and watery in taste are worse in the actual eating, but
also worse concocted, bad for the stomach and unwholesome. This is
why people prepare them with oregano.

Some of our own people call the fish produced in rivers 'white mullet',
believing that they are a different species from grey mullet. But in all else
it is in every way the same animal, being a little whiter, with a smaller
head and a more pointed jaw. But the property of the food from it is
as I remarked earlier about the river grey mullet. So that the ambiguity
relates to the name and not the thing. But I shall now also speak of what
is more useful to understand than this.

This fish is also one of those that are pickled, and the variety from
pools becomes much improved when prepared in this way. For it gets rid
of everything in the taste that is slimy and foul-smelling. The recently
salted fish is superior to the one that has been pickled for a longer time.
But a little later there will be a general discussion about pickled fish, as
also about fish that can be kept in snow* until the next day.

25   On sea bass   714

I have not observed this being produced in fresh water, although I have
seen it ascending rivers or pools from the sea. This is why it is seldom
found in bad condition, as grey mullet often is. Nor does it avoid lagoons
and river mouths, although it is nonetheless pelagic. (People use this name
for fish that retreat to the deep sea.) The nutriment from this and the
other fish generates blood that is thinner in composition than that from
terrestrial animals, so that it does not give abundant nourishment and is
quickly dispersed. But since we sometimes use the term 'thinner' in the
case of two things being compared, and at other times in absolute, non-
comparative terms,* you should understand that when things are being
referred to in absolute terms there is an implied comparison with blood at
the mean between extremes. The extremes of defective composition are
that it is thick like liquid pitch, and whey-like in such a fashion that when
it has been drained from a vein, when it coagulates, it has very much
watery liquid floating on the surface. The best blood is that produced 715
precisely between these extremes, from bread that has been very well
prepared, about which there was discussion in the first book; and from
birds – the partridge and those like it. Close to these are the pelagic
species of sea fish.

26 On red mullet

This, too, is one of the pelagic fish and has been prized by men as superior to the rest in tastiness on eating. It has flesh that is firmer than just about all of them and is quite friable, which is the same as saying that there is nothing either sticky or oily in it. At any rate, when well concocted it is more nourishing than other fish. It has been remarked earlier that harder food and food that has a coarser substance and, as one might say, more earthy, is more notably nourishing than moister and softer foods, when, as well as this, it contains substance proper to the body being nourished; the substance itself being distinguished by tastiness. For those foodstuffs that are foreign to the whole natures of the animals being nourished either are not eaten by them at all, or are eaten without pleasure. Nevertheless just as the moister of the proper foods is less nourishing, so it is more easily concocted and distributed. Therefore 716 red-mullet flesh is tasty, being food proper to the nature of humans but, although it is firmer than other fish, nonetheless it can be consumed on a daily basis because it is friable, non-oily and also has some sharpness. For foods that on first eating are immediately oily and sticky are filling and quickly ruin the appetite; and furthermore, we do not tolerate their consumption for very many days in succession.

Now gourmets have marvelled at red-mullet liver on account of its tastiness, but some people hold that it is wrong to eat it on its own, and they make what is called *garelaion* in a container which contains a small amount of wine in which they macerate the organ, so that everything derived from the liver and the previously prepared liquids becomes one fluid that is uniform to the senses. In this they dip the flesh of the red mullet and eat it. But I do not think that it has either the taste or the benefit to the body to justify such esteem; just as neither does the head, and yet the gourmets praise the head and assert that it takes second place 717 after the liver.

Nor again can I understand why very many people buy the largest red mullet, which has flesh that is neither tasty like the smaller ones, nor easily concocted since it is quite firm. Consequently I enquired of one of those who were buying large red mullet at a high price whatever was the reason for his eagerness for them. He answered that while he bought old ones like those particularly because of the liver, he did so because of the head as well. But to have spoken to such an extent about gourmets is sufficient for the practical purpose of this work.

The best red mullet occur in the open sea, as is the case with all other fish, not least because of their food. At any rate those fish that eat crabs are ill-smelling, disagreeable to taste, difficult to concoct and unwholesome. They are distinguished prior to eating by cutting open the belly; but to anyone eating them immediate recognition takes place at the first smell and taste.

27 On rock fish   718

They call them 'rock fish' from the places in which they are found to be living. For they do not lurk or spawn in smooth, muddy or sandy shores, but where there are some rocks and headlands. The parrot wrasse has been thought to be the finest among them in tastiness, and following it the *kottyphos* and the *kichlê*, and then the rainbow wrasse, the *phykês* and the perch. Not only is the food from them easily concocted, but it is very healthy for human bodies, generating blood of mean composition. I call 'mean', blood that is not thin and watery but also not excessively thick. Since there is remarkable latitude to the word 'mean', variations within it will be discussed as the work proceeds.

28 On the goby

This fish is shore frequenting, being itself one of the fish that always remain small. The one from sandy shores or rocky headlands is best for enjoyment, concoction, distribution and a healthy humoral state. But 719 the one from river mouths, marshes and lagoons is not enjoyable to the same extent, nor is it wholesome or easy to concoct. If the water is also muddy or the river is cleansing a city, the goby in it would be very bad, like all other fish living in such waters.

Now it is reasonable that among the rock fish there is no obvious differentiation to be made, one from another, between fish of the same species, since those dwelling in very clear water would always avoid all fresh water and water that is a mixture of fresh and sea water. The same applies to the next after these, the pelagic fish. For they do not vary greatly from one another, as do fish dwelling in both types of water. For of the latter, the ones in very clear water are the best of their species, but the ones dwelling in rivers that clean cities are the worst of all, and the ones in between are an average of these two groups. This has been stated previously when I wrote the section on grey mullet.

However, the flesh of gobies, just as it is firmer than that of rock fish, is softer than that of red mullet. So the bodies of those eating it are 720 proportionately nourished.

29 On fish with soft flesh

In the third book of *On Foodstuffs* Phylotimos wrote as follows about soft-fleshed fish, in these very words:

Gobies, wrasse, rainbow wrasse, perch, Murry eels, *kichlai*, *kottyphoi*, horse-mackerel and again, hake; and, as well as these, bonito, sole, *hêpatoi*, *kitharoi*, maigre and the whole family of tender-fleshed fish are dealt with better in the stomach than all others.

So it is worth wondering how he neglected the parrot wrasse, although they hold first place in the rock-fish family, all of which have flesh that is very soft and most friable when compared with other fish. For some of these are soft-fleshed but have no friability, since they contain a sticky, oily juice; and others that have escaped the stickiness and oiliness, while in this respect the same as rock fish, differ in the firmness of their flesh. Now just about all pelagic fish are like this unless any corrupt their flesh 721 with bad food, as red mullet do when they eat *karkinidai*. These are little animals very like small crabs, yellowish in colour. But rock fish do not make use of a variety of foods, nor different habitats, nor fresh water; and consequently they are always without blemish.

Those that Phylotimos called hake, and others refer to as *oniskoi*, when they use good food and clear sea have flesh that is the equal of rock fish; but when they have made use of defective food and have passed the time in mixed waters – especially waters that are foul – they do not shed their soft flesh but they also acquire some oiliness and stickiness, in virtue of which they are no longer as tasty, and the nutriment that they produce and distribute is fuller of residue.

As I said, it is proper to bear in mind this generalization about all fish, that they are worse in the outlets of rivers that clean out latrines, bathhouses or kitchens, and the dirt from clothes and linen, and from 722 other things that need cleansing in the city through which they flow, especially when it is thickly populated. The flesh of the Murry eel that lives in water like this is also found to be very bad. One does not, indeed, find it travelling up the rivers or being produced in marshes. Nevertheless it is very bad in the mouths of rivers like the one that flows through Rome. Because of this, alone of almost all sea fish, it is sold most cheaply in that city, like those that are produced in the river itself. Some call the latter Tiberines, since they have a specific shape unlike any sea creature. One can learn that the admixture from the city's drains makes them very bad from the fact that fish produced in the river itself before it reaches the city are better. And indeed, another river called the Nar, which empties into the Tiber about three hundred and fifty stadia upstream, has much 723 better fish than the Tiber since right from its source it is a large river, and it stays clear as far as the Tiber because it has a brisk, steep flow; so that nowhere, even briefly, does it form stagnant pools.

Now those whose experience of the native fish comes from habitual use do not need the above features for their recognition. But those unaccustomed to them, whether from another city or locals, should at the outset test them in respect of such features, before reaching an understanding of the nature of each fish through personal experience.

Phylotimos should not simply have made mention of all tender-fleshed fish together, nor indiscriminately mixed up the others with rock fish. For these latter are always the best, but *oniskoi* are not, nor are Murry eels, nor gobies either. In fact, some of these also occur in rivers and marshes and some in the sea; but some occur in so-called lagoons or, speaking generally, in mixed waters where the mouth of a large river joins the sea. Accordingly, when looked at separately, they differ greatly from one 724 another, as for instance grey mullet and Murry eels. And while *oniskoi* differ less than these, they also differ to not a small degree from one another. However, gobies do not have flesh that is soft, as both *oniskoi* and rock fish do, just as neither do *skianides* and *skianai* [*sc.* maigre] – for they are referred to in both ways.

I wonder very much at Phylotimos in connection with the *kitharoi*, for while the turbot is very like them it has softer flesh than they do and is considerably inferior to the *oniskoi*. In fact these and the so-called *hêpatoi*, and the others that Phylotimos connected with rock fish, he understood to stand halfway between the tender- and the firm-fleshed fish. For while not quite firm-fleshed, they fall short of being quite tender-fleshed. Among the latter Phylotimos also neglected the sole, just as he neglected the parrot wrasse among the rock fish; unless, perhaps, he used the name flounder for soles. For in a way they resemble one another; however, they are not precisely the same species. The sole is softer, more pleasant to eat, and in every way better than the flounder. But horse-mackerel, too, are somehow halfway between tender-fleshed fish and the firm-fleshed ones. However, none of the above fish need vinegar, mustard or oregano, 725 as the oily, sticky, firm ones do. Nevertheless some people use them by frying them, others by baking them or preparing them in a pan, as they do the *rhombus* and the *kitharos*.

But, while the preparations from cooking pans are for the most part causes of a lack of concoction, that with white sauce is best for it. This dish is produced when, after ample water has been added, one pours on a sufficient quantity of olive oil and a small amount of dill and leek, and then partly boils it and adds just so much salt that the whole sauce does not appear salty. This is the recipe that is useful for convalescents, but the fried fish is also useful for people in perfect health, and next to this is that cooked on a brazier. But while the latter requires oil and fish sauce with a little wine, it is fitting for the fried preparations to have more wine and fish sauce than these with a small amount of oil poured on. But for those whose stomach is disturbed by this, vinegar containing a little fish sauce and pepper should be readily available. For on changing to a diet with these ingredients they concoct the food better and come to no harm so far as excretion is concerned. Because of this, some people especially 726 consume fish fried with wine and fish sauce, most adding pepper, but some few adding oil.

Some of the above fish, when sprinkled with simple salt and fried, become very pleasant to eat and also better concocted, and are better for the stomach than all other fish recipes. But from all the above fish the nutriment is best for those who are not in training, and the idle, frail and convalescent. People in training need more nutritious food, about which there has been previous comment. It has now been stated often that soft, friable food is best for health, because it is the most wholesome of all foods; and there is no greater foundation for secure good health than a healthy humoral state.

30 On firm-fleshed fish

Phylotimos also wrote about these in the second book of *On Food*, as follows:

Weevers, pipers, sharks, scorpion fish, horse-mackerel and red mullet; and again, sea perch, *glaukoi*, parrot wrasse, dogfish, conger eels and sea bream; and as well 727 as these, eagle rays, great white sharks, hammerhead sharks and all the firm-fleshed fish are difficult to deal with and distribute thick, salty humours.

This is Phylotimos' statement. But let us examine each individual item mentioned, from the beginning.

Now weevers and pipers, to those who have eaten them, clearly have firm flesh. But there is no one species of shark. For the fish that is highly prized among the Romans, which they call *galaxias*, belongs to the family of sharks [*galeoi*]. This fish does not seem to occur in Greek waters, which is why Phylotimos also appears to be unaware of it. However, the name for shark has been written in two ways in copies of his text – in some, *galeoi* with three syllables; in others, *galeônymoi*, with five.* And it is clear that the *galaxias*, which is in high repute among the Romans, is one of the tender-fleshed; but the other sharks are firm-fleshed.

Following on, Phylotimos correctly counted *skorpioi*, horse-mackerel, 728 red mullet, sea perch and *glaukoi* among the firm-fleshed fish. But he is wrong to include parrot wrasse among them, because they belong to the rock-fish. Next he included dogfish, which he ought to have numbered among the cetaceous animals, since they have flesh that is firm and full of residue, and so is cut up and pickled as food for ordinary people. In fact they are unpleasant and gelatinous, and therefore people eat them with mustard, and oil and vinegar, and with sharp dressings compounded of these.

Also of this group are the whales, dolphins and seals. The large tunny come close to them; however, it is not the equal of those in pleasure of eating. For tunny, especially the fresh ones, are unpleasant, but they improve when pickled. The flesh of younger and smaller tunny is not hard to the same degree, and it is manifestly better concocted. Still more so than these, very young tunny after pickling are a match for the finest preserved fish. Most are imported from the Pontus and are only inferior to those from Sardinia and Spain. For indeed this preserved fish, with 729 reason, is highly valued for both tastiness and its soft flesh. Such preserved fish are now usually referred to by all as sardines.* The *mylloi* imported from the Pontus are regarded next after sardines and young tunny, and following them, the *korakinoi*. However, let us take these remarks about preserved fish as by the way.

Among the firm-fleshed fish Phylotimos gave favourable mention to the hammerhead sharks, but he should also have remarked on their unpleasant taste, and similarly that of the saupe, which he completely ignored. But he correctly stated that conger eels, sea bream, lamia sharks and eagle rays are firm-fleshed. As he himself said, there are also other firm-fleshed fish whose names he did not mention because people do not use them much; for which reason it is better to examine their properties and let their names be.

Now Phylotimos was correct when he said that firm-fleshed fish are more difficult for the body to handle than soft-fleshed ones. For concoction in the stomach, conversion to blood in the liver and veins, and 730 assimilation in each part being nourished is easier in the softer fleshed and more difficult in the harder. For these phenomena occur when they are undergoing change, and the softer ones are more easily changed because they are more readily affected; change is the name given to the effect of things being changed. So he was correct when he said that they are difficult to handle, and correct, too, when he said that the firm-fleshed fish produce thick juice. For firmer food has a thicker substance, and softer food a thinner.

One must next examine whether firmer food also produces salty juices. For Phylotimos, like his teacher Praxagoras, says that salty juice is produced from foods that undergo longer heating. I do not think that one should refute this in general terms, but by making use of distinguishing criteria. And since the argument is common to all firm foods, let us consider it next under a specific heading.

31   Do all firm foods produce salty juices on boiling?

Phylotimos and Praxagoras believe that not only with firm-fleshed fish, but also with every other hard food, salty juice is produced on prolonged 731 boiling, and not only do they specify it as salty, or saline, but also alkaline. I myself observe that the decoction of most foodstuffs (of all, if you like) always becomes more salty in relation to the time it is boiled; but that sometimes it later also becomes sharp, when they want it to. However, I also observe that the solid matter, when boiled in water, gets rid of its original quality in the water during that time, and becomes bland (as it is called) and watery, with neither saltiness, nor sharpness, nor bitterness, nor astringency. You will realize the truth of what I say more clearly if you ever transfer whatever you wish into different water and boil it. You will find that the boiled solid matter itself gets rid of its particular quality and that the water receives it. Lupins, you will find, make the water sharp since they themselves also possess an innate sharp quality. So too do bitter vetch, *abrotonon*, wormwood [*apsinthion*]* and hulwort, and others that are sharp. But the boiled-down material 732 itself seems less sharp. And if you transfer the material into different water and repeat the boiling, you will find, as I just said, that the sharpness has been removed even more than before; and if you transfer it into different water a third and a fourth time, even still more so than previously. So that in time you will find that all sharpness has been removed.

In the same fashion, with bitter things like garlic, onions and leeks, the water in which they are boiled clearly develops bitterness, but their own substance retains less of it. And if you keep transferring them into different water they get rid of the bitterness completely. Moreover, astringent apples, medlars and wild pears, while they themselves become sweeter in relation to the amount of boiling, produce a decoction that is astringent. But if you boil only the juices themselves, at first they become more salty, and subsequently also sharp. This is why one must concede that while Phylotimos and Praxagoras know about the juices, one must consider the reverse to be the case with the solid parts. For, as I said a little earlier, if one transfers them from the first into a second water, and after that into a third or even a fourth, he will discover that they 733 completely get rid of the original flavour, so that they appear watery and bland to the taste. But when they have not been transferred into different water, it is inevitable that the decoction first becomes more salty and subsequently sharp. Especially, I think that the Praxagorean school were deceived by the fact that the sauce becomes more salty during boiling, not recognizing that since the salt and fish sauce in the original dressing had been introduced into the water, inevitably as boiling proceeds the juice becomes more salty of itself, just as if you were to mix the smallest amount of salt with clean sweet water without introducing any solids. For this becomes salty on heating, too. And what wonder? For this finest water, when boiled for a longer period, eventually takes on a salty quality also.

32 On molluscs

Since, in everybody, what surrounds the whole of our body, like some garment we are born with, is called skin, and the covering in whelks, 734 purple shellfish, oysters, clams and others of the sort is analogous to it, for this reason they are called pottery-skinned animals. At any rate, the covering that surrounds them externally is very like pottery or stone. Now, it is a common feature of all such animals that in their flesh they have salty juice that moves our bowels. But the range in both quality and quantity in this juice is specific to each animal.

For oysters' flesh is the softest of all the molluscs, but small clams, razor-shells, mussels, purple shellfish, trumpet shells and others of the sort have firm flesh. So it is understandable that oysters empty the stomach more while providing less nutriment to the body; and that the firm-fleshed molluscs are more difficult to concoct but are more nourishing. All these last are boiled, but people eat oysters unboiled; some people also fry them.

Just as firm-fleshed molluscs have flesh that is difficult to concoct, so is it also hard to corrupt, and consequently we often administer them 735 to those who are corrupting food in the stomach due to an unhealthy state of the humours that flow down into it from the liver, or are contained within its coats. As I said, all molluscs contain a salty juice that promotes gastric emptying, but the firm-fleshed ones contain less than the oysters. This is why we give them to people who are corrupting food, after boiling them two or three times in the best water and transferring them into clean water when the previous water now appears salty. A great deal of so-called crude humour is produced from them, and from the soft-fleshed ones, mucus too. So as well as being difficult to corrupt, when they have got rid of the salty juice so also does the flesh become costive to the stomach. Similarly, if one dresses them with salt and fish sauce (as they usually do with clams) and drinks the resulting sauce, the stomach is adequately emptied but the man's body gets no nutriment from it.

33   On crustaceans

Lobsters, *pagouroi, karkinoi,** langoustes, prawns, freshwater crays and those others that have a surrounding shell that is thin, but like mol- 736 luscs in hardness, while they have less salty juice than molluscs, even so they have a good deal of it. All of them are firm-fleshed and so are both difficult to concoct and nutritious, that is to say, when they have first been boiled in fresh water. Their flesh also, like the flesh of oysters, acts to check the stomach contents when, as stated, it gives up the salty juice in the water after it has been first boiled. Accordingly, like the hard molluscs, these are hard to corrupt.

34   On cephalopods [*malakia*]

The animals with skin that is neither scaly nor rough, nor pottery-like, but soft as in man, are called cephalopods. These are the polyps, cuttlefish, squid and the others that resemble these. They appear soft when touched because they have a covering that is neither scaly nor rough, nor like pottery. They are firm of flesh, hard to concoct, and in themselves have a small amount of salty juice. However, if they are concocted they contribute quite a lot of nutriment to the body. They also produce a very great quantity of crude humour.

35 On cartilaginous fish [*selachia*] 737

The skin of such animals is rough and shines in the night. This is why some say that the cartilaginous fish have themselves taken their name from the fact of possessing brightness [*selas*]. Among them the electric ray and the stingray have flesh that is soft, as it is also tasty, passing in the stomach with moderate ease and being concocted without difficulty. But it is also moderately nutritious like all other soft-fleshed fish. A feature common to just about all of these is that the parts at the tail are more fleshy than the middle parts. Especially is this the case with the electric ray. For you see, the middle parts of these animals seem to have within themselves what is very like soft cartilage. Skates, rays, monkfish and all like them are firmer, more difficult to concoct and contribute more nutriment for the body than the electric ray and the stingray.

36 On the cetaceous animals

Something has been said previously about the cetaceous animals in the sea, among which are the seals, whales, dolphins and hammerhead 738 sharks, and the large tunny;* and as well as these, dogfish and other such creatures. But now one must say about them, in summary, that all animals like these have flesh that is firm, unwholesome and full of residues. Because of this, people for the most part bring them into use by first pickling them, making the nutriment which they distribute to the body more fine in substance, and with this the potential for it to be concocted more rapidly and to be more readily converted into blood. For, you see, fresh flesh, when it has not been very well concocted, accumulates the greatest amount of crude humour in the veins.

37 On sea urchins

People eat them with honeyed wine, and with fish sauce to move the bowels, and they prepare dishes from them by adding eggs, honey and pepper. They are one of the poorly nourishing foodstuffs that are of average property as regards thinning and thickening the humours.

38   On honey

Up to this point the entire matter of foods has been encompassed by two
classes, one of them belonging to plants, the other to animals. But honey   739
is separate from each of them. For it occurs upon the leaves of plants, but
is neither their juice, nor their fruit, nor a part of them but, while being
of the same class as dewdrops, it is neither so regularly nor so equally
abundant as they are. But I am aware that once in summer such a great
deal of it was found on the leaves of trees, shrubs and certain herbs that
the farmers said jokingly, 'Zeus rained honey.' The previous night had
been pleasantly cool, as happens in summer (for it was summer at the
time), but the day before there had been a hot and dry blending of the
air. Accordingly, those with expertise in nature thought that vapour from
the earth and the waters, having become quite thin and baked from the
sun's heat, accumulated from condensation due to the chill at night. In
our region this is rarely seen to take place, but in the Lebanese mountains
it occurs very often each year; so that by spreading skins on the ground
and shaking the trees they collect on them what flows off, and fill vessels
and pots with honey, calling it honeydew or air-honey.*

Now it is clear that the material for the production of honey is some-   740
thing of the same type as dewdrops, but it appears that something, for
good and bad, has been added to it by the plants upon whose leaves
it is being collected, and as a result it is finest where thyme and certain
other herbs and shrubs that are hot and dry in blending occur in greatest
quantity. For that very reason honey produced on such leaves is of very
fine substance, and so is easily changed to bile in warm bodies. But it is
most suitable for cold bodies whether they are in such a state through
age, disease or their own nature. Further, these latter bodies are naturally
nourished by the honey's being converted into blood, since in hot bodies
it is converted to bile before it can become blood. Being fine in substance
it necessarily has some bitterness, as a result of which it stimulates gastric
emptying. So by removing this feature from it we make it more suitable
for both distribution and nutrition. The best way to do this is by first
mixing it with a lot of water, and then boiling it until foaming ceases.
Of course one should remove the foam from it as soon as it forms. For
with such preparation it loses its bitterness and, the bowel no longer   741
being stimulated to excretion, all is quickly distributed.

But *melikraton* that has been boiled briefly, or not at all, is evacuated
before it can be concocted and distributed to, and nourish, the body.
A further difference between them lies in the fact that the incompletely

boiled one generates some wind in the stomach and intestines, but the one that has got rid of all froth on boiling is non-flatulent and also diuretic. But if one licks up the honey on its own, unmixed with water, it is less nourishing but more aperient. If one takes more of it, it usually provokes the upper alimentary tract into vomiting. When boiled without water, it is neither emetic to the same extent, nor aperient, but is better distributed and more nourishing. This latter stimulates urine flow less than the one boiled with water.

However, not even when they are nourishing do they provide a worthwhile nutriment to the body, so that some have thought that they are not nourishing at all. But enough was said in the third book of Hippocrates' *On Regimen in Acute Diseases*, which some entitle *Against the Cnidian Maxims* 742 and others *On Ptisane*, although both are in error, as indicated in my commentaries* upon it. But in the present work it is better to say no more about it than I have already said. To summarize, this was that it is suitable for the aged and, generally speaking, those with a cold body blending, but that it is turned to bile in those in the prime of life and those with warm blending; and that we get a little nutriment when it has not already changed to bile, since if this occurs it cannot then give any nourishment at all.

It is clear that I mean that the pale-yellow bile is generated from it, not the black. For already it has often been said in many passages that it is customary among physicians to call this sort simply bile, with no qualification as regards colour, and to describe all other biles by the name of the colour. All others except the greenish bile are manifestly evacuated with difficulty when the body is ailing. But yellowish bile, and the pale and greenish one, are often vomited and passed in the motions in the absence of illness.

39 On wine   743

Everyone agrees that wine is one of the things that give nourishment, and if, indeed, everything that nourishes is food, one would have to say that wine also would be one of the class of foods. But some physicians assert that one should not call it food. At any rate in their accounts drink, which is also called draught (as food is also called victuals, foodstuffs and eatables) is to be distinguished from food. So because of this they think it wrong to call wine food. However, they agree that it gives nourishment, which is what we require in the present context. If they had conceded that some other substances are nourishing but that they baulked at calling them foods, we could have collected instruction about all of them in a single book. But since they only think it wrong to call wine a food although it gives nourishment, they will concur with my appending the discussion about it, brief as it is, to the work on food. For the properties of wine about which Hippocrates wrote in *On Regimen in Acute Diseases* are not properties *qua* food, but rather properties *qua* medicament. Now I have explained these in the third of my commentaries on that book; in my treatise *On the Therapeutic Method*; and in my *On Hygiene*. But starting from that point, in the present work I shall speak of the features that 744 distinguish wine in the giving of nourishment.

The thick, red ones are the most useful of all wines for the production of blood,* since they require the least change into it; and after these are the wines that are dark and at the same time sweet and thick; then the ones that are dark red in colour and thick in consistency, combining with these features some astringent quality. The white, thick, harsh wines are less nourishing than these, and the wines that are white in colour but thin in consistency are the least nourishing of all, very close, I suppose, to the water that is appropriate for what is called *hydromêlon*.* Their nature indicates, and experience bears witness to the fact, that thick wines are more nutritious than thin ones. But the sweet wines are more concocted in the stomach and better distributed than the harsh ones, since they are warmer in property. The thick ones are much more slowly concocted, just as they are more slowly distributed; but when they chance upon a strong stomach, so that they are well concocted, they provide more nutriment for the body. It is clear that, just as they are better than the 745 thinner wines for nutrition, so are they worse for the production of urine.

40   On things that have been omitted from the discussion up to now

I have been putting off to the end of this work speaking about pickled foods and neutral foods. So that I do not neglect these, now is the time to discuss the properties of each separately.

On pickled foods

The bodies of animals with flesh that is firm and full of residue are suitable for pickling. As was stated in an earlier comment, I mean by 'full of residue' fleshes that have interspersed within themselves a moisture that is rather full of phlegm. And to the extent that this is greater in amount and thicker, so is the flesh better when pickled. But animals with either a very soft or very dry and residue-free state of the body are unsuitable for pickling. For the property of salt, as shown in my treatise *On Simple Drugs*, is compounded from the dispersion of surplus moisture 746 from whatever bodies it comes into association with, and from reducing and contracting them. While foam of nitre and loose nitre foam* can reduce and disperse, they cannot contract or compress.

Accordingly those bodies that are naturally dry become withered and inedible when sprinkled with salt. Anyone who has tried to pickle hare produces what looks like mummified weasels! But the flesh of pigs that are at their prime, and fat, is suitable for pickling since it has avoided each of two faults – the dryness of aged pigs and the disproportionate moistness of young pigs. For just as dry bodies resemble hides when pickled, in opposite manner those that are extremely moist liquefy and are melted away in the presence of salt. For this reason not even those fish that are soft-fleshed and free from residue – like so-called rock fish and the *oniskos* 747 from the open sea – are suitable for pickling. But *korakinoi*, *mylloi*, small tunny, sardines, pilchards and what are called *saxitana*, are suitable. Also, the cetaceous marine animals are better when pickled since they have flesh that is full of residue. But red mullet are bad for pickling, having flesh that is dry and without residue.

From these things it is clear that fish which become hard, tendinous and like skin and hide when pickled, are all difficult to concoct; but that those that are the reverse of this, being themselves fine in their substance, when taken as a meal thin the thick, viscid humours. The finest that have come to my experience are the pickled fish called *gadeirika* by former physicians (present-day physicians call them *sardai*) and the *mylloi* imported from the Pontus. The *korakinoi*, small tunny and the so-called *saxitana* hold second place after them.

41   On neutral foods

Some foods are neutral as regards all of the differentiae that I said existed amongst foods. For you might find one that is intermediate between those with soft and those with firm flesh, so that it is neither one nor yet the other; and others between what are thinning and what are thickening; or warming and cooling; or drying and moistening.

Foods that are similar to them in nature are suitable for animals that 748 maintain their natural mixture unblemished, but for animals with bad mixture, whether innate or acquired, it is not the consumption of what is like them that is valuable, but of what is the opposite. For what is by nature perfect is protected by what is alike; but those that are unsoundly mixed are brought to their proper mixture by foods that are their opposites. For this reason what is neutral will be specific to the nature of each animal – such and such for a man, such and such for a dog, and such and such for every other animal. And, for a man as a separate individual, such and such as regards age and, as well, differences in occupation, customs and the district in which he has dwelt for a long time.

Commentary

K. 454 Theoretical argument...From this opening paragraph Galen clearly has in mind the epistemological debate about the nature of medical knowledge. On the one hand there was the view that it could be revealed by a theoretical approach, one which we might now call deductive but which at that time was termed Rational or Dogmatic (the Greek *dogma* meaning, among other things, doctrine). The holders of this view, a rather diverse group, stressed the importance of a knowledge of anatomy and physiology, and of understanding the obscure as well as the evident causation of disease. One the other hand there was another view that all therapeutic (and more generally, medical) knowledge was the outcome of experience alone, an approach which we might term inductive, but which then, as indeed now, was referred to as Empirical (from the Greek *empeiria*, meaning experience). And so there were those practitioners who were called *Rationalists* and those termed *Empiricists*. A third group of *Methodists* held quite different views. They did not deny that elements of both the Rationalist and Empiricist positions were of interest, but they did deny that treatment should be based upon them. Instead they postulated three body states, the constricted, the lax and the mixed, which determine the nature of therapy. They also held the view that all of medicine could be learnt in a few months, and required no prior education in philosophy, mathematics and the like. It is little wonder that a physician of Galen's background regarded them with some contempt – 'that mad, unmethodical sect'[1] – although they included in their number such a prominent physician as Soranus of Ephesus, for whom Galen did have respect. Methodism aside, there must have been many physicians who gave whole-hearted allegiance to neither the Rationalist nor the Empiricist point of view, seeing virtues in both and adopting a more or less eclectic approach. However, there is little reason to believe

[1] *On the Therapeutic Method* K. x.51 (Hankinson's translation).

153

that a physician's epistemological stance would have had any significant effect upon his actual practice.

As Frede has pointed out,[2] Galen was an eclectic only in the sense that he saw some virtue in both Rationalist and Empiricist positions. His approach could often be regarded as Rationalist, and much of his *On the Natural Faculties* seems to support this view, but it was a highly qualified approach in that, as he makes clear in this present work, it was available only to a select few, and in any case its conclusions would be vitiated if they were not supported by experience.

In antiquity the situation was described in some detail by the Roman encyclopaedist Celsus;[3] and there is a very good modern treatment in Michael Frede's introduction to the translations in Walzer and Frede.[4]

without demonstration... Galen is using an ordinary word – *apodeixis* – in a technical sense. The role of demonstration is prominently discussed in Aristotle's *Posterior Analytics*:

> By demonstration I mean a scientific deduction; and by scientific I mean one in virtue of which, by having it, we understand something;

and again:

> demonstration depends on universals and induction on particulars and it is impossible to consider universals except through induction... and it is impossible to get an induction without perception...[5]

Aristotle was developing the logical foundations of an axiomatized science, in which knowledge arises from axioms, or first principles. But an axiom (say, that a line is the shortest distance between two points) is certainly not represented in human DNA. What is represented there is perception (the capacity to feel, see, hear and smell), the ability to remember, and the potential for the development of rational thought. This brings out the point of the second half of this quotation, that axioms are derived by a process of induction. Aristotle makes clear[6] that the axioms upon which deduction rests must themselves be the product of (repeated) perception, the preservation of perceptions in memory (since perception without memory has no point in this context), the significance of which is grasped by the *nous*, the application of the intellect, which Barnes[7] plausibly argues is comprehension and not, as many commentators would have

[2] Frede (1981) 70.   [3] *On Medicine* proem 12–17 = Loeb *De medicina* 1, 6–10.
[4] Walzer and Frede (1985) xx–xxxiv.
[5] *Posterior Analytics* 71b17; 81a40–81b1 (Barnes's translation).   [6] *Posterior Analytics* 99b14–100a9.
[7] Barnes (1975) 256.

it, intuition. In other words there has been a process of induction, albeit an inductive process that operates at a different level from what we usually refer to by that name, that requires the application of *nous* (intellect, intuition, comprehension) to bear fruit. The question then arises, what is Galen referring to when he speaks in the next paragraph of 'perception or a clear mental concept'? Frede[8] has pointed to 'a shift in focus' from Aristotle's approach in the *Posterior Analytics*, in which knowledge was less concerned with new things than with the theoretical understanding of things already known, to one which asked how new things are found. To accommodate this shift Galen developed his own logical approach. For only through logical method could truth and falsity be recognized. As to this logical method, Barnes[9] identifies two main parts and one minor one, but that to which Galen is attracted here is the method of demonstration (*apodeixis*) worked out by Aristotle in which, starting from first principles, successive deductions finally lead to proof. In *On the Therapeutic Method*[10] Galen set most store on the demonstrative method, in which the truths of medicine were either primary, indemonstrable, self-justifying propositions, namely axioms, or derivative from them, namely theorems. In fact he went beyond Aristotle who, as pointed out by Ross,[11] had had in mind a fully developed science, beyond the stage of enquiry, like mathematics and, especially, geometry. Galen, however, believed that the method could be applied not only to the 'hard' sciences like geometry, but also to empirical disciplines like biology, and the empirical art of medicine. As Barnes puts it, 'the science of medicine is essentially empirical, and its axioms must include matters of empirical fact...'; and further, 'among the first principles of an empirical science will be propositions known by empirical observation'.[12] This is, in effect, what Galen says in *On Mixtures*,[13] when he states that the starting-points of any demonstration are 'those related to both clear perception and clear comprehension' (*ta pros aisthêsin te kai noêsin eisin enargê*). He puts it with more precision in his *Introduction to Logic*:

As human beings, we all know one kind of evident things through sense perception and another through sole intellectual intuition (*noêsin*); and these we know without demonstration but things known neither by sense perception nor by intellectual intuition, we know by demonstration...[14]

---

[8] Frede (1981) 75.   [9] Barnes (1991) 66–8.   [10] *On the Therapeutic Method* K. x.50.
[11] Ross (1995) 43.   [12] Barnes (1991) 71–2.
[13] *On Mixtures* K. 1.590 = Helmreich 51, 14–15 = Singer (1997) 239.
[14] *Institutio logica* 1.1 = Kieffer 31 (Kieffer's translation).

and he goes on to point out that demonstration is not merely from things already known, but from things already known 'that are proper to what is sought to be demonstrated'; in other words, in the present context, things appropriate to medical science. With the proviso that Barnes would prefer us to read 'comprehension' rather than 'intuition', this is the point of Galen's 'either in perception or in a clear mental concept' in the present work.

455 Diocles...of Carystus in Euboea flourished about the same time as Aristotle and, as Galen implies, was regarded as a leading example of the Rationalist or Dogmatic approach, although it is unlikely that the epistemological split had been formally recognized at that time. Galen's point is that even one with such a viewpoint did not wholly eschew the empiricist approach. There is useful comment upon Diocles in Smith.[15] The work mentioned survives only in fragments such as the one that Galen is about to quote. These were first published by Wellmann in *Die Fragmente der sikelischen Ärtze*, but the definitive edition, which is more complete than that of Wellmann, is now that by van der Eijk, recently published.[16] This very detailed work became available to me only during the final revision of this book, but my own translations have greatly benefited from it. I have not, however, always followed van der Eijk in his identification of the various cereals.

457 indication...*endeixis* – once again, an ordinary word that was used in a technical sense by those of Rationalist persuasion, to identify those signs that allowed one to make inferences from what can be observed to discover what cannot. It is one of the two ways of accounting for phenomena, the other being insight. In his *Introduction to Logic*, Galen asserts that 'men call "indication" the discovery of the truth about the thing in question arising out of the nature of the thing and made through following out the clues given by what is clearly observable'.[17] Kudlien thinks that Galen commonly used the word in the modern sense of 'indication', that is, as related to therapy,[18] but this is only tenuously so in the present context.

Mnesitheos...of Athens, of the fourth century BC. His views were such as to qualify him in Galen's eyes as a Dogmatist. In his *On Venesection against Erasistratus* Galen included him approvingly in a list of proponents of blood-letting as a form of therapy.[19] He was credited by the comic author Eubulus, no doubt with tongue in cheek, as asserting that bile

---

[15] Smith (1979) 181–8.   [16] Van der Eijk (2000).   [17] *Institutio logica* XI.1. (Keiffer's translation).
[18] Kudlien (1991) 104.   [19] *On Venesection against Erasistratus* K. XI.163 = Brain (1986) 25.

was caused to flow at the ninth cup of wine, and madness occurred at the tenth![20] The extant fragments, with an extended essay on the man himself, are to be found in Bertier.[21]

458 distinguishing criteria... *diorismos* – often translated as definition – had a particular technical meaning, the important feature of which is that it is not only *descriptive* of an attribute but includes the explanation or *cause* of it (i.e., in Aristotelian terms, the efficient cause or the 'how'; and the final cause or the 'why').

Erasistratus... of Ceos. One of the two great Alexandrian physicians of whom we have knowledge, the other being Herophilus. An agnostic so far as the humoral theory of disease was concerned, he was a favourite target for Galen's barbs. However, it is apparent, if only from the virulence with which he attacks Erasistratus' views, that Galen held him in considerable respect. None of his works exists in its entirety. The extant fragments have been edited by Garofalo (1988).

melikrat... a mixture of honey and water. The physician Dioscorides describes this at length:

Melikraton possesses the same qualities as *oenomeli* [a wine–honey mixture]... We use it boiled for those who have a feeble pulse, are weak, have a cough, suffer from pulmonary inflammation and are wasted... *Melikraton* is prepared by mixing one part of honey with two of old rainwater and standing it in the sun. Others make a mixture with spring water, then store it after they have boiled it three times...[22]

Patients with weakness, cough and pulmonary inflammation make one think of pulmonary tuberculosis or some suppurative condition of the lung like abscess or bronchiectasis.

even encounter the opposite... Galen here shows his recognition of the phenomenon of human variability – an acknowledgement of the fact that individuals react to identical stimuli in individual ways – which he expresses on many occasions, and which is the antithesis of the more rigidly doctrinaire approach of the true Dogmatist.

459 innate heat... or their natural warmth. The concept of innate or natural heat had been developed in considerable detail by Aristotle in, for example, the group of brief treatises known collectively as the *Parva naturalia*. Its source, he thought, was the heart, and the *psychê* or 'soul' (or, as we might better say, 'life force') was dependent upon it, for in its absence life ceased. As will be seen, it was believed to be an essential

[20] Alfageme (1995) 570.   [21] Bertier (1972).
[22] *On the Materials of Medicine* v.9 = Wellmann III.12–13.

participant in a range of body functions, being analogous in some ways to the modern notion of energy, an analogy made more pointed by the fact that while it was increased by, and was dependent upon, the consumption of food, it was in turn an essential element in the whole 'digestive' process – from concoction within the stomach to the elaboration of humours within the venous system, and the subsequent assimilation of nutrient material for tissue growth or replacement. Here, Galen is looking at it as one component of the individual's natural mixture, blending or temperament, in which it is appropriately balanced by the other active quality, cold, to act upon the balanced pair of the two passive qualities, moist and dry.

460 pottery-skinned animals . . . *ta ostrakoderma*, that is, molluscs, which Galen will deal with in III.32 (K. 734–5).

461 fish sauce . . . *garum*, the Latin name for a condiment which figures prominently in this work, is in Greek *garos*. Prepared from salted fish entrails allowed to stand in the sun and ferment, its closest modern equivalent may be the *nam pla* of Thai cuisine. It was widely used as a condiment over many centuries throughout the Mediterranean world and is mentioned by a number of ancient authors. Dioscorides refers to its pharmacological properties.[23] The definitive modern work is without doubt the exhaustive monograph by Curtis, with copious references to Galen.[24] At a time when food preservation was always a problem it was very popular, and the subject of an economically significant trade.

464 other biles . . . It is not clear what Galen has in mind by these. As described above, in the introduction, of the four traditional humours or body fluids there were two biles, one yellow and the other black. Here he seems to be differentiating the biles not only in terms of colour but of grades of colour, as well as in terms of some unstated relationship to disease. So too, he has just noted variation in types of mucus. Clearly his classificatory system had some flexibility.

handled differently . . . Galen is looking at the question of why the same foods are differently treated in different individuals in respect of the ease or otherwise of evacuation and concludes that there are three reasons. The first is the natural disposition of the alimentary tract (i.e., its innate mixture of qualities) and this is a constant for the individual. The second is the balance of solid/liquid that may reinforce or inhibit the effects of the natural disposition. The third is the presence or absence

---

[23] *On the Materials of Medicine* II.32 = Wellmann I.132.
[24] Curtis (1991), especially chap. 3. See also Dalby (1996) 75–6; 199–200; and Purcell (1995) 132–49.

of bile or mucus, which have the effect of reinforcing what is similar in the natural disposition, and counteracting what is dissimilar.

Epidemics...[25] The actual words Galen uses, which I have translated as eatables, nutriments, foodstuffs and comestibles (but any of similar meaning would be equally acceptable) are, respectively, *edesta*, *trophai*, *sitia* and *brômata*. Galen's point is that they all mean much the same thing and that there is no need to be pedantic about the choice.

466 remain unconcocted...For the word used by Galen, *meteôra*, LSJ has a primary meaning of 'off the ground', 'suspended in mid-air', but it may also have a sense of 'unsettled, fermenting, undigested'. Jones's 'rumbling', in his translation of the Hippocratic *Aphorisms*,[26] goes even further.

467 bowel evacuation...or, perhaps less likely, gastric emptying. This is a good example of the ambiguity associated with these words.

barley water...Galen uses the term *ptisanê*, that is, a ptisan, or decoction of barley, either barley water or barley gruel, highly regarded for its medicinal properties in his time, and valued as a standby in home nursing until quite recently.

Hippocrates...The source of the quotation is *Nutriment* 19 – 'In nutriment purging excellent, in nutriment purging bad; bad or excellent according to circumstances.'[27]

468 qualitative alteration...That is to say, food *qua* nutriment alone is not to be regarded as a drug, since nutrition is purely a physiological activity. But if it results in something which is not a normal physiological activity – and this seems to be the case with abnormal warming, and so forth – the action is to be regarded as pharmacological. It seems likely that Galen did not intend us to regard such action as necessarily pathological (it could be therapeutic) but clearly this could be so. He deals at greater length with what he believed was the essential distinction between drug and food in *On Mixtures*[28] This is that a food undergoes assimilation into the body tissue; a drug does not. A drug affects the body; but a food is affected by the body. The distinction may be absolute but commonly the substance can be both food and drug. Before it is assimilated it may act *qua* drug (it may be heating, for example); but the final process of assimilation sees it acting *qua* food (it may take part in growth, for example). In the terms of a modern pharmacologist,

[25] *Epidemics* 11.2,11 = Loeb *Hippocrates* vii, 34; vi.6,2 = Loeb *Hippocrates* vii, 262.

[26] *Aphorisms* iv.72 = Loeb *Hippocrates* iv, 155.

[27] *Nutriment* 19 = Loeb *Hippocrates* i, 348 (Jones's translation).

[28] *On Mixtures* K. 1.681–4 = Helmreich 107–9 = Singer (1997) 283.

Galen's discussion covers both pharmaco-kinetics, the effect of the body on the drug/food, and pharmacodynamics, the effect of the drug/food upon the body. The physico-chemical detail of necessity is lacking, but one cannot fault Galen's conceptual thinking.

471 the mouth of the stomach... phlegm... One must assume that this patient had complained of epigastric pain or discomfort, and that this would usually have indicated a 'mouth of the stomach' or cardio-oesophageal problem, to Galen, but that something in the patient's history had led him to what he believed to be the correct diagnosis of an accumulation of phlegm.

473 in that work... He is referring here to his *On the Mixtures and Properties of Simple Drugs*.[29]

all men of old... Philistion of Locri Epizephyrii in southern Italy (early fourth century) has been thought to have influenced Plato. His fragments have been edited by Wellmann; Ariston is mentioned by Galen on several occasions; Euryphon was a Cnidian physician whose views on the noxious effects of nutritional residues are mentioned in the *Anonymus Londinensis* (sometimes referred to as the '*Menon Papyrus*'); nothing seems to be known of Philetas.

On Regimen... It is easy for confusion to arise here. Galen is referring to the Hippocratic works which we now know as *Regimen I, II, III* and *IV*, the last, also known as *Dreams*, being taken by him as part of the third book. The work he refers to as the second part of three books is *Regimen I*, and the alternative opening words are at chapters xxxvii and xxxix of the modern version (numbering begins with *Regimen I*), the former being the preferred one today. It is this book which, standing alone, he calls *On Regimen*. When the books are taken as one, this was called, he says, *On the Nature of Man and Regimen*. However, in antiquity a different Hippocratic *Nature of Man* was associated with a work called *Regimen in Health*. By the time of Galen these two works were treated as different entities as they are now, and in fact Galen wrote separate commentaries, which have survived, about both works. Wilkins deals authoritatively and at some length with the matter of *Regimen II* in his foreword to the present work, to which reference should be made. There is also discussion by W. H. S. Jones in the Loeb edition of Hippocrates, and also by Smith.[30] Smith seems to think that Galen was himself the cause of some ambiguity, giving examples of the way in which,

[29] *On the Mixtures and Properties of Simple Drugs* K. XI.359–XII.377.
[30] Loeb *Hippocrates* IV, xxxviii–xxxix; Smith (1979) 59; 116–17.

over a period, he was inconsistent in the way he identified the various *Regimens*.

476 bitter aloes...copper ore...*aloê* is aloe vera. The copper compounds are respectively, in the Greek, *chalkos kekaumenos, chalkanthos, anthos chalkou, lepis* and *chalkitis*. All are listed and more fully discussed by Dioscorides,[31] who deals with their pharmacological properties at length. Pliny the Elder has a good deal on copper in its various forms in his *Natural History*. Pharmacologically, it is evident, as Galen implies, that the useful property of all the compounds was their astringency, which was employed in the reduction of granulation tissue (the 'proud flesh' which can be a cause of slow healing of wounds), and in exuberant tissue in other sites such as the nose or the anus. It also found a place as a topical application in ophthalmology. Until quite recently, and even occasionally today, it had an acknowledged place in the therapeutic armamentarium for the treatment of granulation tissue – Douthwaite[32] remarked upon its astringent and haemostatic effects in dilute solution. LSJ gives 'rock alum' for this particular instance of *chalkitis*, but there does not seem to be any justification for this. Pliny the Elder is quite clear in his own mind that it is an ore from which copper is obtained by smelting, and the Loeb editor suggests that he is speaking of copper pyrites, which is a sulphur compound, and that *chalkitis* contained copper, pyrites and marcasite.[33]

477 Herakleides of Tarentum...flourished in the first half of the first century BC, and was a pupil of Mantias, himself a pupil of Herophilus. The extant fragments have been most recently edited by Guardasole.[34] The same author, in an earlier article, emphasizes his importance in the development of the Empirical school.[35] There are frequent references to him as a 'renegade Herophilean' in von Staden's account of Herophilus and the Alexandrian school.[36]

478 sweet fish sauce...Curtis expresses some puzzlement about this. He thinks that it may have been made by the addition of honey.

such dispositions...Here and in the succeeding paragraph Galen is saying that an understanding of the disposition of the individual patient should be prior to the use of any food or the application of any therapy, the latter view being at the root of the 'modern' preoccupation with holistic medicine. There are some interesting aspects to this. Clearly, Galen is as wary of a rule of thumb approach to nutrition, as he is to

---

[31] *On the Materials of Medicine* v.76; 98; 77; 78; 99 respectively.   [32] Douthwaite (1963) 359ff.
[33] Loeb *Natural History* IX, 214; and see Bailey (1932), part II, 164–7; Healy (1978) 309; 317–19.
[34] Guardasole (1997).   [35] Guardasole (1995).   [36] Von Staden (1989), s.v. Herophilus.

the same in therapeutics. He again insists that there is variability in the human condition, in this case in the disposition, which we know from elsewhere may be an acquired or an innate state (nowhere does he say that an innate disposition is inherited, however). The discussion in these and the following paragraphs depends upon Galen's use of the verb *diorizein*, which variously means distinguish, define, delimit. In an interesting article van der Eijk[37] states his belief that Galen used the word, in its various forms, to insist that experience of a condition or testing of a theory only have validity if qualifying factors such as age, or environment, or disposition, are taken into account. So that where, in the next paragraph, I translate *diôrismenê peira* as 'defining test' he would prefer 'qualifying experience'. If I have understood him correctly, we are, in effect, speaking of the same thing, which is the need to define, or subsequently diagnose, a disease by relating the results of observation to all significant (internal or external) variables.

480 naked wheats... or free-threshing, as opposed to hulled. The classification of the varieties of wheat, and to some extent of wheat derivatives, has been a source of discussion since antiquity. The ancient sources for this discussion include the Greek Theophrastus and the Romans Pliny the Elder and Columella, to name but three. Modern views stem from the work of Jasny, were developed by Moritz and later Jardé, and have been set out most recently, and I believe authoritatively, by Zohary and Hopf.[38] One can identify several sources of confusion, of which the most important has been the plethora of classificatory criteria that have been used over the years – such as, to mention the chief ones used, whether the grain was hulled or free-threshing; whether the seed was sown in spring or autumn; the number of rows in the ear of grain; whether the seed was soft or 'vitreous' (and thus its milling potential); the colour. Thus there developed a corresponding plethora of spurious 'species'. Progress in developing a better-based taxonomy has resulted from a more secure understanding of the ancient sources (for example, the recognition that autumn sowing was the norm, as Hesiod had pointed out in his *Works and Days* long ago, and that spring sowing was merely an emergency procedure when the autumn crop had failed); and from a classificatory rationalization arising from advances in the study of genetics. Zohary and Hopf[39] have dealt with the subject in detail, and Sallares[40] gives a complementary account of great value. It is due to these

[37] Van der Eijk (1997).
[38] Jasny (1944); Moritz (1958); Jardé (1979); Zohary and Hopf (1994).
[39] Zahary and Hopf (1994) 18–54.   [40] Sallares (1991) 316–32.

authors that we can now say with some assurance that Galen intended the following:

a. *sitos* was, non-specifically, 'cereal', although which sort of cereal may often be inferred from the context.
b. *tiphê* was domesticated einkhorn wheat (*Triticum moncoccum*) and hulled.
c. *zeia* and *olyra* were two varieties of emmer wheat (*T. turgidum* varieties) and hulled. Throughout this translation I refer to them as emmer^z [*zeia*] or emmer^o [*olyra*], according to the text.
d. The *pyroi* were the two species of naked wheat – durum (*T. turgidum*) and bread-wheat (*T. aestivum* or *vulgare*) and this seems clear from the present text.

As to 'spelt', which is a primitive, hulled variety of *T. vulgare* and often mentioned in modern translations, Sallares believes that, although it is certainly present in palaeobotanical studies, it is difficult to identify in the ancient sources.

This leads to the question of the classification of flours, with which Galen will deal shortly. There were two main types, corresponding to the two species of naked wheat. From durum wheat came *semidalis* (Latin *triticum*), whilst from bread-wheat came *silignis* (Latin *siligo*). As Galen points out, this loan word was late entering Greek. The alternative name from earlier times was *sêtanios*. A difficulty with *semidalis* arises from an ambiguity in the English language, since it is often referred to as *aristos* and this can be translated as 'finest'. In the context of flour-milling, that word suggests a physical characteristic. However, as pointed out elsewhere,[41] it was in fact used to describe the bread made from it in terms of its supposed nutritive value. Indeed, durum wheat could not have been milled to produce a fine flour comparable to that from bread-wheat.

482 should not be baked ... kneading ... The interval between kneading and baking, during which gas produced by the action of the yeast or leaven causes the dough to expand or 'rise', is what we now speak of as proving. The word that I have translated as kneading – *malaxis* – is more literally softening, and this is a fair description of the change in the consistency of the bread dough as kneading progresses. Due to changes in the gluten component it also becomes more elastic or, as here, tenacious. The tenacity of dough is an indication of the amount of gluten it contains. The more tenacious, the higher is the gluten content, and the presence of gluten is necessary to bake a properly risen bread.

486 depletion of the body ... This is clearly an important passage for an understanding of Galen's physiology of digestion, but it is

[41] Sallares (1991) 323.

nonetheless something of a puzzle. Plainly, Galen believes that the body which is depleted of food (as a temporary phenomenon; he does not here imply starvation) takes up nutriment more aggressively than the body that is not so depleted. So it seems that the alimentary tract is not just a passive participant in the transfer into the portal venous system of the concocted, partially concocted or unconcocted contents, but has an active role. The means by which this role is expressed is unfortunately not stated. Nor does Galen explain the nature of the troublesome illnesses, or the mechanism of their production.

487 pankration...a particularly savage contest which combined boxing, wrestling and almost every other form of brutal attack – but not, according to *OCD*³, biting or eye gouging, except at Sparta!

488 glutinous humours...The opportunities for confusion that this paragraph offers are great, and stem from the following facts: in Greek *trophê* can refer to the food itself or to the nutriment derived from its concoction; *chymos* also has an even wider range of meanings; and humours, as we use the term, do not exist in the food but are formed within the body. It seems that we are to understand, firstly, that when Galen refers to *trophê* from glutinous humours he is referring to the nutriment that is provided by them; and that elsewhere he is speaking of foods with the *potential* to produce such humours. The important point seems to be that these athletes require foods that are the reverse of 'normal' foods, in which difficulty of corruption allows for more efficient concoction and distribution. The matter of the physical characteristics of the humours – their degree of thickness or thinness – is one to which he often alludes. On this and crude humour, see the note on K. 491.

489/90 as to the breads...Galen describes three different baking techniques. The most satisfactory makes use of the pottery *kribanos* or *klibanos* – the same as the Roman *clibanus* or *testum*. There is a good account of this, with line drawings, by Cubberley.[42] Essentially it was a bell-shaped cover standing on a plate, and heated from underneath. From the dimensions given it must have been for domestic use. The *ipnos*, also translated in LSJ as 'furnace', must have been on a larger scale for commercial (or perhaps communal) use. The word that I translate as ash-hidden – *engryphias* – describes the baking of the loaf on a pottery tile placed in the coals. The particular virtue of the *kribanos* seems to have been that the pottery from which it was made took up moisture from the dough.

[42] Cubberley (1995) 55–68.

490 in respect of those features only...This is an example of Galen's intuitive grasp of a fundamental principle of statistical inference, namely, that a variable under investigation must be dealt with in abstraction from other variables. There are other examples in this work, not the least interesting being his father's experiments with contaminants in wheat and barley, related in 1.37 (K. 552).

tagênitai **and** *têganitai*...The essential feature is that they are cooked in a pan called a *tagênon* – a frying pan. Whether Galen is speaking of pancakes, as some have thought,[43] or some type of fritter or flapjack, one really cannot go past Grant's neat translation of *tagênitai / têganitai* as 'griddle/girdle',[44] which I give here, even though Galen does not give enough information to say whether his flour and water mixture was a batter or a dough. Indeed, in the absence of any binding agent like oil or honey one could be forgiven for wondering if the result was merely a disintegrating mess!

491 crude humours...Galen commonly refers to a humour as crude (*ômos*). The translation could equally well be 'raw', 'uncooked' or even 'unconcocted'. The point seems to be that the humour as first elaborated in the body requires further concoction to become good or healthy humour (for example, the *chrêstos haima* or useful blood to which Galen often refers), and that, as in the present case, certain foods produce a humour that is difficult to take past the crude, poorly concocted stage

493 *On the Thinning Diet*...[45] 'I myself know that in the case of kidney complaints and many joint problems (where the joints have not yet been found to be full of stones), some have been shown to remit completely on this sort of diet, and others moderately so.' In spite of the title in English translation this is not a book on slimming, but is to do with thinning the humours or body fluids. Thick humours were seen as causes of illness. See the comment by Wilkins in the foreword.

494 light bread...The adjective used – *plytos* – has a primary meaning of washed. But for this specific reference, where it qualifies *artos* (loaf or, generically, 'bread'), LSJ has 'light'. Certainly it is difficult to see how washed would suit the context. The last sentence seems to say something about the ordinary bread of the times! The part of the paragraph that has been translated literally (airy and earthy) could imply light in texture, and dense or heavy. However, it is important to note that the words Galen is using refer to two of the four traditional elements that underlie

---

[43] Dalby and Grainger (1996) 38.   [44] Grant (2000) 82.
[45] *CMG* v.4.2,433; and see Singer (1997) 305–24.

all matter – earth, air, fire and water. Which is not to say that he would have thought that earth had actually entered into the bread, so much as that the four elements were inescapable components of his reasoning, even if he would not necessarily have taken them literally.

495 the weakest sites... This is an important statement, which is no less true today. One can instance the development of osteoarthritis as a consequence of football knee; or the occurrence of bacterial endocarditis upon a previously damaged heart valve. Even with the idea of superfluous material we think of the disordered metabolism which results in gout, when uric acid, accumulating in excess because it is not dealt with by the body in the usual way, is deposited in joints, especially joints which are under stress.

496 wheat family... For a more precise identification we can turn to Dioscorides, who says that groats are obtained from 'so-called *dikokkos zea*', that is, emmer[z] (*Triticum turgidum*, previously *dicoccum*).[46] Galen, however, quite clearly is using the term here to refer more generally to 'wheat' regardless of species. Foxhall and Forbes believed that in some instances the *chondros* of antiquity was identical with the modern Cretan variety, namely, ground wheat boiled with milk to the point at which all milk is absorbed, then sun-dried and stored.[47] Whatever the validity of this view it seems not to be what Galen had in mind on this occasion.

honey-wine... Dioscorides[48] describes two types. The first – *melitês* – consisted of five parts of old wine to one of honey, which was fermented after the addition of salt. The second was that which Galen is presumably describing – *oinomeli* – in which the proportions were two of new wine to one of honey, sometimes boiled together, but with no suggestion of fermentation.

ptisan(e)... Daremberg's translation of 'préparé à la ptisane', in the commentary in the Helmreich edition, seems 'right', although it required slight emendation of the Greek text.

Hippocrates... nutritious... In fact Hippocrates says rather more (and less!): 'Wheat is stronger and more nourishing than barley, but both it and its gruel (*chylos*) are less laxative. Bread made from it without separating the bran (*synkomistos*) dries and passes; when cleaned from the bread it nourishes more but is less laxative.'[49] This passage nowhere mentions groats (*chondros*), and the superior variety is in fact

[46] *On the Materials of Medicine* II.96 = Wellmann I.86; and see also Isager and Skysgaard (1992) 21.
[47] Foxhall and Forbes (1982) 66, n. 84.
[48] *On the Materials of Medicine* v.7–8 = Wellmann III.12–13.
[49] *Regimen* II.42 = Loeb *Hippocrates* IV, 310 (Jones's translation).

white bread; which suggests that here, as he does from time to time, Galen is interpreting Hippocrates to suit his own argument.

501 same potential as wheat...which is also what Hippocrates had said (see preceding note), and one may ask how correct they were. Nutritional data for modern cereals are available from various sources (e.g. the United States Department of Agriculture) but although these are useful, a degree of caution may be necessary when transposing them to ancient times, certainly where bread-wheat is concerned. For it is obvious that there is, and perhaps always has been, great intra-specifc variability with *T. aestivum*, although this does not seem the case with durum wheat, barley, rye or oats. But, although available energy in the harder North American varieties is roughly the same as that in the softer varieties of Britain and Australia, the sources of that energy can vary considerably. This is brought out in the following table, adapted from that given in USDA Nutrient Data Base for Standard Reference (for convenience I include rye and oats):[50]

	Protein	Fat	Carbohydrate	Available energy
	(expressed as grams/100 grams)			(as kilocalories)
Wheat, bread-				
hard red	15.4	1.9	68.0	329
soft white	10.3	1.6	71.2	331
Wheat, durum	13.7	2.5	71.1	339
Barley	12.5	2.3	73.5	354
Barley, pearled	9.9	1.2	77.7	352
Rye	14.8	2.5	69.8	335
Oats	16.9	6.9	66.3	389

Of course these are not the only nutritional components (there are vitamins and minerals, for instance) but it is they that are necessary to permit growth, tissue replacement and energy for all purposes. To the extent that these data reflect the position in antiquity, both Hippocrates and Galen were wrong, for barley is clearly superior to wheat, especially as a source of energy. But of course that is only a part of the story. As Galen would have agreed, the nutritional value of a foodstuff is represented by food preferences as much as by cold figures. In classical antiquity, as Garnsey for one has pointed out, wheat was Roman and barley was Greek (not least because mainland Greece was suited to its cultivation),

[50] USDA (1999), Nutrient Data Base for Standard Reference, Release 13.

but over time and for a variety of reasons Greek preference shifted in favour of wheat.[51] 'The data' may point in one direction for the individual, but for a people the combined preferences of all individuals may well point in another.

503 Hippocrates ... extent ...[52]

504 stickiness ... That is, the flour contains less gluten, or less gluten with the appropriate colloidal properties, which is the essential component for producing a risen bread.

ptisane ... In fact in *Regimen in Acute Diseases* 15, Hippocrates merely said that ptisane should be made from the best barley and should be very well boiled.[53]

505 natural moisture ... Galen is making a distinction between residues of moisture that have become surplus to the plant's requirements; and that moisture which is in accord with its nature, innate, and an integral component of the living plant.

506 barley meal ... *alphita* – usually, as here, in the plural. Moritz[54] makes it clear that the word referred to meal or flour, and particularly to its degree of fineness, and was at first applied to flour from any grain and only later specifically to barley. The term covers *krimna*, where the meal is coarser, and the finer *aleura*.

507 *siraion* ... boiled-down new wine; but also sometimes translated as 'must', which is new wine, or wine in the early stage of manufacture before fermentation is complete.

wheat ... Galen uses the word *sitos*. It may be that this is an example of its identification being determined by context, as mentioned earlier. However Sallares, when referring specifically to this passage, believed that it shows that, for Galen, *sitos* was naked (and by implication) bread-wheat.[55] Some two hundred or so years later, he adds in a footnote, *sitos* had replaced *pyros* in the Egyptian papyri. The latter word has disappeared from modern Greek, where wheat is *sitari*.

508 the openings of the veins reaching down ... the openings in the wall of the stomach and small bowel where the veins were thought to terminate. Galen had to provide an answer to the question of how the concocted material, the *chyme*, entered the veins to be concocted further before being distributed to, and passed on to, and (eventually) assimilated into the tissues.

---

[51] Garnsey (1999) 119–22.   [52] *Regimen in Acute Diseases* 10 = Loeb *Hippocrates* II, 70.
[53] *Regimen in Acute Diseases* 15 = Loeb *Hippocrates* II, 72–4.   [54] Moritz (1958) 149.
[55] Sallares (1991) 348.

5 10 Praxagoras...of Cos of the fourth century B C was an important figure in Greek medicine. He was not only the teacher of Phylotimos but also of Herophilos. None of his works survives except as fragmentary references in other authors, especially Galen. They have been collected and published by Steckerl (1958), who also included the fragments of Phylotimos, among others. Praxagoras is said to have believed in a humoral theory of disease, although he counted a larger number than the eventual canonical four of the Hippocratic *Nature of Man*. The word which I have translated as 'glassy' – *hyalôdê* – is translated by Steckerl as 'vitreous'. But this risks confusion with the modern vitreous humour of the eye.

triptên...The word Galen uses for barley-cake is *maza*, which comes from the verb *massô* – to knead, to press in a mould. The word the Athenians are said to have used is derived from the word meaning to rub – *tribô* – and is probably qualifying an understood *maza*.

5 14 rye [*briza*]...is characteristic of the temperate areas of the Old World, being winter hardy and drought resistant. Given its climatic preferences it is no surprise that it was grown hardly at all in southern Greece. Dioscorides does not mention it, and neither does Theophrastus. It seems that Galen thought that Mnesitheos was describing rye under the name of emmer[z].

5 15 Homer...*Odyssey* IV.604.

the cities...Prusa and Nicaea – in Bithynia, close to the present Sea of Marmara; Crateia (also called Flaviopolis) was a Bithynian city between Claudiopolis and Ancyra (modern Ankara) in Galatia; Claudiopolis and Iuliopolis – in Cilicia, that is, south-west Asia Minor; Dorylaeum – in Galatia, central Asia Minor.

5 16 Theophrastus...The excerpts are from his *Enquiry into Plants* VII.9.2. Aegilops [*aigilops*] is the wild grass which donated the gene that conferred bread-making potential on the bread-wheat *Triticum aestivum*.

Herodotus...*Histories* II.36, where he is describing the cultural characteristics of the Egyptians. The Penguin translator, de Sélincourt, translates *zeia* as spelt, but this is incorrect.

5 17 Dioscorides...[56] Clearly, Dioscorides was astray in his belief that einkhorn was a type of emmer[z], although he recognized the relationship of emmer [*zeia*] and emmer [*olyra*].

5 20 *tragos*...to Dioscorides, this was a form of groats much the same as that derived from emmer[z]. He considered that because of its chaff content it was less nutritious. Jasny[57] thought that it was 'nothing else

---

[56] *On the Materials of Medicine* II.89 83 = Wellmann I.171–2. [57] Jasny (1944) 54–5; 115.

than hulled wheat without the hulls'. The use of 'genus' and 'species', whilst a literal translation, of course does not have the same meaning as it does in our present Linnaean binomial system of classification.

522 Andromache...*Iliad* VIII.188.

524 pulse...All the items listed, with one curious exception, are legumes (or pulse). The exception is rice. This plant has nothing in common with pulse, although it is true that it is a cereal from which bread is not produced. It seems to have been regarded as of little importance. Like Galen in this work, Dioscorides dismisses it in two lines, calling it 'a type of grain grown in marshy and damp sites. It is moderately nutritious and constipating.'[58] As Heiser points out, the legumes constitute 'an extremely large and cosmopolitan family'.[59] Not all plants called beans are legumes (he instances the castor-oil bean), but many different legumes are called beans, peas or pulse. It may be helpful at this stage to list what seems to be an up-to-date version of legume taxonomy. The numbering corresponds to Galen's chapters.

16 – *ospria* (plural) – pulse of all kinds. *SOED* says pulse is the edible seeds of leguminous plants, but the word can also refer to the plant yielding those seeds. It is of interest that there are also two words in Theophrastus, which he seems to apply indiscriminately (in successive lines at *Enquiry into Plants* VIII.1) – *ta ospria* and *ta chedropa*. Galen uses only the first in this work.

18 – *phakos* – lentil – *Lens culinaris*.

19 – *kyamos* – faba bean; broad bean – *Vicia faba*.

20 – *kyamos Aigyptios* – Egyptian bean – *Nelumbium speciosum* (so LSJ). It may be that this is the regional variation of the faba bean for which the modern vernacular alternative is in fact 'Egyptian'. Indeed, since *V. faba* is thought to have originated in the Nile Valley, the faba bean may be a regional variant of the Egyptian!

21 – *pisos* – pea – *Pisum sativum*.

22 – *erebinthos* – chickpea – *Cicer arietinum*.

23 – *thermos* – lupin – *Lupinus albus*.

24 – *têlis* – fenugreek – *Trigonella foenum-graecum*.

25 – *phasêlos* – cowpea – *Vicia unguiculata* (previously *V. sinensis*). *ôchros* – birds' peas – *Lathyrus ochrus*.

26 – *lathyros* – grasspea; chickling vetch – *Lathyrus sativus*.

27 – *arakos* – wild chickling; bird vetch – *L. annuus*.

28 – *dolichos* – LSJ says calavance – *Vigna sinensis*, which is the identical translation given for *phasêlos*. Galen also seems to have been confused.

---

[58] *On the Materials of Medicine* II.95 = Wellmann I.73. [59] Heiser (1990) 119.

He may have been correct in thinking that the two are one and the same.

29 – *horobos* – bitter vetch – *Vicia ervilia.*

36 – *aphakê* – dwarf chickling – *Lathyrus cicera.*
    bikion (so **LSJ** for this reference) – vetch – *Vicia sativa.* Modern Greek for vetch is *bikos.*

526 elephantiasis...We are in something of a nosological wilderness here! Elephantiasis, as the term is used today, refers to a condition in which the extremities in particular become grossly swollen and indurated due to obstruction of the lymphatic channels, classically by microfilariae in the condition known as filariasis. Grmek[60] is almost certainly correct in his view that in antiquity the term was used to refer to leprosy (Hansen's disease). This disease, in its lepromatous form, when advanced produces great thickening and induration of the skin of face and extremities.

dropsical disorder...I have used this for the Greek *hydatôdês kachexia* – literally 'watery disaffection'. Dropsy is a non-specific term (now obsolete) which implied fluid retention due either to cardiac or renal disease.

female flux...This could be menorrhagia, which is an excessive and prolonged menstrual blood loss with, usually, a hormonal basis; bleeding *per vaginam* due to malignancy; or leucorrhoea, which is a persistent whitish vaginal discharge of multiple aetiology. One might guess from the context that the first is the correct translation, but it remains a guess.

528 the same things...constitutions...This paragraph illustrates the pervasiveness of the theory of mixtures of qualities, as well as its intimate relationship to the humoral theory of disease. Moreover, it applies not only to humours, but to the foods themselves and, most importantly, to the environment. The purpose of Galen's recommendations is to ensure that the different sets of mixtures are properly matched, although it is not entirely clear how this is being achieved.

530 bean flour...'freckling'...Skin colour in slaves would have been of no concern, and one must assume the aim was merely to smarten up the product before putting it on the market. The words translated as 'nitre' and 'light nitre' are both given the same meaning by **LSJ** – sodium carbonate, or what we commonly refer to as washing soda. The statement about the removal of moles and freckles is an example of the way a belief which is manifestly incorrect can persist in the mind of even an intelligent and observant physician such as Galen. This is not a failing restricted to antiquity.

---

[60] Grmek (1989) 168–73.

541 *The Merchant Ships*...A play that has not survived.

arachos...with a *chi* (χ) and not a *kappa* (κ), thus ἄραχος [*arachos*] instead of ἄρακος [*arakos*]. The word Galen uses for 'throw away' – *rhipta* – is translated by LSJ for this particular reference as 'winnow'; the Latin version in Kühn uses *detergeo*, which means 'cleanse', amongst other things. Both versions suggest that the bad or useless part is being discarded to leave the useful part. The use of axeweed for comparison suggests that 'throw away' is more appropriate. Just the same, according to Dioscorides (III.130) axeweed was not merely a weed, although it grew as a contaminant amongst wheat and barley, for it was used as an antidote (he does not say against what), was good for the stomach, and when used before intercourse was believed to be contraceptive.[61] So that there would have been some point to winnowing it. Galen returns to axeweed in 1.37 (K. 553), when he discusses his father's experiments on contaminants. See also John Wilkins's earlier comment.

542 mildew...or rust. The passage is at *Enquiry into Plants* VIII.3.2 (Hort's translation here).

543 reed...ink...*kalamos* is a reed, any one of a variety of species, whose name is applied to, amongst other things, the flute, a fishing pole, an arrow shaft or, as here, a writing instrument. Ink is *melan*, the neuter of *melas*, which simply means 'black'.

Hippocrates...*Regimen* II.45.

544 dolichos...This plant appears to have been as much a mystery to Galen as it is to us. His inference seems to be that the juxtaposition of *dolichos* and *ôchros* (birds' pea) indicates a close botanical relationship between the two; and because this comes immediately after mention of peas and beans, the further suggestion is that all four are part of a single family.

546 Ceramos...on the shore of the Ceramicus Gulf (modern Kökova Körfezi) in south-west Asia Minor, east of Halicarnassus.

force of necessity...Hippocrates asserted that they cause painful knees; Dioscorides, that they caused haematuria, amongst other things.[62]

552 in order to understand...The problem was whether the contaminants arose spontaneously as a result of some metamorphoses from the legitimate crops, or were germinated from their own specific seeds, which were contaminants at the time of sowing. It seems to be clear that Galen favoured the first alternative. Unfortunately the conditions of the experiment were inevitably such that external

---

[61] *On the Materials of Medicine* III.130 = Wellmann II.140.
[62] Hippocrates, *Epidemics* II.4,3 = Loeb *Hippocrates* VII, 72; Dioscorides, *On the Materials of Medicine* II.108 = Wellmann I.182–3.

contamination could not have been controlled. The passage is of particular interest because one can sense the origin of Galen's own interest in
experiment, that is, a father for whom he clearly had great respect.

554 seeds of Demeter...or, to the Romans, of Ceres; hence
'cereals'.

558 rising of the Dog Star...in late July according to our reckoning, so that the period Galen identifies is from early July to mid August.
The Dog Star, Sirius, had been the base for the earliest known solar
calendar, in Egypt, when in ancient times its heliacal rising (i.e., when it
first appeared in the east just before dawn) coincided with the inundation
of the Nile. Because of asynchrony between the solar and lunar year the
time of rising steadily changed over a cycle of about 1460 years. A major attempt at stabilization came with the advent of the Julian calendar,
which applied in Galen's time.

561 colocynth...probably the bitter melon, *Citrulus colocynthis*, which
is native to the Eastern Mediterranean. However, another cucurbit, *Mo-
mordica charantia*, also goes by the same name. In the words of Robinson
and Decker-Walters the present nomenclature of the family *Cucurbitaceae*
is a 'vernacular conundrum'.[63] Not the least of the problems is that so
many New World representatives of the group have become household
names in the Old. Even Goodyer, the seventeenth-century translator of
Dioscorides, speaks of 'pompion' at a time when pumpkins had only
recently been introduced into Europe, but no pumpkin existed in the
ancient (European) world. The identifications that I give here for the
various members of the family must be regarded as best guesses.

563 own particular moisture...innate watery quality...
Galen is making a distinction between a water that is particular or proper
(*oikeios*) to it, and a watery quality that is innate (*symphytos*). On the face
of it this may mean that while the latter is a congenital quality, that is,
has been present, or potentially present, from the time of generation, the
former is an acquired quality that is nevertheless specific to the particular
foodstuff.

569 thick humour accumulates...Galen seems to be saying that,
although the type of humour is unaffected by the ease or otherwise of
concoction, excessive consumption can result in what we might call humoral overload, when the accumulation of humour in the portal venous
system outstrips the capacity of the veins and liver to further concoct it
into blood.

---

[63] Robinson and Decker-Walters (1997) 2.

572 quantity of lice [or parasites] ... *to tôn phtheirôn plêthos*. What underlies this remark is impossible to say, but it recurs in his *On Foods Productive of Good and Bad Humours*.[64] Whether it is to be taken literally, or whether it is a metaphor for some disease state, one cannot say. But it is worth remembering that we have already seen (1.55; K. 641) a reference to a belief (not by Galen, in that instance) in the spontaneous generation of scorpions from basil.

580 'seconds' [*deuterias*] ... Dioscorides gives some additional detail.[65] The juice that had been expressed was replaced by water in the proportion of one part for ten, and further reduced by boiling to one third of its volume. Salt was later added, presumably as a preservative, and the final product was stored in an earthenware vessel for one year, but thereafter rapidly weakened.

581 always astringency ... this diverges from Helmreich, who has *epikerastikon* – 'tempering <the humours>', rather than the alternative given in the *apparatus criticus*, *epikratêtikon* – 'astringent'. It is hard to see how the former would fit the context.

584 mulberries ... Galen seems to regard *sykaminon* and *moron* as synonyms, although LSJ restricts the latter term to the *black* mulberry *Morus nigra*.

593 *praikokkia* ... The chapter heading is *Peri armeniakôn kai praikokkiôn*. For the first, for this specific reference, LSJ has 'apricot', but there is no entry for the second. However, André states that *armeniace*, *armeniacum* and *praecoquum* were all alternative Latin names for the apricot, *Prunus armeniaca*.[66] It appears that both names used by Galen referred either to the same fruit or to two varieties of apricot. From what is said later in this section, the latter seems likely.

more pleasant ... this is not the only occasion when Galen anticipates the music hall ditty, 'a little of what you fancy does you good...' The nauseating effect of unpleasant foods is a common experience.

598 astringent apples and pears ... The whole of this section highlights the problem of deciding when Galen is referring to the stomach proper, the belly or the intestines. On what is admittedly a subjective view it is hard to believe that Protos's 'noteworthy' evacuation was not a visible event; in other words a bowel action.

601 all manner of things ... This translation is of the text in Kühn, and differs from that in Helmreich's edition, which presents an anomaly

---

[64] *On Foods Productive of Good and Bad Humours*, K. VI.792–3.
[65] *On the Materials of Medicine* V.6,15 = Wellmann III.10–11.　　　[66] André (1985) 324.

that was pointed out to me by Michael Dyson. The Helmreich version, ἔστι τε γάρ μοι φύσει τοιοῦτος ὁ στόμαχος ἀνατρέπεταί τε ῥαδίως ἐπὶ τοῖς στύφουσιν, translates to 'My *stomachos* is naturally like this and is easily upset after astringent things.' But he goes on to say that he relieves this by taking additional astringent items, and this is surely highly unlikely. The Kühn edition, however, has ἐπὶ τοῖς τυχοῦσιν, as Helmreich indicates in his *apparatus criticus*. The implication of the alternative translation is that the orator has a 'sensitive *stomachos*' which is easily upset after various foods, but which can be helped by consuming some astringent item. This seems a more likely proposition.

602 quinces... Galen appears to recognize two varieties, which differ in astringency. The first name is related to locality, the town of Cydonia in western Crete, but the second is obscure. *Strouthion* means, literally, 'little sparrow', which seems an unlikely name for a quince.

604 Hippocrates...[67] In Galen's version the text goes *palên es rhoiês chylon alphitôn epipassousa*, whereas the Loeb edition has *plên*... and the translator, Wesley Smith, gives 'Nothing relieves it except sprinkling barley meal in pomegranate broth. She survived on one meal daily...'

having heartburn... the whole of this paragraph is full of interest. To take first the matter of terminology, we can see here the origin of our term – cardia – for the part of the stomach surrounding the entrance of the oesophagus; and our 'heartburn' runs parallel with the Greek *kardialgia* (lit. 'heart pain'). Again, we have seen that *stomachos* can indicate the junction of the lower end of the oesophagus and the stomach, and so the Greek used here, *epi tôi stomachôi daknomenôi* (lit. 'in the case of the gnawed-at *stomachos*'), can fairly be regarded as referring to the gastro-oesophageal segment, although I have retained the transliterated *stomachos*. Indeed, the condition described sounds exactly like what is today a very common diagnosis, namely, gastro-oesophageal reflux. Beyond terminology, however, the intriguing question is how the ancients, having indicated by their terminology that confusion with true heart pain was possible (and the modern clinician would agree with this), nonetheless had made the distinction between the two. There are two possible answers to this. First, true cardiac pain must have been very much less common in antiquity than it is today, if only because a shorter expectation of life would have led to a smaller proportion of people in the older age groups and fewer candidates for coronary artery disease; and because the lifestyle of the ancient Greeks, and in particular their diet, must have

---

[67] *Epidemics* 11.2 = Loeb *Hippocrates* vii, 30–1 (Smith's translation).

led to a much lower incidence of coronary atheroma, the precursor of coronary thrombosis, in such candidates as did exist. Second, as anyone who has suffered from gastro-oesophageal reflux knows, in the early stages of the condition immediate relief can be obtained by something as simple as a drink of water, and this surely would have pointed to the alimentary tract as the seat of the disorder.

607 Hierichous . . . modern Jericho.

608 liver . . . obstructed . . . There are two points to make here, the first of pathological interest, the second relating to medical theory in antiquity. Galen is clearly describing the condition of cirrhosis of the liver, characterized by increasing cicatrization of that organ consequent upon destruction of liver cells from a variety of causes. The association of cirrhosis of the liver with palpable enlargement and induration of the spleen is almost a constant feature of the condition, and it is of great interest that this was recognized in ancient times. The second point relates to the matter of obstruction or impaction, which Galen held to be at the root of the problem. Vallance has pointed out that the notion of problems due to the flow of fluids being impeded in the body had a long history in Greek medicine, and that this was related to the idea of the body as a network of pores.[68] He has written at length on Asclepiades of Bithynia who held that obstruction, *enstasis*, of these pores was due to *anarmoi onkoi*, by which term, Vallance believes, Asclepiades meant 'fragile corpuscles'.[69] An alternative and more literal translation (which may have been more in line with Galen's thought) would be 'disjointed particles'. Although Galen was quite critical of Asclepiades, Vallance believes that the main difference between Asclepiades' view and Galen's was that the latter hypothesized that obstruction (he spoke of *emphraxis*) followed unnatural swelling or a foreign body combined with contraction of the pores. However, in a later passage in the present work (K. 687), Galen speaks not of pores but of vessels, the statement being consonant with his account of the anatomy of the liver, in which he describes 'a single large [portal] vein, deriving the others from it like branches from the trunk of a tree' (in the translation of May).[70]

612 Great Alexandria . . . of the various cities so-named, that in Egypt was surely 'the great'.

Beroia . . . modern Aleppo.

---

[68] Vallance (1990) 98–110.   [69] See also his entry in *OCD³*, s.v. Asclepiades.
[70] *On the Use of the Parts* K. 111.341 = Helmreich 1.250.

617 *persea* ... according to LSJ an Egyptian fruit, *Mimusops Schimperi*; but according to *SOED*, a mythological, sacred tree.

619 mast ... *SOED*: 'The fruit of the beech, oak, chestnut, and other forest-trees, esp. as food for swine.' Except when the reference is unequivocally to the oak I have used 'mast'.

622 turnips ... Galen is making two turnips into one – the turnip proper or *gongylis* (*Brassia rapa*), and the related French turnip or *bounias* (*Brassia napus*). Galen returns to the turnip in 11.60 (K. 648). The list of plants that are said to be eaten in famine follows the identifications in LSJ. French carrot for *gingis*, like French turnip, is an unavoidable anachronism.

date palm ... The top, or 'brain' of the date palm (like the 'heart' of the coconut palm) is the growing tip, the removal of which effectively kills the plant.

623 *atrakis* ... about which both LSJ and Durling know no more than that it is the name of a spinous plant.

624 *kibôria; kolokasia* ... according to LSJ the former is the seed pod of the latter. According to Durling, the latter is the root of the Egyptian bean.

abaton ... LSJ – for the present reference, 'a plant eaten pickled'.

627 glueing up the eyelashes ... doubtless to treat ingrowing eyelashes. Its use for this purpose is confirmed in Dioscorides 11.133, where the leaves and stem are also said to have a digestive property.

633 *rhaphanos* ... This was certainly the Attic name for cabbage. Galen, reasonably enough, does not say what the word meant to his contemporary readers. However, Dioscorides[71] says that it was used by some, as *raphanon agria*, for *apios*, the pear. *Rhaphanis* was the radish.

Readily Available Medicines ... *De remediis parabilibus*, K. XIV.311–581. The text we have now is believed to be spurious.

634 sorrel ... There is some confusion here and with the following item (11.48). Hort, in his translation of Theophrastus, translates *lapathon* as 'monk's rhubarb' (*Rumex patienta*) and this is followed by LSJ, which has 'curled dock' (*R. crispus*) for *oxylapathon*.[72] However, Dalby[73] has 'sorrel' (*R. acetosa*) for the former, and this is supported, perhaps, by the fact that the modern Greek for sorrel is *lapatho*. In truth the most that can be said with certainty is that both words indicate plants of the genus *Rumex*.

---

[71] *On the Materials of Medicine* IV.175 = Wellmann 11.324.
[72] *Enquiry into Plants*, Loeb *Enquiry into Plants* 1, 139 (Horst's translation).   [73] Dalby (1996) 85.

635 nightshade [*strychnon*] ... This is most unlikely to be strychnine, as the Greek might suggest. That is the name of an alkaloid derived from the *Nux vomica*. Dioscorides mentions four different varieties of στρύχνον, of which one is said to be cultivated and edible; one appears to be the winter cherry; a third is hypnotic, so most likely to be the deadly nightshade or belladonna (which contains the alkaloids atropine and hyoscyamine); and the fourth is referred to as 'madness-producing'.[74] It is impossible to decide with certainty which plant Galen refers to here, but the deadly nightshade is not unreasonable.

637 whorls ... *sphondyloi* – the circular weights that are used in spinning. These are the flower heads of the artichoke, which is the item we consume today. It is clear that what Galen has been referring to up to this point is the thistle-like artichoke plant.

639 for cooks, tastiness ... This contrast between the physician and the cook was of long standing. As Plato has Socrates say, 'Thus, cookery puts on the mask of medicine and pretends to know what foods are best for the body ...'[75]

641 *asparagoi* ... The term *asparagos* (or *asparagos*) covers a wider range than the vegetable we now call 'asparagus', which in Galen's time was merely one of a number of edible shoots covererd by this term.

Plato ... swim ... spoken by the Athenian stranger in *Laws* 689d, and apparently a well-known adage.

647 Aristotle ... hairs ... *Generation of Animals*, 783a25–6.

652 Hesiod ... *Works and Days* 40.

jaundice ... which suggests that the ancients had made a connection between jaundice and the intra-hepatic obstructions that Galen often postulates. But it would be wrong to see a parallel between Galen's view of jaundice and our own. True obstructive jaundice, as well as the obstructive element that can occur in hepatitis (where the main factor in the jaundice is liver-cell damage) are due to obstruction of the flow of bile in the biliary tree, and not to impaction of material in hypothetical channels in the liver.

656 *aphronitron* ... for Galen's *tou litrou ton aphron*. According to LSJ this is native sodium carbonate (i.e., 'washing soda'), which would undoubtedly be emetic! *SOED* says that *aphronitre* is now saltpetre, but LSJ may be correct for the times we are dealing with.

661 afflictions ... black bile ... This list provides a good example of how there has been a progressive narrowing of definition as medical

---

[74] *On the Materials of Medicine* IV.70–5 = Wellmann II.228–37.
[75] *Gorgias* 464–5 (Hamilton's translation).

terminology has developed, so that a translation that stays with the original sense will often be quite inappropriate. Thus cancer has now a more restricted meaning than the earlier translation of *karkinos*; elephantiasis, a condition which these days is typically the consequence of infestation with the filaria worm, may be adequate for the ancient *elephas*, and indicates leprosy in its lepromatous form. Grmek[76] has much to say on this. But there is little doubt that the *lepra* of the ancients was not, or was not only, leprosy. It included, for instance, the skin condition that we now know as psoriasis, and the similarity of the latter word to *psôra* will not escape notice.

quartan fever...According to the Greek system of ordinals, this is a fever which recurs, in our terms, every third day. We know that quartan malaria, a milder variety of that disease caused by *Plasmodium malariae*, with a greater tendency to chronicity than other forms, occurs now and doubtless occurred then in the Middle East.

melancholia (μελαγχολία)...In his *On Black Bile*[77] Galen says much, some of it confusing, about disease due to a disproportionate amount of black bile. The body's attempts to get rid of this through sweat and insensible perspiration are hindered by the fact that its substance is coarse (*pachymerês*) and so a range of skin lesions can result. The body also may attempt to sequester it in the veins, causing varices and haemorrhoids. Galen recognizes that these visible effects must be replicated in inaccessible parts (such as the intestine) and this leads him to a distinction between the local (and visible) manifestations, and a more general state which he refers to as *melancholia*. Galen also recognized that there was a further, psychiatric dimension to the description of 'black-bile disease', but it is only this aspect which has come down to us. It is plain that our 'melancholia' would be a very incomplete translation.

662 wasting...*kachexia* – literally 'a bad habit of the body'; 'bad disposition'; but in modern medicine a state of wasting, often in terminal illness such as cancer or tuberculosis. This may well be close to the meaning here.

666 *eleios*...according to LSJ 'a kind of dormouse'. Was it the name of one of the numerous species of hamster?

668 *libystikon*...according to LSJ, merely 'a herb'. It appears in Dioscorides as *ligystikon* and *panakon* ('cure-all'). He describes it as a plant growing in the Ligurian Apennines, in northern Italy, with a stem like that of dill, and with similar properties.[78]

[76] Grmek (1989) 168–73.   [77] *On Black Bile* K. v.104–48 = *CMG* v.4.1.1.
[78] *On the Materials of Medicine* iii.51 = Wellmann ii.64–5.

668 terrestrial...This is not an entirely literal translation. Galen is dividing the animal kingdom into 'winged', 'aquatic' and 'footed' (*pezos*) groups, and, as he points out, this last would exclude all land animals without feet, including snails, so these must be treated as 'footed' if they are not to be forgotten. But we have no term in common use other than 'terrestrial', which I use here. Galen is using three parts of Plato's fourfold classification of living creatures in *Timaeus* 40a (he omits Plato's heavenly gods). Wilkins has earlier discussed the social implications of this section.

672 more full of blood...Helmreich's *anaimoteras*, following Oribasius, would give 'more bloodless', which is surely wrong, for the tongue is a notably vascular organ. The *enaimoteras* of the *apparatus criticus* of his edition must be correct.

674 supporting the bifurcations...or 'fixing' – *schiseis angeiôn stêrizontes*; it is not clear what Galen intends here. There are many examples of lymph glands at the bifurcations or branching of blood vessels, but they are in no sense supportive. However, they can certainly appear so if they have become fibrotic from inflammation, and this may be the answer.

675 beside the neck of the bladder...the prostate gland.

679 fig-fed...the word Galen uses is *sykôtos*. It may be noted that in modern Greek *hêpar* is in the main used to refer to liver in a medical context. In a culinary context, *sykôti* for liver recalls this ancient practice.

680 kidneys...referred to in III.5 (K. 675).

681 varies greatly with the seasons...the animals themselves...Galen correctly points out that the composition of milk is affected by a number of variables, not only between different species, but within an individual species and, he might have added, between individual animals within the same species. The two variables he highlights, the season and the time from parturition, are clearly linked in his mind; and perhaps this was inevitable since the two milk-producing animals with which he would have been most familiar, sheep and goats, have a restricted breeding period and so a restricted season for parturition, namely the spring and early summer. However, he is incorrect when he implies that cow's milk is thickest. In fact ewe's milk is significantly higher in both fat and casein content, as well as in total solids, as the following table, which has been adapted from Charley and Weaver,[79] makes clear:

[79] Charley and Weaver (1998) 349.

	Cow	Sheep	Goat	
Total solids	12.6	17.0	13.2	
Fat	3.8	5.3	4.2	
Casein	2.8	4.6	2.8	(as % of total)

683 red hot pebbles...ordinary heating, as well as red hot pebbles or iron discs (the latter described in *On Simple Drugs*[80] as borne on spits) all have the effect of evaporating and concentrating the milk, which is interpreted by Galen as 'exhausting' the whey. In addition, some denaturation and deposition of protein might occur, and warm milk becomes more susceptible to the coagulating effect of lowering the pH (i.e., increasing the acidity).

components...Milk can be looked at in several ways, and Galen correctly points to one – that it consists of three main components: (a) the whey (which contains minerals, lactose, vitamins and colloidally dispersed protein); (b) cheesy material (i.e., the protein casein which is coagulated as the curd); and (c) butter fat.

686 women...nursing children...One can infer first, that the nurse had been suffering from some deficiency disease that manifested itself in cutaneous ulceration; and second, although less securely, that her milk secretion was also deficient in the same way. What the deficiency could have been is unclear. The nurse's condition does not sound like scurvy due to deficiency of vitamin C, resulting from the destruction of that vitamin in the wild herbs by cooking, as it is not very heat stable in the presence of oxygen. But milk itself is a poor source of the vitamin, so that in any case one would expect the nurse's milk to have been low in vitamin C. Nor does the child's state sound like scurvy. Nonetheless Galen's observation that the condition occurred in many nursing women during a famine cannot be ignored. Deficiency is highly suggestive even if its exact nature remains uncertain.

687 impactions...this is an important passage. Reference has already been made (K. 608) to the views of Asclepiades and Galen on the role of impactions in pathological processes. In the present passage it seems that the vessels in the liver were by nature narrower than usual, rather than narrowed as a consequence of swelling.

689 *oxygala*...the preparation of *oxygala* was described in detail by Columella, in a work written perhaps one hundred years or less before

---

[80] *On the Mixtures and Properties of Simple Drugs* K. x11.267.

the present one. Essentially, fresh (ewe's) milk, seasoned with herbs, was held for several days in a vessel with a drain-hole in the base, through which, after several days, the whey was drained off as the milk curdled. This was the result, as we now know, of the action of various micro-organisms which bring about the formation of lactic acid, with curdling influenced by the consequent lowering of the pH. The draining was re-peated at intervals over a number of days, the herbs were then discarded and salt added, doubtless to improve the keeping quality. It was then sealed until required for use.[81] Here we seem to be hearing of a primitive type of cottage cheese, albeit one which must have owed much to chance, since it would have been impossible to control the type of acid-forming organism from the environment which was contaminating the milk; and of course in any event there could have been no recognition of the prob-lem. There is no suggestion in Columella that any starter was used, nor that the milk was pre-heated (as in modern times) to make it more sus-ceptible to the effect of the acidification. An alternative diagnosis might be the production of yoghurt, as Dalby[82] believes to be the case. The choice of cottage cheese, however, is supported by Columella's emphasis upon removing the whey, which in modern domestic yoghurt (even the 'strained' variety) is to a considerable extent retained within the curd. Of course, one cannot ignore the possibility that the method of preparing ancient *oxygala* gave rise to both modern products.

694 cold oxymel... This is a good example of the influence of pre-heating upon the formation of curd when the pH is lowered, in this case by the vinegar (acetic acid) in the oxymel.

very cold water... which Galen says induces curdling. This is quite a different view from that of Dioscorides[83] who speaks of a silver vessel full of water being lowered into milk while it is being heated, to prevent it from boiling over. One may suspect that Dioscorides' information was the more reliable.

696 cheese... Once again we must turn to Columella, who goes into cheese-making at some length. The rennet, he says, should be from a lamb or kid but he points out that other things act similarly. Like Galen, he mentions fig sap (where the active ingredient, we now know, is the enzyme *ficin*), but he also speaks of wild-thistle flowers and safflower seeds. He describes the expression of whey with weights, forming cheeses in moulds, and 'hardening' it in brine. Cheeses that have been dried and

---

[81] Columella xii.viii = Loeb *On Agriculture*, iii, 203–5.   [82] Dalby (1996) 66.
[83] *On the Materials of Medicine* ii.70.

sprinkled with salt, he says, were suitable for export.[84] The whole passage would not seem out of date to a modern cheesemaker.

700 Homer also knew... *Odyssey* XVIII.45.

707 stifled eggs... the Greek is *ta pnikta*, for which LSJ has 'strangled, 'air-tight', with a secondary meaning 'baked' or 'stewed'. From the description of the cooking and its 'moderately thick' result, it sounds very much as though Galen is describing what we would now refer to as coddled egg.

713 kept in snow... Given that the fish came mainly from the sea, and snow mainly from the mountains, this statement adds point to the view of many, most recently Garnsey,[85] that Galen and other authors described the tables of the well-to-do.

714 non-comparative terms... these alternative meanings hinge on the Greek comparative (here *leptoteros*), which can be translated either as a comparative in the strict sense – 'thinner' – or, in a non-comparative way, merely as 'rather thin', which, as Galen points out, carries an implied comparison with some absolute sense.

727 galeoi ... galeônymoi ... galaxias... (the first two in plural form). Although Thompson refuses to identify the first (he says that some believe it to be the lamprey), he identifies the second and third as dogfish.

729 sardines... Galen is clearly confused here. He gives the impression that the fish from Sardinia and Spain (and those from the Pontus) are but a very early stage in the development of mature tunny (*thynnoi*), and are 'referred to by all as sardines'. But the fish from Sardinia (*sardai*) are surely true sardines, 'probably, as nowadays' in Thompson's words,[86] pilchards. But even this does not entirely resolve the problem since, quoting Thompson again,[87] 'Young Tunny no bigger than a sardine are caught in winter at Toulon.' To add to the confusion, later on (III.40; K. 746) Galen will speak of both *sarda* and *sardinê*, apparently as separate entities, although both Thompson and LSJ regard the words as synonymous. *Mylloi* and *korakinoi* in the following sentence are unidentified.

731 abrotonon, apsinthion... wormwood (*Artemesia spp.*). LSJ has entries for both ἀβρότονον and ἀψίνθιον, respectively *A. aborescens* and *A. absinthium*. Ps.-Dioscorides regarded them as alternative names for the same plant.[88]

---

[84] Columella VII.viii = Loeb *On Agriculture*, II, 284–9. [85] Garnsey (1999) 115.
[86] Thompson (1946) 229. [87] Thompson (1946) 83.
[88] Ps.-Dioscorides III.24 = Wellmann II.34.

735 *pagouroi, karkinoi* ... Neither Thompson nor LSJ distinguishes between the two, identifying each as 'the common edible crab' (*Cancer pagurus*). Possibly Galen is describing local variants of the same species.

737 seals ... hammerhead sharks ... tunny ... Galen is well astray here. Seals (*phôkai*) are not members of the order *Cetacea* nor are they, strictly speaking, marine mammals. Hammerhead sharks should be included with the cartilaginous elasmobranchs, as should dogfish, and tunny are unequivocally fish.

740 honeydew ... Mynors, in his commentary on Virgil's fourth *Georgic*, makes the point that the ancients believed that honey came ready-made from honeydew[89] which, as Galen says here, was precipitated from the atmosphere onto leaves and flowers. This belief, according to Crane in her recent encyclopaedic work on the history of bee-keeping, almost certainly had stretched back for centuries.[90] Indeed the notion that the substance was atmospheric in origin persisted until the close of the eighteenth century. However, the earliest account that has come down to us is in Aristotle's *Enquiry into Animals*, books V and IX (there are some inconsistencies between the two).[91] Aristotle's (and Galen's) view was that the honeydew, having been collected by foraging bees, was regurgitated into the cells of the comb. We now know that honeydew is the excretions of plant-sucking insects like aphids and various scale insects and, with nectar from flowers, is taken back to the colony by foraging worker bees, where the young workers convert it to honey by enzymatic action. What the material was that Galen reports being collected from the trees of the Lebanese mountains is anybody's guess. It is hard to believe that it was honeydew. Perhaps it was the resinous, exudative 'tears' which collect on the bark of some trees and shrubs (mastic is an example) and which, in fact, do provide the propolis or stop-wax that bees use at the entrance of hives.

742 in my commentaries ... *Against the Cnidian Maxims* is published as *Regimen in Acute Diseases (Appendix)*, in Loeb *Hippocrates* VI 262–327.

744 production of blood ... The passage has two points of theoretical interest. First, as often elsewhere, the physical appearance of the food has a causal relationship to the end-product after concoction. The thick red wine gives thick red blood. Second, and associated with this, blood production is clearly a measure of the nutritive quality of a food.

---

[89] Mynors (1990) 258.   [90] Crane (1999) chap. 52.   [91] *HA* 553b24; 623b24.

hydromêlon...according to LSJ 'a drink of water and *mêlomeli*' – the latter is 'honey flavoured with quince'. According to Dioscorides, *hydromêlon* was a fermented preparation of one part sweet juice from the quinces and two parts water.[92] *Mêlomeli* was a preparation of quinces packed into honey and kept for a year. One should keep in mind the distinction between *hydromêlon* and *hydromel*, earlier called *melikrat*, which is honey and water (or sometimes milk).

746 foam of nitre...loose nitre foam...LSJ is little help in distinguishing between what were apparently two forms of sodium carbonate.

---

[92] *On the Materials of Medicine* v.21–2 = Wellmann iii.20.

APPENDIX I

List of plants with Greek and botanical names

Where the Greek names for plant and fruit differ, this is indicated. Where there are alternative Greek names, that used by Galen has been chosen. Modern botanical names, in the main, are those given in Wiersema and León (1999); Zohary and Hopf (1993); Williams, J. T. (1993; 1995); and elsewhere as indicated in the commentary.

Chapter	English name	Greek name	Botanical name
1.2	wheat	πυρός	
	(naked) bread wheat	"	*Triticum aestivum*
	(naked) durum	"	*Triticum turgidum*
9	barley	κριθή	*Hordeum vulgare*
13	other wheat types:		
	einkhorn	τίφη	*T. monococcum*
	emmer variety	ὄλυρα	*T. turgidum*
	emmer variety	ζειά	*T. turgidum*
14	oats	βρόμος	*Avena sativa*
15	broom millet	κέγχρος	*Panicum miliaceum*
	foxtail (Italian) millet	ἔλυμος; μελίνη	*Setaria italica*
16	pulse	ὄσπρια (plural)	(various)
17	rice	ὄρυζα	*Oryza sativa*
18	lentil	φακός	*Lens culinaris*
19	broad (faba) bean	κύαμος	*Vicia faba*
20	Egyptian bean	κύαμος Αἰγύπτιος	(see commentary K. 524)
21	pea	πίσος	*Pisum sativum*
22	chickpea	ἐρεβίνθος	*Cicer arietinum*
23	lupin(e)	θέρμος	*Lupinus albus*
24	fenugreek	τῆλις	*Trigonella foenum-graecum*
25	cowpea	φάσηλος	*Vigna unguiculata*
	birds' pea	ὦχρος	*Lathyrus ochrus*
26	grasspea or chickling vetch	λάθυρος	*L. sativus*

▶

Chapter	English name	Greek name	Botanical name
28	calavance (?)	δόλιχος	(see commentary K. 524)
29	bitter vetch	ὄροβος	*Vicia ervilia*
30	sesame	σήσαμον	*Sesamum indicum*
	rocket	ἐρύσιμον	*Sisymbrium* spp.
31	poppy	μήκων	*Papaver somniferum*
32	flax	λίνον	*Linum usitatissimum*
33	sage	ὅρμινον	*Salvia officinalis*
34	Indian hemp	κάνναβις	*Cannabis sativa*
35	chaste tree	ἅγνος	*Vitex agnus-castus*
36	dwarf chickling	ἀφάκη	*Lathyrus cicera*
	common vetch	βικίον	*Vicia sativa*
37	darnel or tare or poison rye grass	αἶρα	*Lolium* spp.
11.3	colocynth (bitter melon)	κολοκύνθη	*Citrullus colocynthis*
4	gourd	πέπων	? *Cucurbita pepo*
5	melon	μηλοπέπων	*Cucumis melo*
6	cucumber	σίκυος	*Cucumis sativus*
8	fig (fruit)	σῦκον	*Ficus carica*
9	[wine] grape	σταφυλή	*Vitis vinifera*
10	raisin	σταφίς	. . . .
11	mulberry	συκαμίνον or μόρον	*Morus* spp. (e.g. *M. alba*; *M. nigra*)
12	cherry (fruit)	κεράσιον	*Prunus* spp. (*P. avium; P. cerasus*)
13	bramble	βάτος	*Rubus* spp.
	blackberry	βάτινον	*Rubus fruticosus*
14	dog rose (white rose)	κυνόσβατος	*Rosa canina*
15	juniper	ἅρκευθος	*Juniperus communis*
16	cedar [Syrian]	κέδρος	*Cedrus* spp. (*C. libani*)
17	pine cone	κῶνος	*Pinus* spp.
18	myrtle	μύρρινος (μύρσινος)	*Myrtus communis*
19	peach	μῆλον περσικόν	*Prunus persica*
20	apricot	μῆλον ἀρμενιακόν	*Prunus armeniaca*
	"	[? πραικόκκιον]	(see commentary K. 593)
21	apple	μῆλον	*Malus pumilus*
23	quince	κυδώνιον μῆλον [στρούθιον μῆλον]	*Cydonia oblonga* " "
24	pear	ἅπιον	*Pyrus communis*
	pomegranate	ῥόα	*Punica granatum*

▶

Chapter	English name	Greek name	Botanical name
25	medlar	μέσπιλον	*Mespilus germanica*
	sorb-apple or fruit of the service tree	ὄον [οὖον]	*Sorbus domestica*
26	date palm	φοῖνιξ	*Phoenix dactylifera*
	date	φοινικοβάλανος or καρπὸς τῶν φοινίκων	
27	olive	ἐλαία	*Olea europaea*
28	walnut	κάρυον βασιλικόν	*Juglans regia*
	walnut, or nut generally	κάρυον	. . . .
29	almond	ἀμυγδάλη	*Prunus dulcis*
30	pistachio	πιστάκιον	*Pistacia vera*
31	plum	κοκκύμηλον	*Prunus domestica*
32	jujube	σηρικά (pl.)	*Zizyphus jujuba*
33	carob	κεράτια	*Ceratonia siliqua*
34	caper	κάππαρις	*Capparis spinosa*
35	sycamore (fruit)	συκόμορον	*Ficus sycomorus*
36	*persea*	περσέα	?
37	citron	κίτρον	*Citrus medica*
38	oak (tree)	δρῦς	*Quercus* spp.
	oak mast	τῶν δρυῶν βάλανοι	. . . .
40	lettuce	θριδακίνη	*Lactuca sativa*
	lettuce (cos)	"	*L. sativa* var. *longifolia*
41	chicory	σέρις	*Cichorium intybus*
	endive	ἴντυβος	*C. endivia*
42	mallow	μαλάχη	*Malva* spp.
	tree mallow (LSJ)	"	*Lavatera arborea*
43	beet	τεῦτλον	*Beta vulgaris*
44	cabbage	κράμβη	*Brassica oleracea*
45	blite	βλίτον	*Amaranthus blitum*
	orach (garden orach)	ἀτράφαξυς	*Atriplex hortensis*
46	purslane	ἀνδράχνη	*Portulaca oleracea* var. *sativa*
47	sorrel	λάπαθον	*Rumex acetosa*
48	curled dock	ὀξυλάπαθον	*Rumex crispus*
49	nightshade	στρύχνον	*Solanum dulcamara* *Atropa belladonna*
51	celery	σέλινον	*Apium graveolens*
	alexanders	ἱπποσέλινον	*Smyrnium olusatrum*
	water-parsnip	σίον	*Sium latifolium*
	Cretan alexander	σμύρνιον	*Smyrnium perfoliatum*

▶

Chapter	English name	Greek name	Botanical name
52	rocket	εὔζωμον	*Sisymbrium orientale*
53	nettle	ἀκαλήφη or κνίδη	*Urtica ferox*
54	cress	γιγγίδιον or λεπίδιον	*Lepidium sativum*
	wild chervil	σκάνδιξ	*Anthriscus* spp. (? *A. cerefolium*)
55	basil	ὤκιμον	*Ocimum basilicum*
56	fennel	μάραθον	*Foeniculum vulgare*
57	asparagus (see commentary K. 641)	ἀσπάραγος	*Asparagus officinalis*
60	turnip	γογγυλίς	*Brassica rapa*
61	arum (cuckoopint)	ἄρον	*Arum maculatum*
62	edder-wort	δρακόντιον	*Dracunculus vulgaris*
63	asphodel	ἀσφόδελος	*Asphodelus* spp.
64	grape-hyacinth	βολβός	*Muscari* spp.
65	carrot	σταφυλῖνος	*Daucus carota*
	wild carrot	δαῦκος	. . . .
	caraway	καρώ	*Carum carvi*
66	truffles (*T. cibarium* or *T. melanosporum*)	ὕδνον	*Tuber* spp.
67	mushrooms (fungi)	μύκης	Numerous species
		βωλίτης	*Boletus* spp.
		ἀμανῖται (pl.)	*Amanita* spp.
68	radish	ῥαφανίς	*Raphanus sativus*
69	onion	κρόμ(μ)υον	*Allium cepa*
	garlic	σκόροδον	*Allium sativum*
	leek	πράσον	*Allium porrum*
	wild leek	ἀμπελόπρασον	*Allium ursinum*

List of fishes with common names in English and Greek, and Linnaean taxonomies

Except where indicated English identifications are those of Thompson (1946). Amended Linnaean taxonomy is from Papakonstantinou (1988) and Whitehead *et al.* (1989).

Chapter	English	Greek	Thompson	Amended
III.24	grey mullet	κέφαλος	*Mugil cephalus*	*Mugil cephalus*
25	sea bass	λάβραξ	*Perca labrax* or *Labrax lupus*	*Dicentrachus labrax*
26	red mullet	τρίγλη	*Mullus barbatus*	*Mullus barbatus*
27	parrot wrasse	σκάρος	*Scarus cretensis*	*Sparisoma (Euscaris) cretense*
	kottyphos	κόττυφος	*Labridae sp.* (? *L. merula*)	*Labrus merula*
	kichlê	κιχλή	" (? *L. turdus*)	*Labrus viridis*
	rainbow wrasse	ἰουλίς	*Coris iulis*	*Coris julis*
	wrasse	φυκίς	? *Labrus mixtus*	*Labrus bimaculatus*
28	goby	κωβιός	*Gobius sp.* (? *lata*)	*Zosterisessor ophiocephalus*
29	sea perch	πέρκη	*Serranus scriba*	*Serranus scriba*
	Murry eel	σμύραινα	*Muraena Helena*	*Muraena Helena*
	horse-mackerel	σαῦρος	*Caranx trachurus*	*Trachurus mediterraneus*
	hake	ὄνος (ὀνίσκος)	*Gadus merluccius*	*Merluccius merluccius*
	sole (or flounder)	ψῆττα	*Pleuronectidae sp.*	*Pleuronectidae*
	hêpatos	ἧπατος	?	? ?
	kitharos	κίθαρος	?	
	maigre (meagre)	σκιαινίς	*Sciaena aquila*	*Argyrosomus regius*
30	weaver (weever)	δράκων	*Trachinus draco*	*Trachinus draco*
	piper	κόκκυξ	*Trigla sp.*	? *Trigla lyra*; ? *T. lucerna*
	shark	γαλεώνυμος (= γαλεός)	*Squalus blainvilli*	*Squalus blainvilli*
	sculpin (Fr. crapaud)	σκορπίος	*Scorpaena sp.*	? *Scorpaena scrofa*
	horse-mackerel	τράχουρος[a]	*Caranx trachurus*	*Trachurus mediterraneus*
	sea perch	ὀρφός	*Serranus gigas* or *Polyprion Cernium*	*Epinephalus guaza* *Polyprion americanus*

▶

Chapter	English	Greek	Thompson	Amended
	glaukos	γλαῦκος	?	? ?
	dogfish (various)	κύων	*Galeus canis* or *Scyllium canicula*	*Galeorhinus galeus* *Scyliorhinus canicula*
	conger eel	γόγγρος	*Conger vulgaris*	*Conger conger*
	sea bream	φάγρος	*Pagrus vulgaris*	*Pagrus pagrus*
	eagle ray	ἀετός	*Myliobatis batis*	*Myliobatis batis*
	great white shark[b]	λάμια	*Carcharodon Rondeletii*	*Carchardon carcharias*
	hammerhead shark	ζύγαινα	*Zygaena malleus*	*Sphyrna zygaena*
	tunny	θύννος	*Thynnus thynnus*	*Thunnus thynnus*
	'sardine' (pilchard)	σάρδα	(not stated)	*Sardina pilchardis*
	myllos	μύλλος	?	? ?
	korakinos	κορακῖνος	?	? ?

[a]Thompson (1946: 263) believed that this was identical with the σαῦρος of III.29.
[b]Identification from Whitehead *et al.* (1989, 1, 84).

Ancient sources

Texts and/or English translations to which reference is made in the commentary.

Anonymus Londinensis (the '*Menon Papyrus*'), ed. and trans. Jones, W. H. S. (1968), *The Medical Writings of Anonymus Londinensis*, Amsterdam.

Aristotle
The Complete Works of Aristotle: the Revised Oxford Translation, ed. Barnes, Jonathan (1984) (various translators; 2 vols.), Princeton and Oxford.
De anima (*On the Soul*), trans. Lawson-Tancred, Hugh (1986), Harmondsworth.

Athenaeus
Deipnosophistai (*Dinnertime Philosophers*), trans. Gulick, Charles Burton (1927–41) (Loeb, 7 vols.), Cambridge, Mass. and London.

Celsus
De medicina (*On Medicine*), trans. Spencer, W. G. (1971–79) (Loeb, 3 vols.), Cambridge, Mass. and London.

Columella
De re rustica (*On Agriculture*), trans. Ash, H. B., Forster, E. S. and Heffner, B. (1941–75) (Loeb, 3 vols.), Cambridge, Mass. and London.

Diocles of Carystus
A Collection of Fragments and Translation and Commentary (vol. 1), ed. and trans. van der Eijk, Philip J. (2000), Leiden, Boston and Cologne.

Dioscorides (Ps.-Dioscorides)
De materia medica (*On the Materials of Medicine*), ed. Wellmann, Max (1958) (3 vols.), Berlin.

Galen
De alimentorum facultatibus (*On the Properties of Foodstuffs*) – K. VI.453–748, ed. Helmreich, G. (1923), *CMG* V.4.2, Leipzig and Berlin.

De atra bile (*On Black Bile*) – K. v.104–48, ed. de Boer, W. (1937), *CMG* v.4.1,1, Berlin.

De bonis et malis alimentorum sucis (*On Foods Productive of Good and Bad Humours*) – K. vi.749–815, ed. Helmreich, G. (1923), *CMG* v.4.2, Leipzig and Berlin.

De methodo medendi (*On the Therapeutic Method*) – K. x.1–1021.

De naturalibus facultatibus (*On the Natural Faculties*) – K. 11.1–204, trans. Brock, Arthur John (1916) (Loeb), Cambridge, Mass. and London.

De placitis Hippocratis et Platonis (*On the Doctrines of Hippocrates and Plato*) – K. xv, 181–805, trans. De Lacy, Ph. (1984) (3 vols.), *CMG* v.4.1,2, Berlin.

De pulsibus ad tirones (*On the Pulses for Beginners*) – K. viii.453–92.

De remediis parabilibus (*On Readily Available Medicines*) – K. xiv.311–581. The text that has come down to us is not by Galen.

De sanitate tuenda (*On Hygiene*) – K. vi.1–452, ed. Koch, K. (1923), *CMG* v.4.2, Leipzig and Berlin;
  trans. Green, Robert M. (1951), *A Translation of Galen's Hygiene*, Springfield, Ill.

De simplicium medicamentorum temperamentis ac facultatibus (*On the Mixtures and Properties of Simple Drugs*) – K. xi.359–892; xiii.1–377.

De temperamentis (*On Mixtures*) – K. 1.508–694, ed. Helmreich, G. (1969), Stuttgart;
  trans. Singer, P. N. (1997), *Galen. Selected Works*, 202–66, Oxford.

De usu partium (*On the Use of the Parts*) – K. iii.1–933; K. iv.1–366, ed. Helmreich, G. (1968), Amsterdam;
  trans. May, Margaret Talmadge (1968), *Galen. On the Usefulness of the Parts of the Body*, Ithaca, N.Y.

De venae sectione adversus Erasistratum (*On Venesection against Erasistratus*) – K. xi.147–86, trans. Brain, Peter (1986), *Galen on Bloodletting*, 15–37, Cambridge.

De victu attenuante (*On the Thinning Diet*) – not included in Kühn edition; ed. Kalbfleisch, K. (1923), *CMG* v.4.2, Leipzig and Berlin;
  trans. Singer, P. N. (1997), *Galen. Selected Works*, 305–24, Oxford.

In Hippocratis de natura hominis (*On Hippocrates' 'On the Nature of Man'*) – K. xv.1–173, ed. Mewaldt, J. (1914), *CMG* v.9.1.89–113, Leipzig.

Institutio logica (*Introduction to Logic*) – not included in Kühn edition; trans. Kieffer, J. S. (1964), *Galen's Institutio Logica. English Translation, Introduction, and Commentary*, Baltimore.

Protrepticus (*Exhortation to Study the Arts*) – K. 1.1–39, ed. Marquardt, I., *SM* 1.103–29;
  trans. Singer, P. N. (1997), *Galen. Selected Works*, 35–52, Oxford.

Thrasybulus sive utrum medicinae sit an gymnasticae hygiene (*To Thrasybulus: Whether Health Belongs to Medicine or Gymnastics*) – K. v.806–98, ed. Helmreich, G., *SM* iii.33–100;
  trans. Singer, P. N. (1997), *Galen. Selected Works*, 53–99, Oxford.

Hesiod
Theogony and *Works and Days*, trans. West, M. L. (1999), Oxford.

Hippocrates
Works, trans. Jones, W. H. S., Potter, Paul and Smith, Wesley D. (1923–95) (Loeb, 8 vols.), Cambridge, Mass. and London;
   trans. (into modern Greek) Mandelaras, B. (1992), ΙΠΠΟΚΡΑΤΗΣ ΑΠΑΝΤΑ, Athens.

Plato
Charmides, trans. Jowett, Benjamin (ed. Hare, R. M. and Russell, D. A.) (1970), *The Dialogues of Plato*, vol. 11, London.
Gorgias, trans. Hamilton, Walter (1960), Harmondsworth.
Laws, trans. Saunders, Trevor J. (1975), Harmondsworth.
Republic, trans. Grube, G. M. A. (1974), Indianapolis.
Timaeus, trans. Lee, Desmond (1971), in *Timaeus and Critias*, Harmondsworth.

Pliny (the Elder)
Naturalis historia (*Natural History*), trans. Rackham, H., Jones, W. H. S. and Eicholz, D. E. (1940–63) (Loeb, 10 vols.), Cambridge, Mass. and London.
   Healy, John F. (1991), *Pliny the Elder: Natural History. A Selection*, Harmondsworth.

Rufus of Ephesus
On the Nomenclature of the Human Body; *On the Parts of the Human Body* in *Oeuvres de Rufus d'Ephèse*, ed. Daremberg, Ch. and Ruelle, Ch. E. (1851, repr. 1963), Amsterdam.
   Quaestiones medicinales (*Medical Questions*), ed. Gärtner, H. (1970), Leipzig.

Soranus
Gynaecology, trans. Temkin, Owsei (1991), Baltimore.

Theophrastus
De causis plantarum (*Account of Plants*), ed. and trans. Einarson, Benedict and Link, George K. K. (1976–90) (Loeb, 3 vols.), Cambridge, Mass. and London.
Historia plantarum (*Enquiry into Plants*), ed. and trans. Hort, Sir Arthur (1916) (Loeb, 2 vols., including minor works on odours and weather signs), Cambridge, Mass. and London.

References

Alfageme, I. Rodríguez (1995) 'La médecine technique dans la comédie attique', in van der Eijk, *et al.* (1995) 569–85.

André, Jacques (1985) *Les Noms de plantes dans la Rome antique*, Paris.

Bailey, Kenneth C. (1932) *The Elder Pliny's Chapters on Chemical Subjects*, part II, London.

Barnes, Jonathan (1975) *Aristotle's Posterior Analytics*, Oxford.

   (1991) 'Galen on logic and therapy', in Kudlien and Durling (1991) 50–102.

   (1997) 'Logique et pharmacologie. A propos de quelques remarques d'ordre linguistique dans le *de simplicium medicamentorum temperamentis ac facultatibus* de Galen', in Debru (1997b) 3–33.

Baum, Michael (1989) 'Radicalism versus irrationalism in the care of the sick: science versus the absurd', *Medical Journal of Australia* 151: 607–8.

Bertier, Janine (1972) *Mnésithée et Dieuchès*, Leiden.

Brain, Peter (1986) *Galen on Bloodletting. A Study of the Origins, Development and Validity of His Opinions, with a Translation of Three Works*, Cambridge.

Bynum, W. F. and Porter, Roy (1993) *A Companion Encyclopaedia of the History of Medicine*, London.

Chantraine, P. (1975) 'Remarques sur la langue et le vocabulaire du *Corpus Hippocratique*', in *La Collection Hippocratique et son rôle dans l'histoire de la médecine*, Leiden, 35–40.

Charley, Helen and Weaver, Connie (1998) *Food: A Scientific Approach*, Upper Saddle River, N.J.

Crane, Eva (1999) *The World History of Beekeeping and Honey Hunting*, London.

Cubberley, Anthony (1995) 'Bread-making in ancient Italy: *clibanus* and *sub testu* in the Roman world', in Wilkins *et al.* (1995) 55–68.

Curtis, Robert I. (1991) *Garum and Salsamenta: Production and Commerce in Materia Medica*, Leiden.

Cushing, Harvey (1940) *The Life of Sir William Osler*, New York.

Dalby, Andrew (1996) *Siren Feasts. A History of Food and Gastronomy in Greece*, London and New York.

Dalby, Andrew and Grainger, Sally (1996) *The Classical Cookbook*, London.

Debru, Armelle (1997a) 'Philosophie et pharmacologie: la dynamique des substances *leptoméres* chez Galien', in Debru (1997b) 85–102.

Debru, Armelle (ed.) (1997b) *Galen on Pharmacology: Philosophy, History and Medicine*, Leiden.

De Lacy, Phillip (ed.) (1978–84) *Galen. On the Doctrines of Hippocrates and Plato* (3 vols.), Berlin.

Douthwaite, A. H. (1963) *Hale-White's Materia Medica, Pharmacology and Therapeutics* (32nd edn), London.

Durling, Richard J. (1993) *A Dictionary of Medical Terms in Galen*, Leiden.

Eijk, Ph. J. van der (1997) 'Galen's use of the concept of "qualified experience" in his dietetic and pharmacological works', in Debru (1997b) 35–57.

  (2000) *Diocles of Carystus. A Collection of the Fragments with Translation and Commentary*, vol. 1: *Text and Translation*, Leiden.

Eijk, Ph. J. van der, Horstsmanshoff, H. F. J. and Schrijvers, P. H. (eds.) (1995) *Ancient Medicine in Its Socio-Cultural Context* (2 vols.), Amsterdam.

Foxhall, L. and Forbes, H. A. (1982) 'Σιτομετρεία: the role of grain as a staple food in classical antiquity', *Chiron* 12: 41–90.

Frede, Michael (1981) 'On Galen's epistemology', in Nutton (1981) 65–85.

  (1985) Introduction to Walzer and Frede (1985).

Garnsey, Peter (1999) *Food and Society in Classical Antiquity*, Cambridge.

Garofalo, Ivan (1988) *Erasistrati fragmenta*, Pisa.

Grant, Mark (2000) *Galen on Food and Diet*, London.

Grmek, Mirko D. [1983] (English trans. 1989) *Diseases in the Ancient Greek World*, Baltimore.

Guardasole, Alessia (1995) 'Per la posizione di Eraclide di Taranto nella storia del pensiero medico', *Koinonia* 19: 63–9.

  (1997) *Eraclide di Taranto. Frammenti: testo critico, introduzione, traduzione e commentario*, Napoli.

Harig, G. (1974) *Bestimmung der Intensität im medizinischen System Galens*, Berlin.

Healy, John F. (1978) *Mining and Metallurgy in the Greek and Roman World*, London.

Heiser, Charles B. (1990) *Seed to Civilization: The Story of Food*, Cambridge, Mass.

Isager, Signe and Skydsgaard, Jens Erik (1992) *Ancient Greek Agriculture. An Introduction*, London.

Jardé, Auguste (1979) *Les Céréales dans l'antiquité grecque*, Paris.

Jasny, Naum (1944) *The Wheats of Classical Antiquity*, Baltimore.

Kudlien, Fridolf (1991) ' "Endeixis" as a scientific term: a) Galen's usage of the word (in medicine and logic)', in Kudlien and Durling (1991) 103–11.

Kudlien, Fridolf and Durling, Richard (eds.) (1991) *Galen's Method of Healing. Proceedings of the 1982 Galen Symposium*, Leiden.

Langslow, D. R. (2000) *Medical Latin in the Roman Empire*, Oxford.

Lloyd, G. E. R. (1983) *Science, Folklore and Ideology*, Cambridge.

McIntyre, Michael (1988) *Herbal Medicine for Everyone*, Harmondsworth.

May, Margaret T. (1970) 'On Translating Galen', *Journal of the History of Medicine* 25: 168–76.

Moritz, L. A. (1958) *Grain Mills and Flour in Classical Antiquity*, Oxford.

Mynors, R. A. B. (ed.) (1990) *Virgil: Georgics. Edited with a Commentary by R. A. B. Mynors*, Oxford.

Nutton, Vivian (1973) 'The chronology of Galen's early career', *Classical Quarterly* 23: 158–71.

(ed.) (1981) *Galen: Problems and Prospects. A Collection of Papers Submitted at the 1979 Cambridge Conference*, London.

(1991) 'Style and context in the *Method of Healing*', in Kudlien and Durling (1991) 1–25.

(1993) 'Humoralism', in Bynum and Porter (1993).

Pagel, Walter (in collaboration with Pyarali Rattami) (1964) 'Vesalius and Paracelsus', *Medical History*, vol. VII, 315; reprinted in Pagel, Walter (ed. Marianne Winder) (1986) *From Paracelsus to van Helmont: Studies in Renaissance Medicine and Science*, London.

Papakonstantinou, Costas (1988) *Faunia Graeciae*, vol. IV: ΚΑΤΑΛΟΓΟΣ ΤΩΝ ΘΑΛΛΑΣΙΩΝ ΙΧΘΥΩΝ ΤΗΣ ΕΛΛΑΔΑΣ (*Check-List of Marine Fishes of Greece*), Athens.

Purcell, Nicholas (1995) 'Eating fish: the paradoxes of seafood' in Wilkins *et al.* (1995) 132–49.

Robinson, R. W. and Decker-Walters, D. S. (1996) *Cucurbits*, New York.

Ross, Sir David (1995) *Aristotle* (6th edn), London.

Ste Croix, G. E. M. de (1981) *The Class Struggle in the Ancient Greek World*, London.

Sallares, Robert (1991) *The Ecology of the Ancient Greek World*, Ithaca, N.Y.

Schöner, Erich (1964) *Das Viererschema in der antiken Humoralpathologie*, Wiesbaden.

Singer, P. N. (1997) *Galen. Selected Works. Translated with an Introduction and Commentary*, Oxford.

Skoda, Françoise (1988) *Médecine ancienne et métaphore. Le vocabulaire de l'anatomie et de la pathologie en grec ancien*, Paris.

Smith, Wesley D. (1979) *The Hippocratic Tradition*, Ithaca and London.

Staden, Heinrich von (1989) *Herophilus: The Art of Medicine in Early Alexandria*, Cambridge.

Steckerl, Fritz (1958) *The Fragments of Praxagoras of Cos and His School*, Leiden.

Swain, Simon (1996) *Hellenism and Empire: Language, Classicism and Power in the Greek World AD 50–250*, Oxford.

Temkin, Owsei (1973) *Galenism. Rise and Decline of a Medical Philosophy*, Ithaca and London.

Thompson, D'Arcy Wentworth (1936) *A Glossary of Greek Birds*, London.

(1946) *A Glossary of Greek Fishes*, London.

Tracy, Theodore James (1969) *Physiological Theory and the Doctrine of the Mean in Plato and Aristotle*, The Hague and Paris.

US Department of Agriculture Research Service (1999). USDA Data Base for standard Reference, Release 13. Nutrient Data Laboratory Home Page http://www.nal.usda.gov/fnic/foodcomp.

Vallance, J. T. (1990) *The Lost Theory of Asclepiades of Bithynia*, Oxford.

Walzer, Richard and Frede, Michael (trans.) (1985) *Three Treatises ON THE NATURE OF SCIENCE: On the Sects for Beginners; An Outline of Empiricism; On Medical Experience*, Indianapolis.

Whitehead, P. J. P. *et al.* (1984) (repr. 1989) *Fishes of the North-eastern Atlantic and the Mediterranean* (3 vols.), Paris.

Wiersema, John H. and León, Blanca (1999) *World Economic Plants. A Standard Reference*, Boca Raton, Fl.

Wilkins, John, Harvey, David and Dobson, Mike (eds.) (1995) *Food in Antiquity*, Exeter.

Williams, J. T. (ed.) (1993) *Pulses and Vegetables*, London.

(ed.) (1995), *Cereals and Pseudocereals*, London.

Zohary, Daniel and Hopf, Maria (1994) *Domestication of Plants in the Old World: The Origin and Spread of Cultivated Plants in West Asia, Europe, and the Nile Valley* (2nd edn), Oxford.

Index

absorption 21–2
acorns *see* famine
aigilops 69, 169
Alcmaeon 10
alektryôn; alektoris see hen
Aleppo *see* Beroia
alexanders 105
Alexandria xi, xiv, 41–3, 64, 94, 96
alkalinity 144
almond 93–4
aloes (aloe vera) 9, 37, 161
alphita see barley meal
anadosis, meaning of 21–2; and *see*
    distribution
anarmoi onkoi 176
anatomy
    human, cultural taboo on 7
    morbid (pathological) 7
Anonymus Londinensis 5
anorexia 87, 90
aphronitron 113, 178
apodeixis see demonstration
apothermos 55; and *see* must
appetite 15, 111
    not indiscriminate 15
    role of cardio-oesophageal region in 15, 92
    role of vagus nerves in 15
apple 86–8
    Armenian *see* apricot
    Cydonian *see* quince
    Medean *see* citron
    Persian *see* peach
    Strouthian *see* quince
apple-melon 33, 71, 74, 83
apricot 34, 86, 174
aquatic animals 135; and *see* appendix 11
    and water quality 135–6, 140–1
    and water type 136
arachos; arakos xiii, 172
Ariston 37, 160
Aristophanes xiii, xiv, 64

Aristotle 9–10, 14, 24, 109, 154–5, 157; and *see*
    faculty; *mesotês*
Aristotle, works
    Generation of Animals 178
    History of Animals 24, 184
    On the Soul 14
    Parts of Animals 24
    Parva naturalia 157
    Posterior Analytics 154
artichoke 178
arum, Egyptian 109–10
Asclepiades 176
Asia xiv, 53, 110
asparagoi 107–8, 178
asphodel 111
assimilation *see* metabolic pathway; nutrition,
    Galen's definition of
astringency 37–8, 62, 86, 88–9
athletes and food 115; and *see* training
Atticizers xiv–xv, xvii, 18–19, 80–2, 91, 94,
    103–4
attribute *see* property
axeweed 172
axioms, development of 154

balanoi see mast
barley 37, 49–50
    barley-cake 50–1
    meal 168
    and *see* bread; ptisane
basil 106
beans, broad (faba) 59–60
    Egyptian 60
beef 31, 115
beet 101–2
    and lentil 38
    as drug 102
Beroia 94
bile, black 12, 58, 115; and *see* melancholia
bile, yellow 12, 31, 33–4
biles, 'other' 33, 149, 158